CADS AND CAVALIERS

CADS AND CAVALIERS
The Gentlemen Adventurers of the Movies

Tony Thomas

Illustrated by John Lebold

South Brunswick and New York: A. S. Barnes and Company
London: Thomas Yoseloff Ltd

A. S. Barnes and Co., Inc.
Cranbury, New Jersey 08512

Thomas Yoseloff Ltd
108 New Bond Street
London W1Y OQX, England

Library of Congress Cataloging in Publication Data

Thomas, Tony, 1927–
    Cads and cavaliers.

    CONTENTS: Douglas Fairbanks, père et fils.—
John Barrymore.—George Sanders. [etc.]
    1. Moving-picture actors and actresses—Biography.
I. Title.
PN1998.A2T5   791.43′028′0922 [B]   72-5177
ISBN 0-498-01192-5

PRINTED IN THE UNITED STATES OF AMERICA

This book is affectionately dedicated to Walter Mitty, a man after my own heart, and to all the romantics of the world—all the dreamers and all the armchair adventurers. In other words, to you and me, in memory of those thousands of flickering images flashing through the darkness of hundreds of hours at the movies.

CONTENTS

FOREWORD

It is no secret that the giant Hollywood studios, especially during those lucrative days fittingly referred to as their Golden Years, have always acted as the most efficient purveyors to an alternately unemployed and wartorn public of the most meretricious of American myths: throughout the Depression and then throughout the war years the dream of success, of striking it rich, remained the screen's single most common panacea for national malaise. "We're in the money," cheered Busby Berkeley's girls, and a decade later Sidney Greenstreet pronounced with stolid fervor a line which could have stood, could still stand, as an emblem for all the works coming out of the moguls' empire at that time: "If you lose a son, it's possible to get another . . . there's only one Maltese Falcon."

Against the money culture, however, burned another culture, intimately interlaced with the pursuit of riches yet somehow oddly antagonistic to success, suspicious of the grand designs of the Warners and Mayers and Cohns, ironically and yet irreducibly wed to a more ancient, aristocratic standard of conduct than that which Mammon, that peculiarly democratic god, laid down. This culture dealt in ungraven images; it had ideals like Honor and Courage, and it was more suspicious of sham and mercantilism than ever a medieval doctor was of usury. It was a culture created by the moguls themselves, and yet it repudiated every plutocratic intention. For the score of years in which it claimed the affections of the moviegoing public, it paradoxically nibbled away at the secret foundations of studio control while entrenching the star system the studios had created, and reintroduced into American life a code of acting, an *esprit,* which had been lost since Raleigh last departed Virginia.

This burning, ironically alternate culture was the old high way of the cavalier and the gentleman adventurer. The American (or Americanized) actors who best embodied the ideals of that culture were John Barrymore, the two Fairbanks, Errol Flynn, Tyrone Power. The actors who, by subverting those ideals, taught us by contrast the value of what was lost were the renegade Englishmen Basil Rathbone and George Sanders. Over two decades these figures bolstered, on the screen, the ancient concepts of dignity and dare in an increasingly pedestrian industrial world. Nearly as well as their counterparts in the Western, they lived epic lives in a merely dramatic era. If the prospector, the kindly old man enslaved to cupidity, signifies the inherent anguish of the Westerner confronting the contradictory demands of a simultaneously bourgeois and puritan culture, then these gay buccaneers, as deeply pure of heart as they were avid for material gain, signified the inherent anguish of the westerner confronting—in Hollywood, in California, in all this guiltily prosperous century—the contradictory demands of meretriciousness and romance. In a merchant's world, they embodied on the screen the whimsical, useless, and unassailable notion of Honor—and Hollywood, needing to believe the myth of Honor, made them rich to prove it. That was the insidious, paradoxical secret of their success, their sickness, and their fall.

As Mr. Thomas's book vividly shows, they were not, many of them, happy men. Barrymore, once acclaimed the greatest actor of his generation, drank himself to death before he was sixty. Flynn did the same, hastening his descent by pumping himself full of drugs as well as vodka. George Sanders committed suicide last year, claiming he was bored. And Douglas Fairbanks, Sr., whose 1920 *Mark of Zorro* started the whole romance cycle, ended his days a gloomy bitter man, old at fifty-six, pining for the boyish revelries of his middle age. They were men who, though crazily linked to death, did not know how to die. They raged against it. They insisted life offer more than the transparent blandishments of yacht, castle, and car. Deeply wed to the money culture, they needed more than that culture could offer them. They were not mocked: they believed the myths, not the makers. They longed to be what they were on the screen—the anachronistic embodiments of nobility, self-assurance, color.

They came to believe. Wear a mask long enough, it becomes you. The elder Fairbanks, a shade ludicrous as a middle-aged Don Juan, still could not himself distinguish what had been created by studio flacks to sell his movies from what was strong and vital deep within him. Mary Pickford said, years later, speaking about his prodigious physical energy, that he was no different around the house. "He was a little boy. He was just as you saw him on the screen."

The eternal boy, unable to get out of costume, resolute against giving in. There is a haunting poignancy to this image of the aging cavalier, a poignancy not superficial but resilient and profound: it is perhaps the poignancy of our own lost nation, exiled now from Raleigh's grand imaginings, cached in easy securities, spouse to a strongbox. What Fairbanks made flesh was the forgotten nobility of an older, probably mythical, order when this was not the case—when to be a man meant to have the silly aristocratic courage of a boy.

The glamor and the panache of the swashbucklers were a disguise only, a sop to the costume departments. What was really engaging about them, through all those years when the twentieth century rumbled toward a fulfillment of its awful promise, was the secret code they enacted, constantly and in the simplest of ways: a gesture, a riposte, the general air of bemused disdain they carried with them like an amulet, let out the happy lie: life was, and still could be, decorative, charming, superb.

What killed Douglas Fairbanks? What killed Sanders and Barrymore and Flynn? They were born, yes, out of their time (maybe it was the time of Man), but it was more than that. I think it was the exhausting tension between their happy acknowledgment, on screen and off, of the high old culture, and their recognition that, in order to emulate that culture, they had continually to go in heat after choice parts and juicier contracts. They were not any of them professional actors: even the divine Barrymore was limited to a modicum of types, and of them only Rathbone could begin to touch the eccentric fire, the desperately precise quality of exact mimesis, which always shines in an Olivier or a Gielgud. They were not intellec-

tuals either—as no true knight could be—but rather, as Mr. Thomas wisely suggests, Gentlemen Actors, paid handsomely for their own social idiosyncrasies, who spent their professional lives with more or less fidelity sketching themselves. But it all happened in the wrong age for them, and that living of the lie is what did them in.

Implacably, what Henry James called the Hotel Spirit has come to be the dominant American social modality in this century: efficiency, antisepsis, cool, now set our tone. Cads or cavaliers, the men here fondly remembered were crucial to the American public as anachronistic models of virtues (and vices) which countered the Hotel Spirit. (Thank the Lord, said Lionel Barrymore, that his brother Jack could not "adjust.") Escapism, this used to be called: more exactly, it was a case of a communal need for a sanative atavism, for a rebirth of any of the old virtues—the virtues of the country's childhood—which, it used to be believed, made life worth living. Not surprisingly, Tolkien first soared to popularity in these years. For what was demanded was really a resurgence of the sacral. It was not merely for the sake of historical exactness that so many of the swashbucklers wore crosses: Holy Mother Church, no less than that benevolent and despotic father the King, provided an essential social construct against which the cavalier ideals could be viewed to mutual advantage. The world of boys, again, with the cavalier as the not yet rebellious son, as skilled for the fantastic demands of the paladin's code as he was obedient to the sovereignty of the parents who enforced that code upon him. A simpler world: a world without generations gaps, and without any of the social and psychological wisdom which democratic benevolence has since foisted upon us. In that world the man was a boy and the boy a man. Anything could be done. Between the rapier pyrotechnics of the Best Swordsman in France and the languorous crispness of a Sanders or Rathbone repartee, anything was possible. It was a world of grace and dignity and effortless brilliance—a world where the Best and not the Largest, the aristocrat and not the moneylender, seized the day.

On the deepest ironic level, such a world survived so long only by virtue of its essential affinity to death. In the world of the gentleman adventurer as in the world of the Western, the drama of death and the boy animated a populace too soon grown old but still too young to die. Flynn thought there were six best ways to commit suicide: it might be said he tried them all, and thus became the idol of a generation. This was not only a case of Byronic overreach by which he hoped to prove his mettle against the strictures of an insensitive universe. It was grandly less than that. It was his way of showing that, alimony and record-breaking salaries aside, he was match for the moguls. His death, serene and ludicrous as it was, proved that Captain Blood was heavier than either water or gold. He was here like James Dean: it would have been just as supererogatory for him to have lived past fifty as for Dean—or Valentino—to have reached thirty-five.

The tremendous and agonizing paradox of Hollywood—that that consumptive, sweaty-sheeted city is the source of all high artifice and grandeur of sentiment in a meanly artificial and trivially sentimental country—was not lost on the true cavaliers. They were indeed men of another century, horsemen of a peculiar American apocylypse, and, in the thick of the gathering sickness of our day, they saw, better than those of us far enough away from Hollywood to retain our illusions, just what form the final collapse of their quixotic ideals would take. Men of grace and brilliance, they were forced to live within the walls of a consumptive city which yet—and precisely because it was consumptive (such an opiate, such a screen, the disease did throw off)—enabled them to enact, for fun and profit, images of that grand old style which, deeply, was their own real style. It was a nasty balance to hold. I think they became, as Unamuno calls Nietzsche, self-envying men. They did not

take it well, and that too is what killed them.

They might have expired as quickly in the cancerous Italy of Catherine de Medici or the gay plot-ridden France of Richelieu. Historically that is relevant, but mythically it is not, and here is the crux of the matter. For it was Hollywood's failure to provide a viable balance, in the adventure epic, between myth and history that spelled its curious inbred richness, and its eventual decline.

The grand age of the adventure epic gave to the American people, as to people all over the world, an image of grandeur and glitter and flair which our own eccentrically stable country could barely approach. Most importantly, it gave a sense of grace. Grace—the ability to make the difficult look easy and the simple look profound—was the stylistic hallmark of the swashbuckler and the gentleman adventurer, be he wicked or pure. In an age in which grace was already passing on, along with the dueling sword and the buckler, to the graveyard of the inutile, that was more than a passing fancy. The image expanded and enriched us.

Mr. Thomas takes us back more years than we might imagine. He casts back not only to the Thrilling Thirties and the Fabulous Forties, but to an age rich in simplicity, ineluctably splendid, thrilling and fabulous in ways that, as the desperate hyperboles here imply, our strange century could only imitate. It was an age, we want to believe, when grace was more than a gift of God.

Thaddeus Tuleja

PREFACE

This book was a pleasure to write and I can only hope it evokes a similar attitude from the reader. If that happens to be the case, I think it might be a pleasure tinged with a certain measure of regret. I am not of the opinion that the past was better than the present—there is plenty of evidence to the contrary—but without delving into a deep sociological dissertation I do lament the passing of one or two aspects of life as it used to be. In particular I feel sorry about the decline of romanticism in motion pictures and the virtual disappearance of actors who might be described as *gentlemen*. I am, of course, speaking in Byronic terms, and I like to think I understand how Lord Byron felt about life in his own era, and how lost and confused he would feel if abroad in these harsh, loud, unromantic times. The educated, man-of-the-world kind of actor personified by Errol Flynn and Douglas Fairbanks (father and son) as heroes, and Basil Rathbone and George Sanders as villains, seems to be in short supply these days, as does the ability to make convincing adventure films on heroic themes. The theme of *Cads and Cavaliers* is, then, *romanticism fondly remembered:* I appear not to be alone in this kind of nostalgia.

ACKNOWLEDGMENTS

In writing a book that is largely an exploration of my own fascination with a certain film genre—the historical romance, the swashbuckling and costumed adventure—I must admit to much help given me by many people. I should begin by doffing my cap to the Canadian Broadcasting Corporation, who, in the dozen years I was their Hollywood correspondent, allowed me to indulge myself writing and producing programs about the film world. I am especially grateful to Harry J. Boyle, a generous and understanding boss.

Much of the writing and, incidentally, all otherwise unidentified quotations, spring from my own interviews and tape recordings with the subjects. However, I met neither Douglas Fairbanks, Sr., nor John Barrymore. In the case of the elder Fairbanks I was helped in my study by Douglas Fairbanks, Jr., whom I also grilled about his own adventures, and by the gracious Mary Pickford. The study was vastly aided by reading and digesting two books of Fairbanksiana: *Knight Errant,* by Brian Connell (Doubleday and Company, Inc., 1955) and *The Fourth Musketeer,* by Ralph Hancock and Letitia Fairbanks (Holt, Rinehart, and Winston, 1953). For help with the John Barrymore section I am grateful to Rudy Vallee and to Samuel A. Peeples, who allowed me to reprint here his own recollections of Barrymore, originally written for the magazine *Films in Review* (May, 1970). That same magazine was also the source of two articles of particular help to me: "Robin Hood on the Screen" (February, 1965), and "Swordplay on the Screen" (June–July, 1965), both written by Rudy Behlmer. I should mention at this point that Henry Hart, who retired in 1972 after editing *Films in Review* for some twenty years, provided a treasure-trove for film researchers by putting together that excellent magazine, and that Mr. Hart was one of the people who most encouraged me to write about films.

In researching the Barrymore chapter I studied Gene Fowler's masterful biography, *Good Night, Sweet Prince* (The Viking Press, 1944), and Hollis Alpert's excellent coverage of the whole family, *The Barrymores.* I also quoted a few lines from Lionel Barrymore's book, *We Barrymores* (Appleton-Century-Crofts, Inc., 1951). Vincent Price kindly allowed me to lift some lines from his *I Know What I Like,* published by Doubleday and Company, Inc. in 1959, and that same publisher agreed to my quoting a section from Basil Rathbone's autobiography, *In and Out of Character* (1958). I am grateful to John Cutts for letting me use part of his Rathbone article for the magazine *Films and Filming* (March, 1969) and to Mrs. Rosemary Warner for providing me with written material by her brother, Errol Flynn. Excerpts from *The Memoirs of a Professional Cad* (copyright © 1960 by George Sanders) were reprinted by permission of G. P. Putnam's Sons.

I am also indebted to Mildred Simpson and her staff at the library of the Academy of Motion Picture Arts and Sciences in Los Angeles. That I am in debt to John Lebold for illustrating this book from his vast collection of film photographs is, I hope, glowingly obvious. And, of course, the book itself is my way of saluting all the actors who played the cads and cavaliers, and brought me enjoyment. Gentlemen, I thank you.

Tony Thomas

1

DOUGLAS FAIRBANKS, PÈRE ET FILS

FILM swashbuckling began in 1920 with Douglas Fairbanks and his decision to make *The Mark of Zorro*. Whatever had been done before in costume and adventure films was instantly rendered lackluster by comparison with the gymnastic verve and the powerhouse vitality of this extraordinary man.

Stardom has never been merely a matter of talent. Fairbanks, like most other great screen personalities, was unique. The mold was seemingly lost or destroyed immediately after the man was fashioned. He set a standard for athletic heroics that has never been matched and he was a titan in an era of film history that will never be seen again.

There are oddities in the story of Douglas Fairbanks, just as there are oddities in the stories of all people of exceptional ability and unusual attainments. It was odd that Fairbanks reached the age of thirty-seven before he made his mark with *The Mark of Zorro;* had he not made this drastic career change from light comedian to dashing adventurer, he would be only a minor figure in film annals. But the oddest thing about Fairbanks, the ever-beaming, effervescent actor, the most ebullient of all the movie cavaliers, was the disparity between his many years of happiness and the two ends of his life span. Fairbanks was the glummest of babies and in the last few years of his life he returned to being glum. But his prime lasted a long, long time and for years it seemed as if he had actually found the Fountain of Youth. He had only one child, a son who would bear his name and follow a similar path, yet—another oddity—he felt nothing paternal for the boy and resented him because he was evidence of age. Fairbanks was a father who didn't want to be called Dad.

I put the obvious question to Douglas Fairbanks, Jr. "What kind of a man was your father?" "Well, I think the best way to answer that is to say he was a perfectly wonderful boy. He was a natural Peter Pan. He always thought of himself in terms of youth and he loved life in terms of youth. He loved play, games, and competition—and that attitude applied to his buisness. He was a shrewd, tough businessman."

Fairbanks Sr. was very much against his son becoming an actor. "He was almost violent on the subject; in fact, things were strained between us for some years because of it. But much later when I had become established on my own, and formed my own company, he not only became reconciled but he was extremely enthusiastic and took pride in telling people I had done it on my own and in spite of his objections He thought that was a fine thing to have done."

The other person to ask about Douglas Fairbanks is Mary Pickford. The line of questioning has to be oblique. Here the relationship was much more strained. The dream marriage that made them the King and Queen of Hollywood for a dozen years somehow petered out despite the great feeling they had for each other. Yet the marriage was every bit as romantic and gleaming and storybookish as their gossamer movies.

Sitting in the little lounge off the big lounge at Pickfair, the Buckingham Palace of Beverly Hills, Mary Pickford looked out over the sloping lawns and thought back half a century. "I remember I wasn't too impressed by him the first time. I saw him on Broadway in a play and I thought he was much too exuberant."

Fairbanks, Sr. with Clare McDowell, Charles Hill Mailes, and Marguerite de la Motte in *The Mark of Zorro*

Mary paused and mused. I couldn't see the expression in her eyes because she was wearing dark glasses. A little smile appeared around her mouth. "He was a little boy. He was just as you saw him on the screen. Did you know he never used a double? He did everything you saw him do on the screen. And he was like that around the house —he'd have you out there jumping around the lawn or climbing that water tower and up on the roof."

Another pause and then, softly, "No matter how many people were in the room, when he left, the room was empty."

There was nothing about Fairbanks as a baby to suggest a presence that would ever be missed. His face was a solemn mask and it never cracked a smile until he fell on his head when he was three. His solemnity was much less of a problem to his mother than his strange fearlessness in climbing trees and climbing onto the roof of the house and staring into space. One of his capers was to try to fly like a bird, the failure of which caused him to be knocked unconscious. When he came to, he at first looked surprised and then, for the first time began to laugh. From then on Fairbanks was a smiling, happy, bouncing boy who grew into a smiling, happy, bouncing man—and remained so until he reached his late forties. Then, past the peak of his popularity and no longer able to hide his age, the latent streak of sadness reappeared.

He was born Douglas Elton Ulman in Denver, Colorado on May 23, 1883. Five years later his father, Charles Ulman, his business ventures having collapsed, walked out on his wife and three sons and never returned. Some years later the mother reverted to the name of her previous husband John Fairbanks, who had died of tuberculosis not long after their marriage.

Douglas Fairbanks soon decided what he wanted to do in life—be an actor. Actually he never really became an actor in the literal sense because he was never, on the stage or screen, anything other than himself. Fortunately for his acting aspirations, Fairbanks was a three-ring circus. He was a man of enormous ebullience who loved cavorting before an audience, and he did it so well people were fascinated by him, although it took some years before he could control and skillfully use his Saint Vitus-like energy.

In the summer of 1899 the esteemed actor-manager Frederick Warde brought his stock company to Denver to present a series of plays. At some point, probably not long after he hit town, Warde was cornered by a bright-eyed, highly personable sixteen-year-old lad who told him how much he wanted to get into the theater. Warde was impressed by the barrage of enthusiasm and told the boy he would hire him if he ever got to New York, probably thinking it was a safe promise to make a boy he would never see again. He was wrong. Douglas Fairbanks turned up in New York the following year and held Warde to his word.

Any young American beginning a career in 1900 no doubt considered it the most auspicious of times: a new century looming before the most promising nation on earth. Fairbanks made his debut in Duluth in September, playing a lackey in a costume drama. No lackey ever bounced into a scene with such vigor. A few weeks later, Warde gave Fairbanks the role of Laertes in *Hamlet* because the actor who regularly played the part was ill. The critics noted that Warde's supporting company was pretty poor stuff, and that by far the worst was the young clown playing Laertes. By the end of 1900 Warde suggested to Fairbanks that it might be better if he left the company and acquired a little more education. Fairbanks spent the first half of 1901 at Harvard, distinguishing himself only in the gymnasium. He spent the summer of that year working his way around Europe.

Fairbanks tried unsuccessfully to get theatrical work upon his return to New York. For a while he worked as a clerk in a brokerage house on Wall Street, from which he was fired when it became obvious there was no knowledge of finance behind the beaming personality. The following February he landed a small part in a short-lived Broadway play. It wasn't much, but at least it was his New York debut. His next job came half a year later when he persuaded a touring company to hire him. From then on, Fairbanks managed to eke out a living in the theater although there were times when his merry tirelessness, his lack of discipline, and his love of playing practical jokes on the other actors during performances brought him close to being dumped.

In 1907 Fairbanks met and fell in love with Beth Sully, the daughter of millionaire Daniel J. Sully, who had made his fortune the hard way as a cotton manufacturer. Mr. Sully was in no way pleased at the prospect of his daughter's marrying an actor, particularly one whose efforts had brought him no fame and no money. The young couple were adamant in their mutual ardor and Sully finally agreed to sanction the marriage, but only if Fairbanks would quit the theater and become a businessman, to which end he was willing to lend his considerable aid. Fairbanks was under contract to producer William Brady at the time. Brady accurately pointed out to the love-smitten actor that he was making a mistake in leaving the entertainment business because it was the only business in the world to which his talents and temperament were suited. Fairbanks laughingly tossed off the advice and Brady let him go, but not without first stipulating that, should he ever return to the theatre, he would be legally bound to resume his contract with Brady.

Fairbanks was away from the theater for only a year. His father-in-law set him up as an executive of the Buchan Soap Corporation, but fate stepped in to make a few decisions. Daniel Sully suffered disastrous business setbacks the year after his daughter's marriage, and one of the companies that went down the drain was the soap company. Fairbanks now found it quite necessary to return to his former craft. Odd as it may seem, the play in which he resumed his acting career in August of 1908 was called *All for a Girl*. Now twenty-five and more responsible than before, Fairbanks applied himself to his work and quickly became one of Broadway's favorite young comedy actors. Over the next seven years he built a solid repuation as an amusing actor of unflagging energy, one who could always be relied upon to enliven his roles with gymnastic leaps and bounds.

Fairbanks's film career began fortuitously. A newsreel cameraman spotted the popular Broadway actor strolling with his wife and young son in Central Park, and asked him to besport himself for the camera. Fairbanks performed a little athletic foolery over and around the park benches and went his way. A month or so later a man from a newly formed film company came to see Fairbanks and told him that he and his partners had seen the newsreel footage and that in their opinion he was a natural film actor, that his personality and his dexterity were perfect for the movies. Fairbanks, like most stage actors of the period, looked upon films as little more than claptrap, and he told the man he was not interested. The man then told Fairbanks they were willing to pay him $2,000 a week. This was more than Fairbanks had ever made or was ever likely to make on the stage; after a few days of thinking it over he decided to go to Hollywood—not to make a series of films, as the offer suggested, but to make one and then consider the verdict.

Douglas Fairbanks never returned to the stage. His first film was *The Lamb,* made in Hollywood in 1915 by Triangle, a company whose name derived from its three famous organizers—D. W. Griffith, Thomas Ince, and Mack Sennett. It was immediately obvious to Fairbanks that these were not claptrap merchants, and that the art of filmmaking was developing rapidly toward a limitless future. It was equally obvious to him that the screen was also limitless in the freedom of movement it offered his bounding body. If ever a man found himself a marvelous niche, Fairbanks found his in Hollywood in these formative years of the picture business.

The quick success of Fairbanks in films was largely due to a very young scenarist named Anita Loos, who would later achieve great fame as an authoress and playwright. Fairbanks was something of a problem to his producers, who soon saw that he was not a man of much dramatic range and that his lack of skill might become tiresome. As they pondered, the happy actor continued to jump around the sets amusing the cast and crew. It was Anita Loos on the sidelines who found and realized the solution—to make the screen image of Fairbanks exactly what the man was himself.

Douglas Fairbanks was well and continuously employed in his first five years in Hollywood. He made twenty-nine pictures in that period; none of them was anything other than light, ephemeral entertainment in which he was pleasing and amusing with his sunny personality and his athletic romps. The titles seem to indicate the caliber of the content:

The Lambs	*The Man from*
Double Trouble	*Painted Post*
His Picture in the	*Reaching for the*
Papers	*Moon*
The Habit of Happi-	*A Modern Musketeer*
ness	*Headin' South*
The Good Bad Man	*Mr. Fix-It*
Reggie Mixed In	*Say, Young Fellow*
Flirting with Danger	*Bound in Morocco*
The Half Breed	*He Comes Up Smiling*
The Case of the	*Arizona*
Leaping Fish	*Knickerbocker Buck-*
Manhattan Madness	*aroo*
American Aristocracy	*His Majesty the*
The Matrimaniac	*American*
The American	*When the Clouds Roll*
In Again, Out Again	*By*
Wild and Woolly	*The Mollycoddle*
Down to Earth	

These films were all successful, in varying degrees, and they made Fairbanks a wealthy man. He was, however, not content with his salary of half a million dollars a year once he realized that some of his pictures were bringing the producing company a million and more each. He formed his own company and in 1919 persuaded three of Hollywood's major figures to come in with him and found a corporation: Fairbanks, D. W. Griffith, Charles Chaplin, and Mary Pickford thus formed United Artists. Already a millionaire at the time of forming the corporation, Fairbanks went on to make fortune after fortune. Griffith dropped out and died in relative poverty, but Chaplin and Pickford soon became, and remained, millionaires.

The Shakespearean observation about the "tide in the affairs of men,/ which, taken at the flood, leads on to fortune" must have flashed in the mind of Douglas Fairbanks like an immense neon sign in 1919. He was about to launch himself on a decade of fantastic success and popularity, such as few men ever experience. It was partly due to his business acumen and partly to his marriage to Mary Pickford, then an equal, if not greater, luminary among Hollywood royalty. The two had first met in New York just before Fairbanks left for Hollywood; it had been a brief social meeting with no significance for either of them. Their paths crossed several times later, and a feeling gradually grew.

By 1918 Fairbanks told his wife that he felt he could no longer live if he could not marry Mary, and that he was willing to sacrifice his fame and wealth, if necessary to do so. This was no mere bleating from a highly romantic man. Pickford was also married, although it was well-known in Hollywood that her marriage with the unpopular actor Owen Moore was a sad one. It can be said about both Fairbanks and Pickford that they were unquestionably moral people, both products of severe Victorian upbringings and each equally appreciative of the general public's low opinion of divorce. But the union of Fairbanks and Pickford seemed such a natural coming together of a man and woman ideally suited to one another that the public not only approved but cheered with joy. Their honeymoon trip to Europe and their appearances in London, Paris, and other cities brought on bewilderingly huge masses of fans and great traffic jams. For some years to come it would seem as if Mr. and Mrs. Douglas Fairbanks were the two most popular human beings on the face of the earth.

Perhaps the only people who disliked Fairbanks were those who met him and instantly felt inferior, or who were irked by his overwhelming confidence and well-being. Fairbanks in his years of super-stardom was an incredible athlete: he boxed, he swam, he fenced, he rode horses, he could run and jump like a track champion, and he was an imaginative acrobat. With it all he also beamed with advice about health and the power of positive thinking. He effused about enthusiasm and vigor and determination and happiness. Fairbanks wrote a number of short books on these topics, with titles such as *Laugh and Live, Initiative and Self-Reliance, Making Life Worthwhile*. There was nothing hypocritical about all this. Fairbanks was the personification of everything in which he believed.

Fairbanks decided to make *The Mark of Zorro* not only because he loved the medium of historical romance but because he clearly saw that a change in his image was necessary. The First World War had caused changes in public taste and in concepts of morality. The super-moral, brave, and clean-cut Fairbanks image would soon appear less interesting, and perhaps look ludicrous, unless he took it out of the present and let it skip back into the fictional past. It seemed to him that in the increasing tempo of modern times, with its noise and confusion, there would be a market for movies of pure escapism. No actor ever made a better decision.

The Mark of Zorro was released in November of 1920, and Fairbanks didn't have long to wait to hear the sound of coins pouring into the box offices. Just in case *Zorro* misfired, he had made another of his typical light comedies, *The Nut*, but it was to be the last of its kind because it proved unnecessary. From then on, Fairbanks was a celluloid cavalier. As Zorro he righted the wrongs perpetrated by a dictator in mid-nineteenth century California, swordfighting like mad and causing havoc among the dictator's clumsy soldiers. He vaulted over walls, swung through windows, and performed somersaults—as he fenced. With *Zorro* a smash hit, Fairbanks could safely move into making *The Three Musketeers*, and play the role he loved most—d'Artagnan. When he invented d'Artagnan, Alexandre Dumas might well have been peeking into the future, taking Fairbanks as his model .

With the success of *The Three Musketeers* and with money rolling in by the ton, Fairbanks bought the site for his proposed studio, on Santa Monica Boulevard in Hollywood, a block that is now the Goldwyn Studio and still the West Coast offices of United Artists. The first project for the new studio had been decided upon. This was *Robin Hood,* with a generous budget for magnificent sets, the biggest ever constructed for a film at that time. Fairbanks was away during the construction, and he recoiled when he first saw the huge castle built by art director Wilfred Buckland—the walls stood 90 feet high, and the banquet room was 450 feet long. Fairbanks was a man of only medium height, around five and a half feet, and he felt dwarfed by the set. It took some persuasion from his staff to have him go ahead with the project. It turned out to be a major success, his most profitable picture, and probably the high-water mark in his career.

In his article "Robin Hood on the Screen" (*Films in Review*, February 1965) , Rudy Behlmer outlined the Fairbanks version:

The first half of this eleven-reel film consists of medieval pageantry, tournaments, court life, the trek to Palestine to defend the Holy Sepulchre, and the treachery involving the king's brother, Prince John (Sam De Grasse) and Sir Guy of Gisbourne (Paul Dickey) . Enid Bennett portrayed Lady Marian Fitzwalter—Maid Marian—who sends word of the treachery to the Earl of Huntingdon (Fairbanks) . He returns to England, learns that Prince John has usurped the throne and is oppressing the people, and dissolves into the character of Robin

In *The Three Musketeers*

In *Robin Hood*

Hood, who, with his band of followers, sets out to thwart John and his minions until the return of Richard (Wallace Beery).

It was in the second half of the film that Fairbanks climbed the mighty drawbridge chain at Nottingham Castle, leapt from battlement to tower, slid down a huge drapery, and engaged in feats of archery and swordsmanship. The heaviness of the film gave way to the free spirit of 'Doug,' but he was still somewhat subdued by the mass of decor.

The problem for Douglas Fairbanks at this time in his life was what to do next. *Robin Hood* exceeded even his own dreams of success. The film ended up grossing five times its cost and the acclaim was almost deafening. The only logical thing to do next seemed to be to take a trip through the Arabian Nights. Hence, his *The Thief of Bagdad* —with, again, an enormous budget and enormous sets. William Cameron Menzies designed the sets; had he done so forty years later he could have sold the entire creation to Disneyland for a complete complex of Disney's fairyland playground. Menzies laid four acres of concrete as the slab on which to build his fanciful Bagdad, with palaces, domes, bazaars, huge staircases, and mosques. Fairbanks

was at his acrobatic best, leaping from balconies onto sundry awnings, climbing ropes, bouncing out of a huge vase into another and another and another, and riding magic carpets. Audiences could well ask themselves if this man Fairbanks was a mortal human or a machine made up to look like a man.

Fairbanks had no choice but to continue with film fantasy and escapism, but he was careful not to overexpose himself. After *The Mark of Zorro* he limited himself to one film a year. These Fairbanks films of the twenties involved months of work, but he was also interested in many other activities, including sailing his yacht and traveling. Fairbanks could never stay in one spot for long— movement was in his nature. He and Mary enjoyed giving lavish parties at Pickfair. He was a humorous man and it gave him pleasure to entertain his guests, who included other film celebrities, politicians, and royalty. These were the years when Fairbanks and Pickford were themselves the King and Queen of Hollywood.

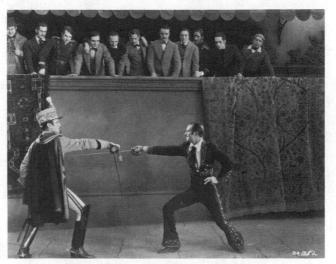

With Donald Crisp in *Don Q, Son of Zorro*

In *The Thief of Bagdad*

In 1925, the Fairbanks film was *Don Q, Son of Zorro,* in which he used a long Australian stockwhip to cut down his enemies, swing from posts and balconies, and climb high walls. The following year, he did the inevitable—he made a pirate picture. He had bided his time about this because he felt such a film should be done in color, then a new aspect of filmmaking. *The Black Pirate* was pure Fairbanks, perhaps because the movie was his own invention. He dreamed up a story about

With Anders Randolph and Donald Crisp in *The Black Pirate*

With Lupe Velez in *The Gaucho*

a young man who avenges the killing of his father by joining the pirates who did it, eventually becoming their leader and leading them into disaster. The simple story allowed for a full array of heroics, much swordplay and swimming, and one memorable stunt in which Fairbanks climbs the rigging of a galleon and then descends the full length of a huge sail by piercing it with his sword and riding the cut all the way down.

Next came *The Gaucho*, with Fairbanks expertly learning to use the Argentine cowboy's version of the lariat—the bola, a devilish contraption composed of three long leather throngs, each with a metal or stone ball on the end. With Fairbanks' bola murderously swishing through the air, no villain had much of a chance of getting away. *The Gaucho* made a profit, but it was far from matching the success of its predecessors. For one thing, it arrived on the market at the time when sound was used in films for the first time. The sound made by Al Jolson's *The Jazz Singer* was pretty elementary, but there was no silencing that crude voice.

In a sly move for something safe and sure to film, Fairbanks returned to Alexandre Dumas. He pro-

With Marguerite de la Motte in *The Iron Mask*

duced *The Iron Mask,* loosely based on the adventures of d'Artagnan and his roistering comrades twenty years after the famous episodes in *The Three Musketeers. The Iron Mask* was a good picture but, as time would tell, a rather sad one because it marked the end of the great Douglas Fairbanks image. For the first time Fairbanks appeared as an older man—he was forty-five at the time and he looked it. The body was still that of an active sportsman, but there was no disguising the thickening features, the slight sag under the chin, and the darkening under the eyes. It was also the first film in which Fairbanks died. Perhaps he realized he was giving up an image: as d'Artagnan dies he sees his already departed old friends Porthos, Athos, and Aramis come toward him from out of the clouds. They laughingly invite him to join them on "the other side" where more adventures lie. The film ends as the spirit of d'Artagnan leaves his body and marches off into the clouds with his fellow cavaliers.

Douglas Fairbanks and Mary Pickford had long thought of making a film together. Now that sound was in, they thought it was a good idea to take an established literary classic and do something of esteem. It was not a good idea. They chose Shakespeare's *The Taming of the Shrew,* something that was beyond the dramatic range of either of them. Fairbanks took a lighthearted approach to the whole thing and never bothered to learn all the lines (perhaps it was beyond him), which he had written on cue cards. His Petrucchio was a scamp rather than a tough shrew-tamer, and Pickford's Kate was a petulant kitten rather than a wild cat—something she openly admits. In fact, no critic was harder on Mary than she herself. She hated the film and said it ruined her career. For all that, the Fairbanks-Pickford version of *The Taming of the Shrew* remains an interesting film museum piece, beautifully mounted and costumed and with one good laugh—not in the body of the film but in the credit titles: the writing credit goes to "William Shakespeare, with additional dialogue by Samuel Taylor." Taylor was the director and possibly a little too close to the project.

The failure of *The Taming of the Shrew* to win wild applause with the moviegoing public hit Fairbanks at a psychologically bad time. Friends had noticed for some time that the famous smiling face had a suggestion of melancholy when not fixed in a smile. The decline of popularity coincided with the arrival of middle age. He had held on to youth longer than any known man, but finally lost it: it

With Mary Pickford in *The Taming of the Shrew*

was a bitter pill to swallow and it might be said he never did swallow it until he was lying on his death bed. In the last ten years of his life, Fairbanks exhausted himself by his refusal to slow down, to quit sports, or to stop staying out late with partying friends.

Fairbanks claimed that picture-making was no longer his main concern. He certainly had no need of income; to the part owner of United Artists the money poured in, and his business managers made other solid investments with it. He made three films during 1931 and 1932—*Reaching for the Moon, Around the World in Eighty Minutes,* and *Mr. Robinson Crusoe,* each more dismal than the last. It was all too obvious that films were no longer his main concern, and people began to ask why he bothered to make them. The only explanation could be that he desperately needed to do *something,* something other than travel, cruise a yacht, play golf, and give parties. What was now also apparent about the man was his restlessness, a certain erraticism, and occasional irritability.

It wasn't until 1930, after ten years of marriage, that Fairbanks made a long trip without taking Mary. He took a sudden trip to Europe, starting

rumors that perhaps all was not well with the ideal couple. His decision to make *Around the World in Eighty Minutes* was also an escape, requiring him to take an extended trip to faraway places to shoot background footage for this glorified travelogue. From then on, the record of his activities shows a man in perpetual motion, obviously driven by some kind of torment. Rumors began to crop up suggesting that he was no longer quite the moral man he used to be. With the implication of love affairs, the relationship between Fairbanks and Pickford grew strained, although there was an emotional tie and an affection that never really died.

By the time he reached his fiftieth birthday in 1933, it was obvious that all was far from well with Fairbanks and his marriage. The famous couple were apart more than they were together, and there were a number of decisions to end the marriage, followed by reconciliations. It seemed that neither wanted to end it, yet neither could hold it together. In mid-1934 Fairbanks was named in London by Lord Ashley as a corespondent in his divorce from young Lady Sylvia Ashley. Fairbanks paid a lot of money to see that the facts in the case were never revealed, but at the end of the year Mary Pickford filed for divorce and received Pickfair as settlement, asking nothing beyond that.

Douglas Fairbanks never became friendly with his namesake son until this period past his peak years. Douglas, Jr. was born in New York on December 9, 1909. Fairbanks was never unkind to the boy, but he candidly admitted he felt no great joy in being a father and was, in fact, rather disappointed that the youngster was fat and dumpy, not the slim and agile little athlete he would have

With Merle Oberon in *The Private Life of Don Juan*

preferred. Ironically, Junior grew to be half a foot taller than his father, and eventually looked even more the dashing cavalier.

The only child of a celebrated film personality might well be expected to behave in a manner different from the norm. In the case of Fairbanks, Jr., the behavior was marked by a measure of bumptiousness, but his personality was generally pleasant and he was kept in line by a strict mother. Beth Sully Fairbanks was, in fact, a woman concerned with social decorum, and she maintained an appearance of affluence that was sometimes not justified by her actual assets. At the time of their divorce, Fairbanks made a settlement of half a million dollars on her and the boy. Had this sum been wisely invested it would have been sufficient for a life style of considerable substance, but Mrs. Fairbanks made an unwise and rather hasty marriage to a stockbroker. Either his judgement or his luck was poor, and much of the Fairbanks money was squandered on falling stocks. The marriage ended after little more than a year.

Fairbanks, Jr., began his transatlantic life at an early age. He was in England and Europe several times as a boy and when, in the early 1920s, his mother's money began to dissipate, she and Junior moved to Paris, where her American dollars allowed for higher living appearances at less cost. She had not been able to admit to Fairbanks, largely because of pride, that much of the settlement money had slipped away. However, by 1923 the strain on her resources was so severe that she gave in to the overtures she had been receiving to allow her son to be used in films. Fairbanks, Jr., had by the age of thirteen reached the height of six feet, and he looked several years older. It was an obvious commercial ploy to capitalize on his name, since his father was by now at the height of his fame with mammothly successful pictures.

The relationship between Douglas Fairbanks and his son had, until the time of the boy's entry into films, been a cool one. Fairbanks had shown no anger or resentment to the boy, but neither had he shown any interest. Junior was eight at the time of his parents' divorce, and once Fairbanks was married to Mary Pickford and making his super-films he saw little of the boy at all. In the summer of 1923 he visited Paris and dropped in to see his son and ex-wife. It was then revealed to him that Junior had had an offer from Hollywood and that it had been accepted. Fairbanks turned almost apoplectic—there were moments in the life of this genial and buoyant man when he showed astonish-

ing flashes of rage and jealousy. Neither Junior nor his mother would admit to financial strain, which left the father to assume that the move was based on ambition. The forty-year-old Fairbanks had managed to conceal his son from the public, as well as giving the impression of being much younger. Thirteen-year-old Junior was too naive to realize he was being exploited and too callow to understand his father's fiercely negative attitude. He was in the strange predicament of having a father who was idolized, hero-worshipped, and imitated by millions of boys, and although he felt much of this admiration himself he could not communicate with the famous man.

Recalls Fairbanks, Jr., "I was starred in a picture called *Stephen Steps Out*. Unfortunately it came out at the same time as my father's *The Thief of Bagdad*, and there couldn't have been a worse comparison in the world. My film was a dreadful dud and so was I. The publicity campaign suddenly disappeared, the talk of a glorious second generation quickly stopped, and I was fired. So we went back to Paris, although I was too innocent to realize how bad I'd been and I was anxious to return to Hollywood. The whole thing, of course, was based on my name, which was both an advantage and disadvantage. At first there was an element of curiosity, but once that curiosity was satisfied, you were on your own. In business, years later, the name was of some value in opening doors, but the door wouldn't stay open very long, and the slamming-shut would be that much harder."

The return to Hollywood in 1924 was motivated by the dire need for income. The fourteen-year-old Douglas was now pushed into the position of earning money to support his mother and several relatives, among them his once wealthy and now impecunious grandfather Daniel Sully. Fairbanks, Sr., had vowed to cut the boy out of his will and to oppose his every attempt to find work in Hollywood. His opposition actually never went further than his speaking contemptuously to anyone who hired the boy. He had no real reason to feel jealous. For two years Junior worked only as a bit player and an extra, and made less money the second year than the first. Junior was nonetheless determined to prove himself; at fifteen he was tall and slim and looked much older; in fact, the first role in which he showed promise was that of the young lover in the 1925 version of *Stella Dallas*, for which it was necessary to wear a pasted-on moustache. He continued playing small parts in numerous pictures, but it was a stage play that brought Junior into focus: the John Van Druten play *Young Woodley*, staged in Los Angeles shortly before his eighteenth birthday. The notices were good and even Senior was impressed; he actually beamed at Mary after one performance and said, "You know, he really can act."

Mary Pickford: "It's not true to say that Douglas didn't love his son. It's just that he was such a boy himself he didn't know how to play the father. Actually the two of them got along quite well after a while, especially when Junior became an active sportsman. Douglas was rather shy about expressing emotion and affection—to anyone; he and Junior got around the father-son relationship by just being friends. They worked out a way of addressing each other—Junior called his father Pete and Douglas called him Jayar, meaning Junior. By the time Douglas died, the two were quite close."

Fairbanks, Jr., was a precocious young man. When Hollywood changed over from silent pictures to talkies in 1929, he was one of the few youngsters able to take advantage of the change. He was cultured beyond his years and although his formal education had been derailed by his career, he had received coaching at the hands of some good tutors. His speaking voice was even then transatlantic, partly due to his anglophilia and his fluency in French. But wisdom cannot be forced onto young shoulders, no matter how worldly the shoulders appear to be, and Junior took himself a wife at the age of nineteen. His bride was Joan Crawford, a few years his senior and equally, if not more, ambitious for success on the screen. Fairbanks, Sr., was opposed to the marriage and tried to warn his son that marriage at that age, and especially between a film actor and a film actress struggling to build their careers, was doomed. Such advice is, of course, never taken. The marriage lasted two years, with young Fairbanks and Crawford parting company on a fairly amicable basis. Crawford has never denied the fact that her ambition made her marriages virtually impossible. During the marriage, she and Fairbanks made only one picture together: *Our Modern Maidens,* a follow-up to her own successful picture *Our Dancing Daughters.*

The film that established Douglas Fairbanks, Jr., as a film actor of some skill and promise was *The Dawn Patrol,* made by First National in 1930. This was the story of the Royal Flying Corps in the First World War, directed by Howard Hawks, who had himself been in the U.S. Army Air Service. It was one of the best of the films dealing with early wartime aviation, and it was remade by Warners eight years later with David Niven playing the part in which Fairbanks had made his mark, that of a carefree young flyer who looks upon aerial warfare as fun and games until his young brother is assigned to the same squadron and shot down the next day. Richard Barthelmess played the harried flight commander, the role that Errol Flynn did in the remake.

The Dawn Patrol brought young Fairbanks a term contract with Warner Brothers. He appeared in six films a year over the next three years, but only a few were anything other than routine product. He played in *Little Caesar* with Edward G. Robinson, *Parachute Jumper* with Bette Davis, and he was loaned to RKO to appear with Katherine Hepburn in *Morning Glory.* Neither Warners nor Fairbanks was eager to pick up the option on the contract, and it was terminated in 1933.

After his divorce from Joan Crawford, Fairbanks, Jr., became more friendly with his father, and they made their first long trip together in the spring of 1933. Senior had long been friendly with the royal family and a wide selection of London socialites and entertainment celebrities. On this trip he introduced his son to this milieu, and the son took to it like a duck to water. One of Junior's first royal friendships was with the Duke of Kent, a friendship that was tragically ended with the Duke's death in an airplane crash during the Second World War. Young Fairbanks later became an intimate of Lord and Lady Mountbatten, which assured access to Saint James' Palace and Buckingham Palace. His father also introduced him to Noel Coward, and that assured access to almost anything.

Aside from the opportunity it gave father and son to get to know each other better, the trip to Europe had business reasons. Junior had decided that acting wasn't enough, that being part of the production of films was of far more interest and challenge. In this he was supported by his father, and they both went to see Alexander Korda to speak of setting up an association between Korda and United Artists. Korda had scored a hit with his *The Private Lives of Henry VIII,* in which Charles Laughton threw bones over his shoulder with great style. The meetings were auspicious, and plans were laid for future productions. Sadly, the results were dismal. In 1934 both the Fairbanks returned to London to work on Korda productions. Senior starred in *The Private Life of Don Juan,* but all that he proved was his inability to revive the spark of old. Some critics were rude enough to

Fairbanks, Jr. in *The Dawn Patrol;* at right is costar Richard Barthelmess.

suggest that he looked like a tired American businessman on a binge. The film was ill-timed; by now the crumbling of his marriage to Mary Pickford was widely known, and it was more than rumored that the former paragon of virtue had become something of a roué. Fairbanks was wise enough to see that his *Don Juan* was an unflattering mirror, and he never appeared on film again. Shortly afterwards, Junior's Korda picture emerged: *Catherine the Great*, with Elizabeth Bergner in the title role and Junior as Peter III of Russia. He did well in the difficult role of an addled monarch, but the film was not a favorite with the public.

Fairbanks, Jr., found London, especially high society, more and more to his liking, and he decided to make it his home, at least for a while. His professional activities during 1934, 1935, and 1936

In *Catherine the Great*

brought him just about enough money to enjoy life among the English aristocrats and theatrical circles but little in the way of career advancements. He made the gossip columns fairly regularly in the company of attractive ladies, especially Gertrude Lawrence, with whom he made one film, *Mimi*. He also did two stage plays. Fairbanks tried to follow through on his plans to become a film producer by setting up a company which made four films, all starring himself: *The Amateur Gentleman, Accused, Jump for Glory,* and *Storm Over London*. Only the first made its money back, and after the fourth he and his partners threw in the towel.

The next step up in the Fairbanks, Jr., career came by way of Hollywood. Early in 1937 he received a telephone call from David O. Selznick asking him if he would be interested in the role of Rupert of Hentzau in *The Prisoner of Zenda*. Fairbanks turned to his father for advice and was promptly told that he should accept the part with the greatest possible speed. Junior was loath to give up his life as a gay blade in London society, but he knew it was a life-style that might well begin to buckle unless his career picked up. By now he was seeing a lot of his father, whose restlessness had resulted in his shuttling between Hollywood and London via New York and many other places. Senior married the former Lady Sylvia Ashley in March of 1936 and for the remainder of his life he kept up a destructive pace of travel, entertaining, business meetings, late nights and early mornings. Not surprisingly, his heart began to give clear signs of stress. Blindly, or perhaps with cavalier abandon, he referred to his cardiac problems as the result of indigestion and did nothing to help himself.

The Prisoner of Zenda—Selznick's 1937 version— was a beautiful piece of action-and-costume filming. It was Ruritania unfolded in all its supposed romance, courage, and splendor, and in playing the part of Rupert, Fairbanks, Jr., finally did what he had been scrupulously avoiding—played the kind of swashbuckling role made famous by his father. He had been denying himself and the public too long. Here was the one kind of film acting to which Junior was best suited by virtue of looks and personality and inheritance; it is, perhaps ironically, the only film image for which he is likely to be remembered, despite his attempts at other forms. Fairbanks, Jr., was Rupert to perfection—the cavalier with a twinkle in his eye, the wicked, roguish adventurer, a devil with the ladies and a demon with the saber.

Junior's role in *Zenda* was a secondary one, in support of Ronald Colman and Madeleine Carroll, but the impression he made was strong and immediate. It seemed to the Hollywood Establishment that the twenty-six year old playboy-actor had now jelled into a viable property. Parts in good productions were offered as never before and in 1938 Fairbanks, Jr., earned $200,000 playing leads opposite Irene Dunne in *The Joy of Living*, Ginger Rogers in *Having Wonderful Time*, Danielle Darrieux in *The Rage of Paris*, and Janet Gaynor in *The Young in Heart*.

Historical circumstances began altering the tone of Fairbanks, Jr.'s career in 1939. He made no secret of his ardent love of Britain and his concern for her security and what to him seemed like sure signs of approaching war. He also—and this is something that cast a shadow over his popularity—began making noises about America's future in the event of war, a future he felt should be unequivocally allied to Britain's. To this end he sought parts in films of an obviously pro-British character, some of them flagrantly so. His three 1939 films might well have led Americans to believe Douglas Fairbanks, Jr., had taken out British citizenship: *Gunga Din, The Sun Never Sets,* and *Rulers of the Waves*.

Gunga Din was a rollicking mixture of Kipling's poem about the Indian water boy who yearned to be a soldier, and Kipling's *Soldiers Three*. Fairbanks, Cary Grant and Victor McLaglen played British Army sergeants with more the flavor of Dumas than Kipling. An excellent picture of its kind, it remains amusing and exciting—except to Indians, who rightly criticize the ease with which three English cavaliers polish off hordes of their

With Cary Grant in *Gunga Din*

With Arthur Mulliner, Mary Forbes, John Burton,
Barbara O'Neil, Basil Rathbone, C. Aubrey Smith, and
Virginia Field in *The Sun Never Sets*

brethren. In the first year of its showing, *Gunga Din* also met with some American criticism, especially from isolationists who carped at Hollywood's waving of the Union Jack.

The Sun Never Sets could hardly have been more pro-British had it been made in London instead of the Universal backlot in Hollywood. The film concerned a family long devoted to the Colonial Service of the British government. The patriarch of the family is that personification of all that the Empire stood for—Sir C. Aubrey Smith. His grandsons, Basil Rathbone and Fairbanks, proceed to the Gold Coast of Africa to assume their duties as ministers of His Majesty's justice. They also proceed to outwit Fascists and overthrow a Fascist plot to plunge the world into war.

Rulers of the Sea told the story of British ship engineer John Shaw and his designing of a steam engine for transatlantic navigation. Paramount brought Will Fyffe to Hollywood to play Shaw, with Fairbanks as David Gillespie, the sailor who worked with Shaw to bring about the first steam crossing from Britain to America in 1838. The film brought an official protest from the American National Maritime Commission, who felt that the producers had slighted the merchant marine traditions of their own country by filming a biased account of nautical history.

The year 1939 was a memorable one for Douglas Fairbanks, Jr. Quite apart from his filmmaking, there was the advent of world war, which whetted his interest more than anything else. International politics and diplomacy stimulated the younger Fairbanks. A romanticist at heart, he felt a sense of fulfillment in involving himself in affairs of state, particularly in drumming up American support for Britain at a time when isolationism was a powerful force in American thinking. But there were two personal events of importance for him in 1939—his marriage to Virginia aristocrat Mary Lee Hartford, and the death of his father.

Mary Lee Hartford had married Huntington Hartford, the heir to the A & P grocery store chain, when she was eighteen. The young couple were popular ornaments among the social enclaves of American wealth, but after a few years it was apparent that their marriage lacked any wealth other than money, and they separated. The union of Douglas, Jr., and Mary Lee was enthusiastically blessed by Douglas, Sr. He even welcomed the news that he was to become a grandfather. He and his son now spoke of going into business together.

But Senior never lived to fulfill the plans or to see a grandchild. The Great Cavalier of the Silent Screen had literally worn himself out by his refusal to live quietly or even to get enough sleep. Periods of black despondency and melancholy dogged him in his last years, and his only means of fighting them was to run faster. His death was the final oddity in an odd life. The most hyperactive and gregarious man Hollywood had ever known died peacefully and alone in his fifty-seventh year, feeling exhausted. He took to his bed on December 11, 1939 at his beach house in Santa Monica, attended only by a male nurse. Around midnight, the nurse entered the room to check on the dozing Fairbanks, who then awoke and asked that the window be opened so he could hear the sea. The nurse asked him how he felt and Fairbanks replied with a smile, "I've never felt better." When the nurse looked in a little later, he found Fairbanks dead. Perhaps if he'd returned a few moments earlier he might have seen the ghostly figures of Porthos, Athos, and Aramis inviting an old comrade to join them in the Great Beyond.

Fairbanks, Jr., shares some of his father's characteristics, certainly the romanticism and the love of pageantry, but whereas Senior's whole life was centered around films and athletics, Junior's is not. He says, "I never was a great actor and I never will be because it doesn't interest me all that much. I soon realized that I was limited as an actor because I couldn't really interpret a part—I could play it on skill and experience but an Olivier I could never be; his kind of subtle probing and

exposing of a character is beyond me. My kind of acting relied on the creative interpretation of other people, the director, the editor, the lighting, and after a while the whole thing began to embarrass me."

The war years 1940 and 1941 saw Fairbanks, Jr., more engaged in politics than films. He appeared in *Green Hell, Safari, Angels Over Broadway*, and *The Corsican Brothers* during these two years but he also appeared many times in Washington, D.C. to see President Roosevelt and high officials about support for Britain. The Fairbanks pictures had been banned in Germany and Italy due to their obvious disdain for Fascism and their tub-thumping for the British; there was also evidence of disdain for Fairbanks himself in the United States. Isolationists labeled him a British stooge and a dangerous propagandist, and several Hollywood producers advised him to tone down his remarks. The advice was totally ignored. He relished the role of crusader for Anglo-American cooperation. He collected thousands of signatures on petitions imploring the government to lift the arms embargo and to rescind the Neutrality Act in order to overtly aid Britain. He gave speeches on the need for involvement and the danger of a world in which "Britain is no longer a great power." Fairbanks also backed his words with money, and sent funds to friends in England to set up three small convalescent hospitals for RAF personnel.

Together with Ronald Colman and Charles Boyer, Fairbanks helped found the Franco-British War Relief, with the funds from their stage productions in Los Angeles being sent to various agencies to aid refugees and evacuees. He was frequently heard on the radio in interviews and talks outlining his belief in the need for American backing of Britain, for a lend-lease program, and for the supplying of armaments. He also described his own meetings with prominent Nazis and Fascists in Europe, in which they told him of their plans for world domination, including the take-over of America. The broadcasts brought praise from some and vilification from others. Evidence of Fairbanks' direct involvement with Roosevelt's plans to support the British came in a letter the actor received from Sumner Welles in January of 1941, inviting him to undertake a propaganda mission to South America. The letter read, in part:

The mission would ostensibly be a mission to investigate in a broad way the effects on public opinion in the other American republics of American motion pictures. In reality your mission would be directed principally toward getting in touch with certain national groups in some of the larger countries to the south which are now believed to be veering toward Nazi ideology.

Fairbanks accepted the offer with alacrity. Prior to leaving on the mission he applied for a commission in the United States Naval Reserve, and when he returned two months later the uniform of a lieutenant (j.g.) was ready and waiting to be donned. Before joining the service, Fairbanks was required to give broadcasts and lectures on the success of the South American tour. Some of the criticism was acid; one wag wondered if perhaps the White House had any plans for utilizing the services of the Marx Brothers.

Fairbanks delayed his entry into the navy in order to make one more film. His funds had been strained by his nonprofit crusading—the generous financial inheritance from his father would be a long time in litigation—and he felt he should make an obviously commercial film. *The Corsican Brothers* was his first blatant effort to cash in on the great Fairbanks image of sword-flashing gallantry and costume heroics. Not surprisingly it turned out to be his biggest money-making picture. The film was a loose version of the Dumas tale of two brothers of royal blood—one good and one mean—who grow up to be enemies. Fairbanks played both brothers and, with the aid of trick photography, good brother Mario was able to dispose of bad brother Lucien. Akim Tamiroff was the evil dictator who had to be stopped, and Fairbanks stopped him with a rapier. Their duel is among the best in the annals of movie swordplay,

With Henry Brandon in *The Corsican Brothers*

thanks to the staging and doubling of fencing master Fred Cavens and his son Albert.

The involvement with politics and diplomacy was not a newfound interest on the part of Douglas Fairbanks, Jr. "It might have seemed like that to some people in those early war years, but I actually began studying political and social economics when I was seventeen. One of my tutors was an old gentleman who had been a consultant to President Wilson and had been with him at Versailles. He sparked my interest, and because I travelled a great deal I was able to apply the knowledge to what I saw firsthand. The business and diplomatic world had always fascinated me, partly I suppose because I was brought up on both sides of the Atlantic."

After finishing *The Corsican Brothers* Fairbanks reported for duty with the U.S. Navy, but not before entertaining and playing host for several weeks to his friend Lord Louis Mountbatten, himself in need of a little rest after two years with the Royal Navy. Fairbanks appealed to President Roosevelt during a weekend as a White House guest for a liaison appointment with the Department of Information. Roosevelt recommended it but the Navy turned it down. It was an indication of many moments of embarrassment Fairbanks would suffer with the Navy as a junior officer with very high connections. Many a ranking regular officer would resent the lieutenant from Hollywood and his acquaintance with the Commander in Chief.

After basic training, Fairbanks reported for duty aboard the flagship of the Atlantic fleet, the U.S.S. *Mississippi*, then engaged in escorting British convoys to the 600-mile limit and sometimes beyond. This was one of the measures he and others like him had suggested be instituted as aid to Britain. There were uneasy moments when newspaper photographers spotted him at the various ports at which the ship docked. The captain asked him if he had hired a press agent. The touchiest time of all was one evening when he was the officer of the watch and the film shown to the crew turned out to be *The Corsican Brothers*. "I was curious to see it because I left the studio before it was put together. But these were not the ideal circumstances for a movie hero to sit and watch his mock heroics, not with the crew yelling things like 'Go get 'em, sailor!' and 'Kill him, Doug!'"

After America's entry into the Second World War, Fairbanks was transferred to the Bureau of Ordnance in Washington for an intelligence and public relations assignment. Now he was caused embarrassment by congressmen asking why he was not on active service. After several months of this kind of agitation, the Navy decided to get Fairbanks out of Washington and to sea—the North Sea. He was assigned to the U.S.S. *Washington,* the flagship of the fleet assigned for patrol duty. Fairbanks tried to make himself inconspicuous, but one day at Scapa Flow, King George VI was inspecting the British fleet and accepted an invitation to inspect the *Washington.* On board the American ship, the king was about to walk down the line of officers when he spotted Fairbanks. He then marched straight over to him and said, "Good Heavens, what are you doing here? I haven't seen you since we played golf at Sandringham." As the two shook hands, a press photographer took the picture that quickly appeared in hundreds of British and American newspapers. The amiable monarch then proceeded to greet the captain and his staff.

Fairbanks was next transferred to the cruiser *Wichita,* one of the two American warships assigned to guard the convoy runs to Murmansk, a duty not likely to be forgotten by anyone who took part. The weather was almost always appalling and frequently an arctic nightmare. Recalls Fairbanks, "I was with what became the most disastrous convoy of the war. We started out with thirty-four ships and we lost twenty-six of them before we reached Murmansk. It was a wicked experience because there was little chance for survival in that icy water. Two of our own observers on the *Wichita* fell overboard and they were dead before we could fish them out."

Fairbanks's next adventure came in June of 1942 when Lord Louis Mountbatten asked him to join his Combined Operations headquarters in London. It was a cloak and dagger job for which Mountbatten clearly knew Fairbanks was suitable. The newly organized Chemical Warfare and Deception Department had to invent means and methods of camouflage and subterfuge for raids on enemy territory. His movie-honed imagination proved useful in devising deceptive tactics for parachute drops behind enemy lines, beach landings, and commando raids. A year of this sort of skulduggery assured Fairbanks a part in the North Africa landings. He later took part in the invasion of Sicily and received the Silver Star for bravery in combat, the first Hollywood celebrity to be so decorated. He also took part in the capture of Elba and Corsica; at one point in that operation, when his commander asked for air transportation, an

RAF officer queried the request: "Why, are we to help Fairbanks find his Corsican brother?" But lightly as he may have been taken by some fellow officers, Fairbanks was awarded the croix de guerre by the French government for his participation in the battle to regain Elba, and the Distinguished Service Cross by the British in recognition of his bravery during the invasion of the south of France. With the war in the Mediterranean at an end, Fairbanks was transferred to a desk job in Washington.

Fairbanks spent the last eighteen months of his service with the Strategic Plans Division of the Navy Department. He resumed his acquaintance with President Roosevelt and was several times invited to the White House, although he was advised to make his entry by the back door and as inconspicuously as possible, "as snide comments were again being made by the high brass about the movie star lieutenant commander. Similar comments were made whenever Fairbanks and his wife entertained weekend guests at her home in Virginia, especially when the guests were people like the Duke and Duchess of Windsor, admirals, and prominent politicians. Admired as he was in certain circles, in others he was not. Fairbanks to his detractors was a glory-hound, a taker of advantages, a publicity-seeker and a lover of pomp. Quite possibly he was a little of all these things, while possessing also some very positive qualities. He was, so to speak, to the manner born, and he has carried off his life-style with the happy assurance of a man who knows who and what he is. A close friend says, "Doug likes everything he sees, and he's seen everything."

Fairbanks's active naval service ended in February of 1946, when he was transferred to the reserves. His rank of Commander was upped to Captain by the Act of Congress that specified that officers who had been decorated for bravery in combat should be promoted when retiring from active to reserve duty.

By the time Fairbanks returned to Hollywood, most of the other stars who had served in uniform had already returned, and the cheering for returning heroes had echoed away. Friends advised him not to appear in uniform and not to make any display of his medals. After an absence of five years, Fairbanks was dubious about resuming his film career. He had thought seriously of a diplomatic career, but, somewhat to his surprise, several generous offers came from Hollywood. Fairbanks needed employment, since most of the money left

With Walter Slezak and Anthony Quinn in *Sinbad the Sailor*

Sinbad the Sailor is a fanciful romp into the days of the Caliphs of Bagdad, when Sinbad was making his voyages into the unknown waters of the Indies. In this version Sinbad relates the adventures of his eighth voyage, this one in search of the island containing the riches left by Alexander the Great. The much-grinning, much-leaping Fairbanks looked perfectly at home in this lavish, colorful vehicle, so obviously set in the direction of his father's trail.

The Exile was both written and produced by Fairbanks, who here starred himself as Charles II during the time of the young monarch's exile in Holland. He manages to ward off the Roundheads who are sent to dispatch him because of pretentions to the British throne, and to survive until he is called to London to take up the crown. Unfortunately, he has to leave behind his lovely Dutch girl friend, played by Paula Croset. According to Fairbanks, Charles II must have been a likable lad.

him by his father had been dispersed in support of his family during the war years and in support of many non-paying political activities and charities. Not surprisingly, Hollywood's interest in Fairbanks lay in the heroic image—the image of dashing adventurer conjured up by the family name and bolstered by his own war record and his own breezy manner. This return to stardom would only succeed if he surrendered to this image. Fairbanks made four films in Hollywood in 1946, 1947, and 1948, each a costume fantasy, each well-done, and yet the returns were not large enough to certify him as bankable security.

With Betty Grable in *That Lady in Ermine*

With Henry Daniell and Robert Coote in *The Exile*

That Lady in Ermine was an interesting flop, the last film made by the great Ernst Lubitsch. He died before it was finished and Otto Preminger stepped in to complete it. The story should have been made years before, when the famed Lubitsch touch was still magical. Here the fantasy fails to jell: Fairbanks appears as a romantic young officer of a Hungarian army invading northern Italy in 1861, who billets himself in the ancestral home of countess Betty Grable and falls in love with her, even though he knows they are enemies and the romance is doomed.

With Tom Moore in *The Fighting O'Flynn*

For *The Fighting O'Flynn* again Fairbanks was the producer, this time sharing a writing credit. Light on plot but heavy on swordplay, fisticuffs, riding, and romancing, the story tells of a legendary Irishman who involves himself in a conspiracy to outwit Napoleon's plans to invade the British Isles. Fairbanks cavorted in great bounds of energy and enthusiasm, but neither he nor the film made much of an impression on the public.

By the beginning of 1949 it was clear to Fairbanks that his career as a movie star was largely over. Acting in front of cameras had long ceased to fascinate him, and he was increasingly interested in film production. It was also clear that public taste had been drastically altered during the war years and that television would bring enormous changes in the film industry. International politics continued to dazzle Fairbanks: in these postwar years he was active on behalf of the United States, the Marshall Plan, and particularly the

Cooperative for American Remittances to Europe (CARE). Admirable though these efforts might have been, they also contributed to Fairbanks's alienation from Hollywood, supporting the industry's belief that he was somewhat apart from them and too detached from the average movie-goer.

Something happened in March of 1949 that sealed the impression of Fairbanks as a man apart. He received word from the British Embassy in Washington that he had been made an honorary Knight Commander of the Order of the British Empire. The jeering section could snidely refer to him as Sir Douglas, although as an American citizen he could not use the title. For Fairbanks it was, of course, the crowning citation of them all. Ordinarily, Americans so honored—and there have been several dozen—are invested by the British Ambassador in Washington. But Fairbanks hedged on this; he was about to go to London to make a film for Alexander Korda, and he wanted to receive the insignia of the order from the king himself. This was not protocol, but neither was Fairbanks the average honorary knight: this was one knight with a line to the top. His request was granted although, as an American, the King could only make the investiture informally in a private chamber in Buckingham Palace. The honor was clearly a recognition of Fairbanks's efforts on behalf of Britain in 1940 and 1941, but the thirteen paragraphs of the citation listed his many Anglo-American enterprises, including his work for CARE and the Marshall Plan.

Fairbanks made *State Secret,* a good espionage movie for Alexander Korda, and it was released early in 1950. By now Fairbanks had decided to make London his base, and he purchased an impressive residence in The Boltons, a fashionable Kensington address, for himself, his wife, and their three daughters. The house would see an array of celebrated guests with the passing of the years, including Her Majesty the Queen and Prince Philip. Fairbanks loves entertaining, and he obviously loves to entertain on the highest social strata. He does it with aplomb and ease.

The publicity given Fairbanks's social activity in London tended to give the impression that he had renounced America. Such was not the case. His life now became even more transatlantic, with a constant shuttling between London and New York. He maintained offices in both cities, and worked not only for himself but also for other people in both cities. His last starring role in a feature film was in the 1953 *Mr. Drake's Duck,* a tepid comedy and a feeble last film for any actor. But Fairbanks was too busy to notice. He was involved in the production of a number of films, but by the end of 1952 he had set up his own company to produce films for television. "Douglas Fairbanks Presents" was a popular and profitable series for some years, enabling Fairbanks to make other investments and to continue his multifarious activities in the business world.

The Fairbanks name has been listed on a bewildering number of British and American committees and companies over the past twenty years, leaving onlookers wondering how one man can be so involved and yet remain apparently calm. He admits: "I don't worry too much. If things go well, fine. If they don't, then like Scarlett O'Hara I say I'll worry about that tomorrow. I think the greatest difficulty in dealing with a number of things is to be not *too* concerned about them."

Douglas Fairbanks, Jr., proved that bearing a famous name was not, for him, a burden. That he has been unusually lucky he will not deny. His intelligence has been greater than his talent, and he has been blessed with energy and humour. He says of himself: "I don't take life or myself all that seriously."

Fairbanks' medals and his citations please him but they don't blind him. I politely alluded to his distinctions, such as the rank of captain in the U.S. Naval Reserve. "Don't be too impressed. I never let myself forget the story of the old boy who bought himself a yacht and put on a blue uniform with four stripes and stood before his wife. 'Look, I'm a captain.' She replied, 'Darling, to me you're a captain. To the children you're a captain. To the crew you're a captain. But to a captain are you a captain?'"

2

JOHN BARRYMORE

A PHOTOGRAPH of John Barrymore taken when he was four years old shows a dreamy-eyed little boy with his right eyebrow slightly raised, giving him a simewhat quizzical, faraway look. It was an expression that stayed with him for life. Barrymore may or may not have been the greatest American actor of his time, but he was one of the most individual of human beings, grandly so and sadly so. Barrymore was a supreme romantic of great sensitivity and intelligence, yet a Rabelaisian roisterer who seemed to despise his gifts. He was magic and tragic.

Both John and his brother Lionel became actors because it was the family trade and because they couldn't make a good enough living at anything else. Only sister Ethel looked upon acting as a dignified craft. Lionel's ambition was to become an artist, and at the age of twenty-seven he gave up his acting career to spend four years studying art in Paris. On returning to New York he found it impossible to make money painting and drawing, and he reluctantly returned to the stage. He summarily said goodbye to the theatre when the movies beckoned because the work was easier and the pay better. For the remainder of his long life he cavorted before the cameras in order to subsidize his greater interests in painting, etching, and composing music. Lionel did in fact garner a small reputation as an artist, and some of his canvases brought good money. A few of his compositions were played by symphony orchestras although, with gruff modesty, he doubted that they would have been played if the composer's name had not been Barrymore.

John was far less successful as an artist than Lionel, mainly because he had much less talent

John Barrymore as Don Juan

but also because he was much less pragmatic. John's drawings were the product of a fanciful mind, a psychiatrist might have considered them the product of a wandering, convoluted mind. He was romantic in the true Byronic sense and also in a purely amorous sense—yet none of his drawings reveal any eroticism. Instead, what John Barrymore revealed with his sketches was the darker side of his nature—a subtle morbidity and a hint of madness. At one time late in his life, when he considered playing *King Lear,* he did a line and wash color drawing of himself in the part. The face of his Lear is that of an aged, fear-haunted man with deep sorrow in his bloodshot eyes.

Barrymore's concern with madness stemmed from the death of his father. Maurice Barrymore—actually his name was Herbert Blythe and he invented the other name when he decided to become an actor—was an Englishman born in India. He was a strikingly handsome man with a sense of bravura; he dressed fashionably and spoke elegantly, and it was said of him that he was a swaggering dandy. Maurice Barrymore was, however, not a dandy to be joshed: he was an amateur lightweight boxing champion and a man of courage, as was proven on one occasion in a Texas saloon when he stood up to an armed bully and received a bullet in his shoulder. This was in 1879, four years after his arrival in America and three years after his marriage to actress Georgia Drew, of the renowned American theatrical family.

The parents of Lionel, Ethel, and John Barrymore acted together and separately for various theatrical companies, and the children were more often than not left in the company of the grandparents, Mr. and Mrs. John Drew, probably the two best-loved actors of their time. Mrs. Drew—Louisa Lane before her marriage—was a woman of great character and influence, and adored by her grandson John, who called her Mum Mum. He was more attached to his grandmother than to any other human being in his life, and the emotional consequences of her death when he was fifteen can only be guessed. The probable trauma was doubtlessly aggravated by the death of his mother just three years previously: Georgia had died at thirty-six after a long fight against consumption. Said Lionel many years later, "Jack never felt safe anywhere after Mum Mum died."

Georgia Drew Barrymore was a woman of wit and humor, a respected comedienne. John resembled her in looks and inherited her wit, but in temperament he resembled his cavalier father. Both men had talent and curiosity and both quickly became bored with their achievements. Lionel summed them up: "On stage they were brilliant and poised. Offstage, they invariably stumbled and barked their shins." In 1903 Maurice Barrymore, then fifty-six, suffered a mental breakdown and was taken to Bellevue Hospital in New York where he was diagnosed as having an incipiently para-

lyzed mind. On the pretext of being taken to fulfill a theater engagement, he was taken to a sanitarium in Amityville, New York, where he died two years later. John Barrymore never referred to his father's illness and neither did anyone else who understood John. But an actor, visiting Barrymore in a theater dressing room after a performance, made the tactless mistake of asking him if it was true that his father had died insane. Barrymore turned ashen and in a choked voice said, "I am now going to kill you—you miserable, low, stupid son of a bitch." The other actor made the quickest possible retreat.

Barrymore's capacity for alcohol and his appetite for women were subjects that merited as much attention during his lifetime as his genius for acting. He began drinking at the age of fifteen, and it was at about the same time that he experienced his first sexual adventure with a woman. Unfortunately, perhaps, the woman was his father's mistress, reputed to be ardently sensual. It was noted, some years later, that his scenes as *Hamlet* with his mother, the Queen, were markedly oedipal. Drawn to women though he was (and they to him), he could not maintain a relationship with one. He could neither stay away from them or stay with them. His four marriages all ended because of his indifference, and although he was obsessive about fidelity on the part of his wives, he was himself flagrantly adulterous. But for all his errors and mistakes, Barrymore was an endearing man, capricious rather than malicious, and he was loved and helped by many devoted friends. In fact, Barrymore would never have become famous had it not been for the concern of certain people who forced him to take himself seriously, and who dragged out of him qualities that he hadn't the interest to drag out himself. Barrymore's alert mind was intrigued by books, prints, antiques, ornithology, and wild life, but he never at any time expressed delight with acting, not even in his last years, a time when most actors eulogize their heydays.

One of the friends who dragged Barrymore to fame was the English actress and director Constance Collier, who persuaded him to try *Peter Ibbetson* in 1917 and later helped him stage his *Hamlet* in London. She said: "He was the greatest of all the actors I ever saw. He had a wild soul and no one could discipline him. He had something in his eye, an almost mystic light, that only men of genius have."

It took quite some time for John Barrymore to

reveal anything about himself that suggested genius. After the death of his grandmother he was sent to England in an attempt to bolster his education. He spent a year at King's College, Wimbledon, with no scholastic distinction, and much of the next year at the Slade School of Art. He returned to America in 1899, determined to continue his study of art. He was being supported by his family, who were pleased to see—probably for the first time—evidence of a capacity for hard work and devotion to an interest. Barrymore later worked for several newspapers in New York as an illustrator, but his habits were erratic and his drawings too personal and subjective to allow any real success. The last editor for whom he worked suggested that since all the members of his family were actors he might well follow suit.

It was Ethel who first saw signs of acting ability in John, although his initial appearance with her gave no reason to think she was right. He took over for an ailing actor in Philadelphia in Ethel's hit play *Captain Jinks of the Horse Marines,* and made a fool of himself. The next night the ailing actor was back in his part. Young Barrymore was advised by the stage manager that he might have a future as a comedian if he could acquire a little discipline.

John applied himself to the theater with reluctance, or perhaps with desperation, as the theater was his only possible means of making money. Money was then, and to some extent always would be, a problem for him because he was casual and careless. He played a role in a Chicago play in the summer of 1903 and made his New York debut in December of that year in a play called, most appropriately, *Glad Of It*. It still remained for others to assess his talent. The first person to get Barrymore started was an old friend of the family, comedian Willie Collier. When Collier was signed for the lead in *The Dictator,* a play by Richard Harding Davis, he suggested Barrymore for one of the supporting roles. This kept the errant young actor employed for more than two years, by the end of which time Barrymore had realized a good living could be made from what he was doing. Collier was his mentor and his coach in this first decade of the twentieth century.

By 1910 Barrymore was established as a stage actor with a talent for light comedy and an attraction to the ladies. This was the year of his first marriage. Katherine Corri Harris was one of the many young ladies smitten with the handsome, dashing actor. She was young, beautiful, and a product of New York's high society; it was easy for the amorous Barrymore to fall in love with such a divine creature. All Barrymore wives and girl friends were loved with poetic passion, at least to begin with. What Katherine quickly found out after their marriage was that Barrymore in person was different from Barrymore on stage. She wanted to be seen with him at parties and dances, but he didn't want to be seen in public at all. Once off the stage, Barrymore retreated and became reclusive. He preferred to spend his spare time carousing with friends in shady saloons, or visiting the animals in the zoo. It was noted he had an unusual rapport with animals, especially birds. Many of his haunts and habits appalled the innocent young Mrs. Barrymore, and she was understandably upset when he disappeared for long periods of time without explaining himself.

The marriage to Katherine lasted, or endured, for seven years. Miserable as he may have been as a husband, these were the years of growth for his career. His Broadway plays made him a popular figure, and his popularity was no doubt aided by his reputation as a heavy drinker, his amours, and his bizarre interests. The next important person to step into Barrymore's life and alter its course was a serious young playwright named Edward Sheldon. Sheldon watched Barrymore's performances and saw something beyond the flamboyantly mannered comedian. The two became friends and in 1914 went off on a trip to Europe together, in the course of which Sheldon persuaded the actor to take his career more seriously.

The first evidence of John Barrymore's new attitude toward the theater came when he appeared in *Justice* by John Galsworthy, playing the tragic role of an innocent man condemned to prison. Sheldon had located the play and persuaded a producer to stage it with Barrymore. From then on there was no doubt in the minds of the critics that he was an actor of unusual ability. Sheldon set about writing a play specifically for Barrymore but in the meantime came across another vehicle that he thought would be even better than his own work—*Peter Ibbetson,* a dramatization by John Raphael of the novel by George du Maurier, the grandfather of Daphne. The English play had been brought to America by its champion, actress Constance Collier, who had had no luck persuading any New York producer to touch it. The play was serious and complicated in structure, involving unchronological time sequences revealing instances in the life of a man who had died. Collier happened to discuss the play with Sheldon, who saw its possibilities and set about rewriting it for Barrymore. It opened in April of 1917, ran for seventy-one performances, then went on a long tour.

John Barrymore's film career began in 1914. Between then and 1920 he appeared in twelve movies, all of them made in New York and all of them light comedies of no lasting worth. In these films Barrymore was, like Harold Lloyd, a nice young man getting mixed up in silly adventures. Barrymore hammed the parts and did pratfalls worthy of Charlie Chaplin. For the record:

1914: *An American Citizen*
1915: *The Dictator*
　　　Are You a Mason?
　　　Incorrigible Dukane
1916: *Nearly a King*
　　　The Lost Bridegroom
　　　The Man From Mexico
　　　The Red Widow
1917: *Raffles*
1918: *On the Quiet*
1919: *Here Comes the Bride*
　　　The Test of Honor
1920: *Dr. Jekyll and Mr. Hyde*

Barrymore's attitude toward films was much the same as his attitude toward the stage. He later looked back on these early movies and confessed he had overacted in order to amuse the crews, with results that were, as he said, "woeful and unreal." But in time he would even have to take films seriously. By a coincidence, his first truly creative piece of film acting, as Dr. Jekyll and Mr. Hyde, was made the same time as his triumph as a stage actor of recognized genius, as Richard III. The year was 1920. By now he was thirty-eight and more than halfway through his life; again he had reached a plateau of his career through the guidance and insistence of friends.

One of the people responsible for Barrymore's success was the great critic Alexander Woollcott, who was one of many anxious to enlist Barrymore's considerable talents in an effort to bring lasting prestige to the American stage. A major step forward in that plan was the staging of *Richard III* with Barrymore creating a stunning portrayal of the evil, hunchbacked monarch, moving across the stage like a malevolent black spider. A theory once prevailed, that not to have seen Barrymore on stage as Richard III or as Hamlet was not truly to have understood why the man lingered in the minds of those who did or why he became a legend.

Another person who had great influence on John Barrymore was a poetess who called herself Michael Strange. When she met him in 1917, she was the wife of blueblood diplomat Leonard M. Thomas. She herself was from the social upper crust, a handsome and dynamic woman who joined the league of Barrymore boosters and went one step further than the others by marrying him. By the time of their marriage, August of 1920, Barrymore had agreed, after her considerable encouragement, to play *Richard,* and he was tired from the strain of the hard preparations for the role and from making films at the same time. He would be tired for much of his marriage with Michael Strange because their love was of the tempestuous kind and their many arguments were long and furious.

Barrymore overcame a serious deficiency in his ability as an actor when he accepted the role of Richard. His voice had never been trained for the demands of Shakespeare; it had a rasp to it, and his diction was poor. Fortunately, one of the people interested in promoting his career was Margaret Carrington, sister of Walter Huston and the leading voice coach in New York. With her diagnosis and training Barrymore cultivated the speaking voice that later became one of his most famous assets. He did it in six weeks of concentrated study, mastering breath control and elocution. Mrs. Carrington claimed it was the most amazing feat within her knowledge. With his newfound vocal power and his own fascination with the character, Barrymore gave an electrifying performance as Richard. By now he was an actor of astonishing stage presence, and with the appearance of his film *Dr. Jekyll and Mr. Hyde* it was clear that he could similarly communicate on film. His *Jekyll and Hyde* remains fascinating because he managed to do with face contortions and lighting what later actors achieved only with grotesque makeup.

Seven months after her marriage to Barrymore Michael Strange gave birth to a daughter, Diana. Diana would die thirty-eight years later, having tried and failed to gain fame as an actress, instead gaining notoriety as a drunk. It was tragic and ironic that the love child of two gifted, artistic people should end her own life in such misery. Barrymore could not prevent his own torment from passing to his daughter. Whatever the torment was, it eventually destroyed his marriage to the strong-minded poetess. Perhaps they were both a little too Herculean to coexist peacefully.

It was Ethel Barrymore who hooked John on the idea of playing Hamlet. She merely put the book in

With Louis Wolheim in *Dr. Jekyll and Mr. Hyde*

his hand and said, "Read it, especially the soliloquies." Several hours later he looked up at her with a faraway look in his eyes and quietly announced, "I think I will go and see Margaret Carrington."

Barrymore became possessed with the thought of playing *Hamlet.* He identified with the role, and the philosophy of the soliloquies appealed to him as statements of his own beliefs and doubts and fears. That he played *Hamlet* with poetry and power and conviction is a matter of record. The reason why was suggested by his brother Lionel. "Jack *was* Hamlet. Shakespeare undoubtedly had him in mind when he wrote the part." The play was staged in New York in November of 1922, and Barrymore played the part for 101 performances. It was the last Broadway saw of him until a sorry appearance in a desperate piece of dreck called

My Dear Children in 1939. In between *Richard III* and *Hamlet* he made two films, journeying to England in 1921 to play the lead in *Sherlock Holmes,* with Roland Young as his Watson, and returning to New York later in the year to make *The Lotus Eater.*

After the closing of *Hamlet,* Barrymore went to Hollywood, finally succumbing to the tempting blandishments. He did *Beau Brummell* with a seventeen-year-old Mary Astor as his leading lady. The two immediately fell in love and created publicity that delighted the producers and the columnists. He was still married to Michael Strange but they were separated more than they were together. In November of 1923 he rushed back to New York to fill an engagement as Hamlet at the Manhattan Opera House; after three weeks, he took the play on tour. The tour petered out within two months because Barrymore had now grown weary of the role and felt he couldn't continue. His interest was resparked by the suggestion of his friends that he perform *Hamlet* in London. This was a challenge, the kind that excited Barrymore. For an American actor to play Shakespeare in England in the 1920s was a dangerous risk. But Barrymore did it and won the same enthusiastic notices he had received in New York. He played the Prince of Denmark for three months at the Haymarket and then once again wearied of it, so much that he refused offers to play it in other European cities.

John Barrymore reached a number of conclusions in the summer of 1925, a minor one being to end his spiritually exhausting marriage to Michael Strange. More momentous was his decision to quit the stage, to withdraw at the height of his theatrical fame. Some theatre lovers considered this a sinful retreat from great art, but Barrymore did not share their reverence for the boards. The offers from Hollywood were now irresistible, and once settled in California he spoke rhapsodically about its "fountain of youth" atmosphere. He signed a contract with Warner Brothers for $75,000 a picture, plus expenses. Life began to look good to him, as it would to any forty-three-year-old man offered a generous new lease on it.

The first big project Warners wanted to build for Barrymore was *Don Juan*, an obvious choice for an actor who was himself handsome, charming, elegant, and conspicuously amorous. However, Barrymore was ambitious for more serious movie material and insisted they first do a film of *Moby Dick*, with himself as Captain Ahab. Warners agreed provided they could call the picture *The Sea Beast* and inject a love interest. Barrymore made some rude suggestions about making love to the whale but what Warners had in mind was a girl. Finding a suitable young actress was a problem for a few days. Barrymore arrived at the studio one day to announce that he had just seen "the most preposterously lovely creature in all the world" and that if she didn't get the part he would quit the film. Her name was Dolores Costello and he walked around for hours mouthing her name and saying things like "I shall not eat nor sleep till I see her again."

By the time they had finished making *The Sea Beast* Dolores Costello was as much in love with Barrymore as he was with her. It would have been difficult for any girl to have resisted the ardor of such a romantic suitor. He had insisted on much

rehearsing of the love scenes and numerous takes of them in the filming. During the filming, someone commented to a friend of Barrymore's, complimenting the actor on the quality of his acting in these love scenes. The friend replied, "He isn't acting."

When the time came to make *Don Juan,* Barrymore tried to make Warners use Dolores as the female lead, but they had alread contracted Mary Astor. Miss Astor was rather embarrassed to find her former lover chillingly polite and obviously madly in love with another girl. For all that, Barrymore loved Mary Astor convincingly on the screen and also, trying to be as much like Douglas Fairbanks as possible, leapt through castle windows, climbed battlements, swam a swift river, and engaged in a lengthy, elaborate duel with villain Montague Love. The expensive film was the first to have a synchronized musical score—it was romantic and dramatic, played by the New York Philharmonic—which was considered a major achievement in the cinema. Certainly Barrymore dominated the film, and Warners quickly realized their gamble in hiring him at a high price had paid off.

With Estelle Taylor in *Don Juan*

Barrymore's next picture for Warners was *When a Man Loves,* a treatment of Massenet's opera *Manon* with Dolores as his costar. The film completed his contract with Warners, and he now looked elsewhere for better deals and better pictures. He signed to do three pictures for United Artists but failed to get Dolores into any of them. Barrymore was first a flashy François Villon in *The*

Beloved Rogue; this was followed by adventures set during the Russian Revolution in *The Tempest,* and a silly love story set in Switzerland, *Eternal Love.* Barrymore was not happy with these vehicles and took his time about signing with another studio. In late 1928 he decided to go back to Warner Brothers, now that they had introduced sound on film, and he signed for five pictures to be made over a two-year period, with the contract allowing him choice of material. Not long after that, on November 24, he married Dolores Costello. Thus Barrymore began 1929 with high hopes, a lovely bride, and a new chapter in his career, talking pictures. He bought a big house on Tower Road in Beverly Hills and a 93-foot schooner, *The Mariner.* Barrymore loved the sea. He liked noth-

With Conrad Veidt in *The Beloved Rogue*

With Loretta Young and Baby Jane during the making of *The Man from Blakley's*

With Joan Bennett in *Moby Dick*

ing better than to take his boat and his bride on long cruises down the Mexican coast. The long, detailed logs he kept on those cruises reveal a talent for writing; his humor was delicious, and his observations about life at sea and on land were keen and often poetic.

The first of Barrymore's films under the new Warners contract was *General Crack,* an adventure epic about a soldier of fortune who fights for Austria in the 1830s: he was none too good in this, and his swaggering suggested he had more say about the production than he deserved.

Barrymore thought he would give his public a change of image for his next picture and played Lord Strathpeffer, an English gentleman whose only passion in life seemed to be collecting beetles. The film, *The Man from Blankley's,* was a comedy that only mildly amused the customers.

He next talked Warners into remaking *The Sea Beast,* now that he had the benefit of sound, and insisted on Melville's original title *Moby Dick.* Melville purists had bitterly denounced the distortions of the previous version, but at least it had done well with the public. Nobody much liked the remake.

Then came *Svengali,* one of the most memorable of his movies, in which he cast aside his handsome image, which he despised, and donned hideous makeup, which he loved doing. His Svengali is an evil-looking creature not too different from the Fagin later molded by Alec Guinness in *Oliver Twist.* That he was convincing, with eyeballs that looked like repulsive marbles (he used weird contact lenses), there was no doubt; but the public at large didn't care for his characterization. Escapism and romanticism were the orders of the day.

The last of the Warner pictures was *The Mad Genius,* which was much the same as *Svengali* in theme but even less successful. Warners had reason to regret having allowed Barrymore his own judgment in the choice of material; from a hardnosed viewpoint he had not chosen well. Perhaps it was the Barrymore experience that led Warners to be severe with other contracted stars later on: James Cagney, Bette Davis, Errol Flynn, and others would all have to fight the studio to break typecasting.

Barrymore's choice of screen material suffered from the same fault as his earlier attempts to make a living as an illustrator—the choice was too personal. It revealed an introversion and not a happy one. After leaving Warners he signed with MGM for an even better financial deal, but one that allowed him little say. His first picture for them in 1932 was *Arsène Lupin,* a kind of French *Raffles* with John looking suave and handsome as a refined criminal dogged by a grumbling old detective, played by brother Lionel. The producer responsible for the film was the brilliant young Irving Thalberg. Barrymore later admitted, exaggerating as was his manner, "Thalberg saved me from the breadline." It certainly was Thalberg who put him into more appealing pictures—for example, his next, *Grand Hotel.*

Barrymore was on his best behavior while making *Grand Hotel.* He charmed the aloof Garbo and surprised the crew by the friendliness he was able to bring from her. On meeting her he kissed her hand and said, "My wife and I think you are the loveliest woman in the world." Barrymore knew what he was doing; their scenes together have a tenderness that has rarely been matched in films. She is a lonely Russian ballerina and he an impoverished baron who has taken to thieving jewels. His decision to rob her while staying at the Grand Hotel goes awry when they fall in love. In playing their scenes, Barrymore deliberately muted his own style to allow for hers. Had he been as mannered as Garbo, the scenes would probably have become absurd.

Grand Hotel brought Barrymore back as a viable box office figure. David O. Selznick, then a young producer at RKO, offered him *A Bill of Divorcement.* The role was that of a mental patient who leaves his sanitarium and returns to his home, thinking he has been away for only a short time when in fact it has been a dozen years. He is unaware that his wife has divorced him and is about

With Marion Marsh and Bramnell Fletcher in *Svengali*

With Garbo in *Grand Hotel*

rendered to film, but Ethel was still a major theater star and disparaged the movies. She was, however, in need of money because of tax problems, and Thalberg's offer of $100,000 helped check her disdain. *Rasputin and the Empress* was an ambitious attempt to outline the horrors of the Russian Revolution and the slaughter of the royal family. Ethel was the Empress and Lionel was Rasputin, by far the juiciest part—he fairly wallowed in evil as the power-hungry faith healer who weasels his way into the palace. John played Prince Chegodieff, a character based on the actual slayer of Rasputin, Prince Felix Youssoupoff, who sued MGM and won a costly libel settlement from them. Both Lionel and John tended to regard their sister with awe, but they were not above practicing a little scene-

With Katharine Hepburn in *Bill of Divorcement*

to marry again. Barrymore was touching as the gentle, pitiful man, and the film continues to fascinate audiences, mostly because of the scenes between Barrymore and young Katherine Hepburn, here making her film debut. Stories, probably apocryphal, circulated about friction between the two of them. However, there is no doubt that Barrymore made his customary "pass" at the young lady. Their first meeting is said to have taken place in his dressing room, where she had come to rehearse. Barrymore greeted her affably and said, "Perhaps you'd like to take your clothes off and lie on the couch." Hepburn responded with indignation. Imperturbed, Barrymore quietly said, "I see, then let's just go over the lines." At the end of production Hepburn is supposed to have said to him, "I'll never act another scene with you." His oft-quoted reply certainly sounds like Barrymore: "Really, my dear? I didn't know you ever had."

Irving Thalberg had the inspiration in 1932 to bring all three Barrymores together in a film. Ethel, Lionel, and John had never appeared professionally as a trio. Both brothers had wholeheartedly sur-

stealing on each other. In his close-ups with Lionel, John used the old actor's trick of putting his arm on Lionel as Lionel spoke his lines. Rather than blow up, Lionel left the set on one occasion and telephoned the director, saying: "Will you kindly inform Mr. John Barrymore to keep his hands off me lest at the close of this scene I be tempted to lay one on him."

John, Ethel, and Lionel with Tad Alexander in *Rasputin and the Empress*

Barrymore went back to RKO to do another picture for Selznick, *Topaze.* He gave a restrained performance as the wistful Professor Topaze, an honest but rather tiresome fellow who lectures to his students on Good versus Evil. Topaze is duped into lending his name to worthless tonic water but manages to overthrow his crooked backers, as young Myrna Loy's beauty inspires him to find courage. Next came *Reunion in Vienna,* based on Robert E. Sherwood's play and with Barrymore as Archduke Rudolf, the kind of character he referred to contemptuously as a "sweet-scented jackass." The central character is a lady (played by the exquisite

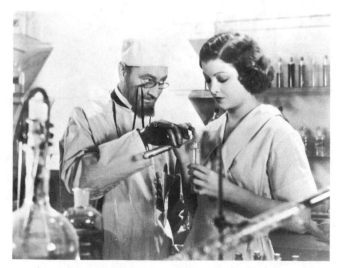

With Myrna Loy in *Topaze*

Diana Wynyard), a former mistress of Rudolf's who as she tours the old palace in Vienna remembers the "old days." For 1933 it was a passable bill of fare.

The moviegoing public had a chance to glimpse John Barrymore in a very self-revealing role in *Dinner at Eight.* In this he played an aging actor addicted to the bottle but trying to keep up his elegant image although he knows his fame has passed. In one scene he bullies a hotel bellhop to find him alcohol, something that must have been easy for Barrymore, now himself never far from a drink. The final scene is also a telling one: the actor decides to end his life by turning on the gas jets in his room, but not before first sitting himself in an armchair, arranging a table lamp to give him dramatic lighting, and running his hand through his hair to make sure it's in place.

Dinner at Eight was David O. Selznick's first film for MGM. His second also called for John Barrymore, plus Lionel, Clark Gable, Helen Hayes, and Myrna Loy; but despite the stellar cast *Night Flight* was a lackluster treatment of the Antoine de St. Exupery novel, involving the Barrymore boys as managers of an airline in South America.

Barrymore next went to Universal to make *Counselor-at-Law,* a good courtroom melodrama that required him to reel off pages of fast dialogue. One evening in October of 1933 he was called to the studio for a retake of a scene. He fluffed his lines on the first few takes. The director, William Wyler, and the crew took this in stride; it was par for the course in picture-making. But as the evening wore on Barrymore continued to fluff lines, even stumbling over simple sentences. Sweating and cursing, he refused to give in. Eventually, after fifty-six abortive takes, Wyler closed the set and asked Barrymore to return the following morning. He did, and then proceeded to perform the scene with one perfect take.

But the previous evening had been a downward turning point in Barrymore's life. He had always secretly feared the mental collapse that afflicted his father, and the lapse of memory seemed to confirm his fear. Actually, Barrymore never did lose his mind; his problems were brought on by his chronic drinking, and a medical specialist later diagnosed him as suffering from alcoholic brain damage, which caused intermittent loss of control. It also caused mind-wandering and a growing inability to memorize his lines. Eventually, Barrymore had to have his lines written on blackboards held beyond the cameras. People who expressed concern about this were informed by the flippant actor, "Well, at least I'm one of the few actors out here who can read."

Barrymore continued to labor hard at film-making. In 1934 he did the easily forgettable *Long-Lost Father,* and the unforgettable *Twentieth Century.* Here Barrymore rose to a fever pitch of frantic comic acting, playing a famed egocentric theatrical producer who must because of a financial predicament sign a certain actress to a contract. The actress, played by Carole Lombard, happens to be a girl he nurtured to stardom but whom he has since alienated by his maniacal behavior. An almost exclusively two-character piece, the whole film takes place on an express train, with the dialogue and the antics of the characters moving just as fast as the train. Barrymore's producer is another knowing piece of business on his part, a savage satire.

Sadly, *Twentieth Century* is the high-water mark in John Barrymore's film career. His health had been deteriorating, largely due to his drinking. Asked why he didn't stop he would say, "It helps me not to worry about the future." His marriage to Dolores had also deteriorated. Once past the age of fifty he seemed to realize the hopelessness of his life. His behavior became more erratic and he seemed to be happy only when away from the business of acting. When boating or fishing, attending to his aviaries, or cleaning the guns in his large collection, he relaxed and seemed content. Anything to do with his work made him edgy, and

With Ralph Forbes, Leslie Howard, and Basil Rathbone in *Romeo and Juliet*

any interest or attention paid his wife by another man brought on fierce rages. Hollis Alpert in his book *The Barrymores,* a beautifully balanced account of the whole family, quotes Dolores as saying, "His jealousy was dreadful to behold." She tells of an evening in which she danced with Selznick at a party, after which Barrymore took her home and kept her up for hours trying to find out what Selznick said to her. He ranted about the infidelity of all women, and he barred the windows of his house to keep out possible lovers.

Dolores helped Barrymore to try to cure his alcoholism, and managed to persuade him to go to a sanitarium. She took the room next to his and became sick herself listening to his behavior. He was abusive and frequently physically violent with the nurses. Dolores was advised to commit him to a mental institution but she hadn't the heart to do so. Instead she decided to retreat, to take their two children and move out of his life, knowing that to continue the marriage would be to invite certain disaster.

Almost two years elapsed between *Twentieth Century* and Barrymore's next film, *Romeo and Juliet.* In that time he spent periods in hospitals and long stretches cruising his yacht. He also took a trip with a friend to India, probably looking, his diary suggests, for some kind of Shangri-la and a panacea in Eastern wisdom. Away from films and marriage, Barrymore's health and frame of mind did improve, but his lack of income, coupled with his expensive life-style and obligations, eventually brought him back to Hollywood.

With Carole Lombard in *Twentieth Century*

Irving Thalberg, ever an admirer of Barrymore, offered him the role of Mercutio in a film of *Romeo and Juliet*, with Thalberg's wife Norma Shearer and Leslie Howard as the young lovers. Since both actors were on the way to middle age, it didn't matter that their Mercutio was also somewhat creaky. Thalberg was confident that Barrymore was capable and signed him without a test. He started worrying when he met the actor; two years had passed since their last meeting, but it seemed more like ten. Drink had made Barrymore boisterous when drunk and vague when not. To help him through the role Thalberg sent for Margaret Carrington, the exacting voice coach and Shakespearean expert who had guided him through *Richard III* and *Hamlet*. It was a wise move; the actor was increasingly suspicious of people, and here was an old colleague he could trust. Not that he took kindly to her whip—he called her "Christ's elder sister." Barrymore also agreed to make his residence during filming a nearby sanitarium. But like other alcoholics he could always find his poison somehow. (On previous occasions he had drunk his wife perfume, and had even siphoned off alcohol from the cooling system on his boat.) Eventually Thalberg decided to get rid of him, and called in William Powell to take over the role of Mercutio. Powell declined, explaining that it was Barrymore who had given him his start in films. Thalberg understood. Later he was glad he had not made a switch. Barrymore's Mercutio was an engaging lecher, prancing and belching and leering at the ladies. There's a delicious naughtiness to his scene with the Nurse (Edna May Oliver) as he tells her that "the bawdy hand of the dial is now upon the prick of Noon."

Somewhat like Mercutio, Barrymore was unable to stay away from women. In February of 1935, while resting in a New York hospital, he was visited by a nineteen-year-old college student who wanted to do a story on him as part of a journalism course. Her name was Elaine Jacobs but she called herself Elaine Barrie, having made that change out of her admiration for the Barrymores. Barrymore became smitten with the girl and, after a well-publicized courtship, married her. Their stormy years together provided much grist for the newspaper mills. And yet this, the most-publicized period of Barrymore's life, was the least worthy of publicity. It was a sad period of decline and of tainted glitter .

Barrymore worked in sixteen films from 1937 until his death five years later; few of the films are worth discussing. He did them out of a desperate need for money to clear his mounting debts. His divorce from Dolores and the provision of alimony for her and support for the children, plus the upkeep on his mansion and his yacht, both of which he was loath to surrender, made the need for money urgent. Yet he was ever sardonic in looking over the wreck of his life; his comment on alimony is a classic: "It's the most exorbitant of stud fees, and the worst feature of it is that you pay it retroactively."

These were the films of John Barrymore in this last stage of his celluloid career:

Maytime (1937): Barrymore as opera star Jeanette MacDonald's manager-husband, so jealous of her affections that he kills her lover Nelson Eddy.

Bulldog Drummond Comes Back (1937): Barrymore took top billing even though his was a supporting role. John Howard played Drummond with Barrymore as Colonel Nielson, a Scotland Yard inspector who comes to the rescue of the dashing government agent when the going gets rough. In this one, Barrymore appeared in several grotesque disguises.

Night Club Scandal (1937): A murder mystery in which Barrymore plays a prominent doctor who kills his young wife and unsuccessfully tries to put the blame on her lover.

True Confession (1937): In this frenetic comedy, Carole Lombard appears as a wife whose vivid imagination gets her involved in a murder case. Her lawyer husband Fred MacMurray extricates her and rescues her from the schemes of crazy, drunken, blackmailing criminologist Barrymore, who steals every scene in which he appears.

Bulldog Drummond's Revenge (1937): Barrymore as the blustering Colonel Nielson again aids the handsome Captain Drummond of British Intelligence.

Bulldog Drummond's Peril (1937): Barrymore refused to continue after this third appearance as Colonel Nielson. John Howard went on to do a half-dozen more films in the series, with Reginald Denny as Algy and Louise Campbell as Phyllis Clavering.

Romance in the Dark (1938): A musical comedy starring Gladys Swarthout and John Boles with Barrymore as an amorous impressario, stealing girls from the tenor he manages.

Spawn of the North (1938): The exploits of fish pirates in Alaskan waters in the early 1900s, with George Raft and Henry Fonda as the heroes who foil the pirates and Barrymore as a garrulous old sailor named Windy. Comic relief. As Hamlet ob-

With Jeanette MacDonald in *Maytime*

In one of his disguises for *Bulldog Drummond Comes Back;* this one gives him a resemblance to his brother Lionel.

served: "That it should come to this. . . . "

Marie Antoinette (1938) : Irving Thalberg's lavish and splendid account of the crushing of the French monarchy with his wife, Norma Shearer, in the title role. Barrymore played the aged King Louis XV and created a brief but memorable cameo of a sad, bewildered old man.

Hold That Co-Ed (1938) : Better than the title might suggest, this was a satire on American state politics with Barrymore as a governor—a cunning old politician out to get votes by backing a needy university as part of his campaign, and seeing to it that their football team wins acclaim.

With George Murphy and Marjorie Weaver in *Hold That Coed*

The Great Man Votes (1939) : Barrymore as a college professor who becomes a drunk after the death of his wife. He goes into decline and ends up as a night watchman, but he becomes rehabilitated by the love and respect of his children. Not a major picture but an interesting one because of Barrymore's playing of the philosophical professor.

Midnight (1939) : Barrymore in support of Claudette Colbert and Don Ameche in a comedy set in Paris. Colbert is a stranded showgirl, hired by Barrymore to distract a playboy's attentions from Barrymore's wife.

The Great Profile (1940) : Barrymore, for the first time, burlesquing himself. In an obvious capitalization on his own stage success *My Dear Children*, he appears as Evans Garrick, a drunken actor fired in Hollywood and returning to the stage, and then in demand again in Hollywood.

The Invisible Woman (1941) : Virginia Bruce was the lady of the title with Barrymore as an eccentric old inventor. He played it fairly straight, probably from sheer lack of either strength or interest.

World Premiere (1941) : Another frenetic performance replete with much mugging. A mad satire on movie moguls, the film lampoons the nonsense of movie premieres with Barrymore playing a conniving, publicity-mad film producer named Duncan DeGrasse.

Playmates (1941) : In his last film Barrymore appeared as himself—not as a guest but as a desperate old actor so eager for work he accepts a job with Kay Kyser and his orchestra at a Shakespearean festival set to swing music. This wretched comedy does have one touching moment, where Barrymore recites Hamlet's soliloquy. During the filming of the scene he stumbled over the lines and stopped. In a choked voice he said, "It's been a long time." He was not alone in his emotion. Several members of the cast and crew had tears in their eyes.

Between *Midnight* in early 1939 and *The Great Profile* in late 1940, Barrymore returned to the stage. The decision might have been brought on by his intense dislike for Hollywood, which he once described in a letter as a "dermoid cyst *Hollywoodus in latrina.*" An equally strong reason would have been the encouragement of his young wife, eager for a career as an actress. At times during their on-again, off-again marriage she had appeared with him on radio broadcasts and in some films, but with little sign of great public interest. She felt a stage vehicle starring Mr. and Mrs. Barrymore might do the trick. Against the advice of all his friends he picked up a tawdry little comedy called *My Dear Children*. Barrymore saw it as a loose format in which the exact learning of lines would be of little importance, one in which he could perform according to how he felt. The fact that *My Dear Children* was a hit was entirely due to the public's curiosity to see the woozy Barrymore stumble his way through trivia and to marvel at his ability to give them their money's worth. He made a fool of himself, but he did it

With Mary Beth Hughes and Lionel Atwill in *The Great Profile*

with flourish and a cunning knowledge of what he was doing. His ad libs were more amusing than the script, and he often kidded the prompters: "Would you mind repeating that, darling, I didn't quite hear."

The plot of *My Dear Children* concerned the flounderings of an aging actor who, while staying at a villa in Switzerland, is descended upon by three grown-up daughters, none of whom he has known since they were babies. The vehicle allowed for Barrymore to appear in Elizabethan costume—his high boots concealing pitifully swollen ankles, causing him to remark on one occasion, with the typical Barrymore elegance of diction, "Strange . . . I've never seen an actor puffed up at *that* end before."

My Dear Children opened at a theatre in Princeton, New Jersey, on March 24, 1939, next moved to Washington, and then went on the road. It played Chicago for almost eight months after which it moved into New York, already a much-publicized vehicle, for four months. It would have played longer, but Barrymore finally could stand it no longer and asked to be released. His film career, considered finished, picked up again due to the publicity he had been receiving. The producers in Hollywood had given up on Barrymore, considering him a poor work risk—drunken, clumsy, moody, unreliable, and too much trouble to bother with. But with the play and the constant newspaper coverage of his noisy marriage, there was no denying the renewed attraction of his name.

Elaine Barrie had played in *My Dear Children* for the first few months, but when her contract expired it was not renegotiated. By then the bickering between her and Barrymore had become injurious to him, and they parted—to everyone's relief. Divorce proceedings were instituted by both parties and by the time he withdrew from the play Barrymore was a free man, free to suffer through what time remained for him.

John Barrymore returned to Hollywood a rapidly aging and increasingly sick man. Alcohol had ravaged his liver and his kidneys; his heart and his circulation began to show signs of great strain; gastric ulcers resulted in frequent hemorrhages and fainting spells. As if to compound the agony, his financial state was as desperate as his body. Barrymore finished the long months of labor in *My Dear Children* with a check for $5,000, which he asked to be made out to his gardner lest some creditor discover this evidence of wealth. Always cavalier in his dealings with people, Barrymore had been flagrantly improvident with money. Added to his genuine debts were those to advantage-takers, those who found it easy to fleece the inebriated celebrity. But Barrymore, with all his faults, was concerned about his debts and now looked around for further employment. As Lionel said, "He was consumed with a passion to remit what he owed."

After completing *The Great Profile* it was clear that Barrymore's future in films could only be a limited one. He looked ill and it was difficult for him even to stand for any length of time. There was no possibility of ever doing another play; consequently, the employment picture was bleak. Salvation came from an unexpected source, radio, and (even more unexpectedly) in the form of Rudy Vallee.

Vallee had long been a top-line radio artist. All through the 1930s his weekly one-hour variety show sponsored by Fleischman had presented him as a singing host to a multitude of guests, many of them newcomers who found the show a springboard to success. In a sense the Vallee show was similar to the kind of thing Ed Sullivan would do on television years later. For his new radio series— to be sponsored by Sealtest—Vallee wanted a change of format, a half-hour program that would stress music and comedy situations. He recalls driving in his car one evening and listening to Barrymore in a broadcast of a Shakespearean play. "I was struck by the quality of the voice that came over the radio, the sonorous sound of it and the image of authority. I had an idea and I talked it over with my producer Ed Gardiner, who later became a well-known performer himself as Archie, the manager of "Duffy's Tavern." We approached Barrymore and put to him the idea of doing a burlesque version of

himself. He jumped at it. Ed and I had our doubts about hiring him but in all the time he was with us he never embarrassed us or let us down. We were criticized by some who thought we were callous turning him into a buffoon, but he didn't think so himself. He realized he had to clown and let the jokes roll off him, and he seemed to enjoy it. He did it so beautifully, and nobody could take offence because you knew that underneath all this we had great respect for him. But it was tragic to see him letting himself be ridiculed; it was simply that he had no choice, there was no other possible way he could earn several thousand dollars a week. There were times when I watched him and remembered seeing him in London, at the Haymarket in 1924, when women swooned as he played *Hamlet*. It was sad to see him mocking himself as an aging, worn-out, hammy actor, but you could only admire him. He was a man doing what he had to do, and doing it in pain."

The Vallee-Barrymore programs invariably had a celebrated guest star who would trade quips with Barrymore. Typical of the better shows was the one in which Groucho Marx was the guest. It was an amusing and acid pairing; both Marx and Barrymore were witty men in person and could probably have done a broadcast even without a script. The Vallee shows employed a staff of top writers—this was a time later to be called The Golden Age of Radio Comedy—but the writers were never named. Hence it is impossible to credit these lines, transcribed from tape:

Marx: Vallee, who is this grotesque-looking creature approaching?

Vallee: Groucho, that's John Barrymore.

Marx: John Barrymore? You didn't tell me he'd be here tonight. What time does the next train leave for Glendale?

Barrymore: Not soon enough. Vallee, do I have to put up with this weird Marxian creature?

Marx: Weird? Weird? Is the pot calling the kettle weird?

Barrymore: Marx, I haven't seen anything as weird as you since I was in Catalina in a glass-bottomed boat.

Marx: Barrymore, it's a wonder that a man with your experience can stand up here and say a thing like that. In fact, it's a wonder that a man with your experience can stand up at all.

Later in the same show Groucho, as an efficiency

expert, outlines a grand scheme to failing businessmen Vallee and Barrymore, and concludes by saying that the scheme is "the greatest proposition ever offered a human being, dead or alive. And that covers both of you." A few lines later Groucho turns to a doubting Barrymore and says, "You'll never get another chance like this if you live to be a hundred—which gives you about three months to look around." ·

Vallee's writers showed Barrymore no mercy. They capitalized on his drinking, his womanizing, and his waning health, touching upon painful truths in great jest. Barrymore never asked for a line to be altered and he responded to every barb. Much of the humor was obviously pointed:

Vallee: John, I've hired an efficiency expert.
Barrymore: An efficiency expert?
Vallee: Yes, you know, a fellow who cuts down your expenses, saves you money, stops you from making mistakes, and keeps you out of trouble.
Barrymore: You mean you can hire a man to do all that for you?
Vallee: Yes.
Barrymore: (to the audience) *Now* he tells me!

In almost two years on the Rudy Vallee program, from October of 1940 to May of 1942, Barrymore earned enough to pay off most of his debts, mainly back taxes. After he died his property was sold to pay the remaining debts. His last show for Vallee was on May 14, 1942, and the show contained a startlingly prophetic line:

Barrymore: Rudy, I'm retiring.
Vallee: Not really? You mean you're leaving acting flat.
Barrymore: Why not? That's how it's left me.

Several of the cast suggested the line be cut but Barrymore laughed, "Nonsense, leave it in. It's just a gag."

During the last two years of his life Barrymore was closely watched over by an illustrious group of friends, among them Gene Fowler, painter John Decker, and actors Alan Mowbray and Thomas Mitchell. Many evenings were spent at Decker's home, where the worldly group held forth with eloquence and wit on all subjects. They affectionately called Barrymore The Monster and checked with each other as to his whereabouts. They watered his drinks to the point where they were almost harmless. Occasionally he would slip away from them and indulge himself, as on the evening he drank twenty martinis before collapsing. That

none of these abuses immediately killed the desperately ailing sixty-year-old Barrymore cannot be explained. His constitution was extraordinary, as was his humor, his courage, and his determination.

Barrymore arrived at the broadcasting studios in Hollywood on May 19, 1942 for a rehearsal of the Vallee programme. After the rehearsal he left the studio to make his way back to his dressing room, but a wave of great illness now washed over him. He stumbled along the corridors trying to find his room, to the amusement of some tourists who assumed the celebrated actor was drunk. In his confusion and his need to lie down, Barrymore settled for the nearest dressing room he could find. Ironically, this was the room assigned to an actor whose admiration for Barrymore was so strong it had clearly affected his own style of speech and theatrical manner—John Carradine. Carradine was out when Barrymore stumbled in, but he returned to find his idol asleep on the couch. Barrymore pretended to be well and spoke at some length to Carradine about the work the younger actor was doing on the stage and screen, at one point advising him never to read his notices, either the good or the bad. The advice suddenly came to an end when Barrymore gasped and lapsed into semi-consciousness.

At the Hollywood Presbyterian Hospital Barrymore was found to have bronchial pneumonia. At last the amazing body had capitulated, yet it lingered for another ten days before the heartbeat stopped and the strange spirit left for what Barrymore called "the Grampian hills." He believed in a life after death, and he told Gene Fowler that after his death he would make a ghostly visitation. Barrymore died at 10:20 P.M. on May 29, 1942. Fowler had vowed to set the hands of an old cuckoo clock in his study at the hour of his friend's death. He didn't remember the vow until two years later, but when he went to the clock then he found it unnecessary to touch the hands: the clock had stopped and the hands stood at 10:20.

Many comments were made about John Barrymore after his death, but none more knowing than that of his brother Lionel. He had authorized an autopsy, "but no medical or literary scalpel revealed, or could reveal, I regret to say, the sources of the revolt, the uncertainties, and the always-questioning consciousness of unfulfillment which impelled Jack Barrymore to his death. The greatly gifted are not the fortunate persons of this world. Today we are forced to read all these astute papers in the magazines about the values of 'adjustment'. We must all, it seems, 'adjust' ourselves to the world and to exerybody else. How fortunate, I say, for the sheep who can munch in unison and adjust. How painful for the artists, the statesmen, the pioneers, the musicians, and the actors who fail to keep time—but what a gift for us that they do fail."

Barrymore: A Personal Recollection

BY SAMUEL A. PEEPLES

I saw John Barrymore in the flesh just twice.

The first time was in San Francisco when I was a boy of ten or eleven, and the year was '27 or '28. A newspaperman friend of my mother's had taken me in tow for the day. I still remember the smell of ink and newsprint in his office and the ungodly clatter of the newsroom. (Years later, when I worked on a daily paper myself, I learned there is order beneath the bedlam.) I also still remember wondering whether we were ever going to eat, for we didn't go, until quite late, to lunch at a dingy hangout of newspapermen where steam beer and mustardy cornbeef-on-rye sandwiches were the staples.

While we were eating another reporter came in and said to my guardian-of-the-day: "Jack Barrymore's in town." My mentor's face lit with pleasure and he slapped me on the back and exclaimed: "I'm going to introduce you to the best damned actor in the whole damned world!"

I don't remember to which San Francisco hotel we took one of the high-backed Yellow Cabs but I like to think it was the Palace, which it well may have been. The suite of rooms we entered was crowded and smelt of whiskey. I was thoroughly familiar with theatrical types and realized at once the suite was full of them. An amiable sort put a glass full of light brown liquid in my hand but my *loco parentis* whiffed the glass and dumped the contents into one of those potted plants which in those days always stood in the bay windows of hotel suites.

He got me a glass of ginger ale poured from a newly opened bottle and almost immediately was sidetracked by a girl in a bright red dress that didn't reach her knees. (I remember seeing the top of her rolled stockings.) Left alone, I found a corner that also had a window. I drank my ginger ale and stared out of the window and suddenly heard a growly voice—I don't know why the adjective "growly" has stayed with me all these

years—mutter in my ear something about was I tired of watching the animals in the zoo. I turned and saw a thin, somewhat elongated face on which one eyebrow was cocked mockingly. I recognized John Barrymore instantly—I'de seen several of his silent films.

Tom Mix had made me speechless with awe when I first met him, but Barrymore saw to it that he didn't have that effect on the little boy he must have been surprised to find in such a gathering. He winked, and his voice wasn't the ranging boom of the "dramatic players" I'd heard in tent shows, but sharp, precise, devoid of affectation, but with a wonderful edge to it.

Barrymore was carrying a drink in one hand and a small, leather-bound book in the other. He put the drink on a table and began pointing at people and likening them to different kinds of animals. I was captivated, for his eye was unerring and he would spot an expression or a movement so patently typical of the animal he then mentioned that I laughed aloud. I particularly recall a thinnish girl half on the arm of an overstuffed chair and half on the lap of an overstuffed man, whose pink bloomers had frilled bottoms that reminded Barrymore of the fluffy tailfeathers of an ostrich. To think I've remembered *her* for 40 years!

My newspaperman joined us and Barrymore said he was working on a speech he had to give on the radio. They retired to a bedroom and I followed. A girl came out of its bathroom, waved, and went off. I remember how Barrymore eyed her departing back, and how he then began pacing up and down, up and down, practising the speech he had to give. I can still remember his voice, but not, of course, his words.

As the years went by I saw almost every movie John Barrymore made. My favorite is *Svengali*, although I'd be hard-pressed to say why. I've seen quite a few of the great Hamlets on stage and screen—Maurice Evans, John Gielgud, Laurence Olivier, Peter O'Toole, Richard Burton, Michael MacLiammoir, Christopher Plummer and even Robert Vaughn (don't snicker—the Man from U.N.C.L.E. acquitted himself very well). But apart from Olivier, who has the voices (note the plural) to match character moods, none spoke for the Prince of Denmark so movingly as Barrymore. I own a recording he made of one of his radio performances of *Hamlet* (my copies are probably taken from glass 'masters'). His voice possessed the dynamics actors achieve when they feel the tragedy they are called upon to express.

All too soon Barrymore's roles became travesties, and even self-parodies, and I began to think my fond idea of his greatness was the persistence of juvenile hero worship. Also, I saw him in the flesh again.

It was during World War II and I saw him from a seat in the theatre in which he was appearing in *My Dear Children*. He was bemused and floundering, garbled his lines, and his voice had become shrill and cracked. But occasionally a line would be remembered, and be spoken with the old magic. But most of it was an alcoholic mumble.

I saw, or resaw, many of his talkies on television during the '50s. I still found excellent *Svengali*, *A Bill of Divorcement* and *Grand Hotel*, and, to a lesser degree, *Topaze* and *Counselor-at-Law*. But the self-caricatures in *The Great Profile* and similar films were painful to see.

In the Spring of 1970 the Los Angeles County Museum of Art began a series of motion picture presentations in cooperation with the American Film Institute and the Library of Congress. Among the films to be presented was *The Beloved Rogue* ('27), one of the Barrymore silents I had never seen (*Sherlock Holmes*, alas, is another).

The Beloved Rogue was shown on a Friday night to a large audience. A very fetching young lady in a micro-mini-dress, which exposed delectable legs, sat next to me. She was 20, and, by her standards, sophisticated, and, by mine, a bit brassy. As soon as the film began she started to squirm, which caused the micro-mini-skirt to edge higher and higher—a somewhat distracting display in a none-too-dark theatre. However, I kept my eyes on the screen, and within a very few minutes *The Beloved Rogue* had defeated the young lady's legs.

According to the program notes *The Beloved Rogue* had long been thought lost, as the result of a negative-destroying fire in United Artists' vaults. The print being shown had been given to the American Film Institute by Edgar Bergen, and it's a beautiful, tinted, release version. Only its last two reels show any evidence of decomposition.

The camera work in *The Beloved Rogue* is exquisite and the lighting is flawless. The production values are superb—William Cameron Menzies had few peers in art direction. The story may seem tame when appraised by today's gamey standards, but it's a good story, and the sequences tell it

beautifully. I was surprised, seeing Barrymore between Slim Summerville and Mack Swain, who play his two comic pals, to observe how small a man Barrymore really was. And I was surprised by his athletic prowess à la Doug Fairbanks—even to doing a tumbler's roll down a snowbank.

François Villon, played by Barrymore, is elected King of Fools in fifteenth-century Paris and dons a clown's motley for some frolics. Barrymore's clowning pantomime while this is being established is the first intimation that this film is not just another costumer. He is funny, graceful, and a wholly believable Villon. I noticed that, despite the passage of almost half a century, he had caught, and was holding, the attention of the audience.

In the midst of the revels King Louis XI, played with relish and much eye-rolling and gesturing by Conrad Veidt, appears. There's an exchange between him and Villon and he orders Villon to be exiled from Paris—with the penalty to be death if he dares to return. The King rides off; the revels subside; the revelers depart. Barrymore, as Villon, is alone, at the base of a large equestrian statue. The sentence has struck him hard. With sad, resigned movements he begins to remove his clown makeup. The half-melon of his "bald" pate goes first, then the rubber nose, and then tears well into Barrymore's eyes (all this in one take). When the clown makeup is completely off we see a face of stark tragedy.

Barrymore uses no theatrical gestures, no over-emphasis, and no mugging—just a weary, beaten twist of the body, and the blink of tear-filled eyes. Alone in front of the camera, and of course without sound, he convinces us he is experiencing François Villon's sorrow and pain and fear.

I glanced at the young lady beside me and was astonished to see she was crying.

I treasure moments of great theatre and that long sequence of Villon being sentenced to exile from his beloved Paris is one of them. The proof of this is the effect it had on that audience of several hundred young, "today" people, who reacted exactly the way Barrymore intended audiences to react.

Seeing *The Beloved Rogue* was a wonderful experience and so was watching that youthful 1970 audience be captivated by the acting of John Barrymore.

3

GEORGE SANDERS

"*I* WAS beastly but I was never coarse. I was a high-class sort of heel." Thus George Sanders neatly summed up more than thirty years of playing cultured cads. No other actor ever quite matched Sanders's way with a sneer or his air of insouciant meanness or his ability to deliver disdainful dialogue in an elegant, cello-like speaking voice. Sanders also used that voice to sing—in a rich baritone—but by the time he got around to singing on the screen (to Ethel Merman in *Call Me Madam* in 1953) hardly anyone would believe the voice was his. The lack of acceptance was greeted by Sanders in characteristic manner, with a barely stifled yawn of indifference.

George Sanders was a corroboration of the commonly held view in the film industry that movie stars are born and not made. He didn't look, sound, or behave like any other actor, but had a distinct image, which is what movie success is largely about. Sanders was, by his own description, an unfettered soul. He could be witty and charming but also snide and impolite, and he could do it all in fluent English, Russian, German, or Spanish. All actors live behind a facade of their own creation but when Sanders said "I find it pleasant to be unpleasant" he was telling the truth.

Sanders was eccentric, most often in a mordantly amusing way. He never sought publicity, which made him a rarity among actors, but he was always shrewd enough to make remarks that got quoted. Some years ago, when he was at Twentieth-Century Fox, he asked the studio to redecorate his dressing room, which he felt was in need of paint and repair. An executive visited him in the dressing room and told Sanders they would be pleased

George Sanders with Hurd Hatfield in *The Picture of Dorian Gray*

to do as he asked if he would do a favor in return—stop making vulgar remarks about the head of the studio. Sanders thought for a moment and then declined. "No, it isn't worth it." And the dressing room remained as it was.

Interviewers were given a particularly rough time by Sanders. On the few occasions when he submitted himself to questioning, he answered either tersely or tartly. One lady who was curious to know what he slept in he informed: "An Inverness cape and a fur parka." To another who wondered why he had never had any children, he said he had no time for "grubby little brats." Hedda Hopper once remarked that Sanders was seldom seen at Hollywood parties. To Hedda, whom he liked more than any other reporter, he explained: "It's useless to go to a party unless you can reasonably expect a good time. I look around at has-beens and would-bes who work so hard at being charming and amusing at parties. Nothing doing! Casting is done at the studios."

With Jeanette MacDonald in _Bitter Sweet_

As he grew older George Sanders became even less tractable, especially to interviewers. Rex Reed, one of the sharpest eyes on the film scene, tackled Sanders in July of 1969 for the _New York Times_, just after the actor had arrived from working in London on John Huston's espionage thriller _The Kremlin Letter_. Reed was invited to Sanders's hotel by a Twentieth Century-Fox publicist, a poor soul who spent the interview period twitching and grimacing and trying to smooth the troubled waters. Reed began by asking Sanders if he enjoyed making _The Kremlin Letter_. Replied George, "No." He then asked Sanders if he had any fond memories of any of his films. The instant reply was "No." Sanders became a little more expansive when Reed wondered if perhaps a lot of the fun had gone out of filmmaking today. "I

think all the fun has gone out of _everything_, but I'm not qualified to comment on films because I never see them. I loathe movies and I loathe the theater." Reed, remembering Sanders's singing voice, tried another tack: "Do you sing around the house to keep your wonderful voice in shape?" In his famous weary way, Sanders drawled, "No. I'm dying now, so I never sing around the house or anywhere else." According to Reed, Sanders looked to be in fine health. As Reed was about to leave Sanders brightened a little: "I'm a cynic. Our values are all false and life is simply a matter of pretense. I don't know where society is going and I don't care. I'm just happy I won't be around to see it."

Whereas most film careers come about by dint of ambition and much promotion, Sanders's seemingly happened without any great strain. Acting was something he turned to when all else had failed, and he never kept secret the fact that money was the chief motivation of his becoming an actor. "In films, one makes more money with less effort than in any other job or profession I know."

Studio executives and producers were seldom offended by Sanders's jaundiced views, because they somehow fit the image of the man. That image is the kind the producers want most—the image of the human being who is a natural for films. That natural affinity is a rare quality which no amount of training can produce.

George Sanders's image was molded by a particular way of life. He was born in Saint Petersburg, Russia, on July 3, 1906, in circumstances he described as plush: "My family epitomized the decadence of the upper classes under the Czar." It was a world that was soon to disappear, but by the time it did it had left its mark on young George—the mark of the aristocrat, with wealthy relatives in high places, servants, ballrooms, and property. Aside from their town house, the Sanders family had a summer house in Estonia and an estate in Finland. "The estate was to prove a godsend when the time came for my parents to flee from the Bolshevik revolution."

Sanders's father was a manufacturer, and his mother was an horticulturist of some reputation, as well as being the heiress to a fortune. Both were of British stock. Sanders described his father as one of the best amateur balalaika players in Russia; he himself was put to studying the violin, but he failed to master it. The musical background of his childhood, however, paid dividends later, when he organized a dance band in college and played the piano, saxophone, and guitar. But in looking back on his childhood in Russia, Sanders said what he remembered most were the winter sports and the summer months of swimming and boating. For him the idyllic life ended in early 1917, when he was sent to school in England. By the end of that year his parents joined him in England, having escaped the Bolsheviks and having left behind their property and their funds, none of which were ever redeemed.

George and his brother Thomas, who later turned up in Hollywood and acted under the name Tom Conway, were enrolled in Bedales School in rural Hampshire. This was the only school Sanders ever enjoyed, because it was coeducational and the discipline was lax. Both boys were difficult to manage, and when Tom brandished a loaded pistol in the classroom he was expelled. George was pulled from the school some time later and sent to Dunhurst Preparatory in order to improve his scholastic record and qualify him for college. In 1921 he was enrolled in Brighton College, spending the next four years with "poor food, uncomfortable beds, sordid scenery, irascible, acidulated teachers, frequent beatings, no girls, no fun, nothing but pimply-faced boys of all shapes and sizes." Apparently, Sanders excelled only in swimming and boxing—and in inventing gadgets. Sanders was, in fact, an inventor with several patents to his credit, but he played down the practical side of his imagination lest it interfere with his image as a languid, lazy cad.

With no discernible ambition, Sanders left Brighton College and went to Manchester Technical School to learn a trade. His first job was working for a textile company in that city. He was dismissed after a year when the management discovered he and another employee were studying the company books and records in preparation for setting up a rival company. Through the influence of his father, Sanders next worked for a cigarette manufacturing company—it seemed a wise move for all concerned because it required him to leave England and move to Argentina. After some time at the main plant in Buenos Aires Sanders was sent to the hinterland as a surveyor-salesman. His apathetic disinterest in cigarette manufacturing and selling left him when he was able to employ his inventiveness and ingenuity. Travelling through the wilds of Patagonia by railroad, car and horse, Sanders devised ways of peddling cigarettes to the natives. He found the farmers and the sheep ranchers friendly once he was able to establish the fact that he was not a bandit. His Argentine adventures spanned three years, which Sanders says he enjoyed because of the healthy life in the primitive wilds and the contrast of occasional hedonism in Buenos Aires. The job came to an end when he embarrassed his boss by arriving at a dinner party one hour late, having assumed, wrongly, that his Latin host and his two dozen guests would commence their formal meal without him.

Another tobacco company was now graced with the services of salesman George Sanders; the job change required him to move to Valparaiso. He then took trips through the wilds of Chile, coming up with some good ideas for sales promotion, the best of which was his scheme for flying over the lush farmlands in an open plane and dropping free samples (with some of the packages containing prizes) of cigarettes hung on miniature parachutes. The plan worked well and brought Sanders praise from his employers; his career in South American cigarette sales promotion might have continued for many years had it not been for his getting drunk one night and challenging a rival for a certain lady's charms to a duel. In the middle of a dark night, Sanders and his opponent went through the ritual of standing back to back, marching ten paces with pistols raised, then turning and firing. Sanders won, his bullet piercing the man's neck but fortunately missing the vital organs. He quickly recovered, but a fraction of an inch would have made a fatal difference. Said Sanders, "I have not owned a gun since then and never will. I can never look back on that night without a cold shiver running down my spine." The resultant scandal caused Sanders to be dismissed from his company and to return to England.

George Sanders reached his twenty-eighth birthday in 1934 with little reason to celebrate. He was still a man of no real trade or profession, and he was finding it increasingly hard to land a good job. Through the efforts of a friend he was taken on by the advertising branch of Lever Brothers Company in London, but that lasted for only a few months— he was sacked for treating the job lightly. But Sanders's fling in the advertising business was not useless: working in the next office was a beautiful redheaded young lady named Greer Garson who belonged to an amateur theatrical company and who persuaded Sanders to read for a part in a play they were doing. At about the same time Sanders's Uncle Sacha, who had been an opera singer, prevailed upon him to study singing. To these two people belongs the credit for putting George Sanders into show business.

Sanders's first job as an entertainer sprang from

his singing and playing the piano at a party. A producer among the guests liked what he heard and offered Sanders a part in a revue. This led to work in radio drama for the BBC, where his fine speaking voice found him more work than he would have found as an untrained stage actor. Sanders appeared in more than fifty BBC productions, at the same time being occasionally employed in plays, mostly as an understudy. His first work in films was in 1936, when he played a mounted god in a sequence of *The Man Who Could Work Miracles.* "The part called for me to ride half-naked and slimy with grease, at four o'clock in the morning during one of England's coldest winters, on a horse which was also coated with grease. Torin Thatcher and Ivan Brandt were the other two greasy gods." Such was the start of a long and profitable screen career.

Sanders made three more screen appearances in 1936, in *Things to Come, Strange Cargo,* and *Dishonor Bright,* and did sufficiently well to get a contract with the British and Dominion Studio. But this studio was shortly thereafter consumed by a raging fire and its assets sold to Twentieth Century-Fox, who also took an option on its contracts, Sanders's among them. He was immediately sent to California because Darryl F. Zanuck was making *Lloyds of London* and needed British actors, particularly one to play Lord Everett Stacy, a cold-hearted, imperious fellow. Sanders proved a perfect choice, his air of patrician hauteur being precisely what the role needed. A major movie villain was born as Sanders treated his wife (Madeleine Carroll) callously and then calmly shot and fatally

With Madeleine Carroll and Tyrone Power in *Lloyds of London*

wounded her young lover (Tyrone Power). It was this initial Hollywood appearance that set the tone of his career; thereafter Sanders would seldom appear in a sympathetic light.

After putting him in small roles in *Slave Ship, Love is News,* and *The Lady Escapes,* Zanuck took a chance on Sanders and gave him the lead in *Lancer Spy.* The film called for good acting and Sanders proved he had learned something of the craft in the few years he had been plying it. The story was set in the First World War and concerned military espionage, the point of the plot lying in the acute resemblance between a captured German army officer and a British naval officer, both played by Sanders. British Intelligence seizes upon the resemblance as a means of sending a spy into Germany—with the British officer assuming the identity of the German after studying his character and background. *Lancer Spy* is an excellent minor war film, crisply directed by Gregory Ratoff, with fine work from Sanders. With the success of the picture his future in Hollywood was assured.

George Sanders did little else but work in films during his first decade in Hollywood. Twentieth Century-Fox had him under contract but they frequently loaned him to other studios; Sanders had for some years the odd distinction of being a star of RKO Radio's *The Saint* series while at the same time playing second leads in Fox pictures. Fox used him in *International Settlement, Four Men and a Prayer,* and *Mr. Moto's Last Warning* (with Peter Lorre as the Japanese detective), and in early 1939 made the deal with RKO that turned Sanders into Leslie Charteris's suave private investigator The Saint. He did five *Saint* pictures before asking to be released from the assignment: *The Saint Strikes Back, The Saint in London, The Saint's Double Trouble, The Saint Takes Over,* and *The Saint in Palm Springs.* After this RKO allowed Louis Hayward to take over the role. In between his *Saint* duties, Sanders player a Nazi spy in *The Confession of a Nazi Spy,* the British Army officer who sneered at frontiersman John Wayne in *Allegheny Uprising,* and the German Army officer who escorted *Nurse Edith Cavell* to her death before a firing squad during the First World War. Sanders always looked superb in uniform and he was one of the few Hollywood actors who could wear a monocle and sport a spiked helmet with genuine style. His knowledge of German and his background as a European aristocrat served him well during the war years.

It was Hitchcock's *Rebecca* in 1940 that gave Sanders his chance to show just how mean an up-

With Anna Neagle in *Nurse Edith Cavell*

per-crust English cad could be. As Jack Favell, the blackmailing cousin of the deceased lady of the title, Sanders was in cahoots with Mrs. Danvers (Judith Anderson, looking rather like a druidess), the evil housekeeper of Manderley. With slightly foppish charm and a drawling old-school-tie accent, Sanders cut a figure the moviegoers found pleasure in hating. More than one leading man would be heard to complain in the years to come that Sanders made his cads so fascinating that he drew attention away from the other characters.

Sanders put in more time as a Nazi in *Manhunt*, making life painful for Walter Pidgeon, and in *Sundown*, as a German assigned to set up part of Africa as Hitler's domain. In a weak moment

In *Rebecca*; the gentleman impatiently waiting to use the phone is Alfred Hitchcock.

Sanders was persuaded to return to playing the gentleman detective—perhaps he agreed in order to escape the Nazi image—and he signed to do *The Gay Falcon*, followed by *A Date With the Falcon* and *The Falcon Takes*. Again he screamed to be let out. Sanders said he would do one more Falcon picture provided he died in it, and someone came up with the bright idea of calling in Sanders's brother Tom Conway to take over from George in a story to be called, with simple logic, *The Falcon's Brother*. Tom then carried the series for a while. His career, as a second-rate star lasted a dozen years, eventually petering out and tragically ending in alcoholism and destitution. He and Sanders were never close friends and their relationship gradually drifted into estrangement.

Among Sanders's rare opportunities to be nice were his roles opposite Ingrid Bergman in *Rage In Heaven* and with Norma Shearer in *Her Cardboard Lover*. It was after appearing in the latter in 1942 —this was Norma Shearer's swan song at MGM-- that Sanders received a message from Louis B. Mayer that he would like to have lunch with Sanders and talk about the possibility of developing him into a romantic star. Sanders felt this might have had something to do with the drain the Second World War was creating on the ranks of Mayer's leading men. Sanders declined the luncheon and the chance to alter his screen image. In his autobiography, *The Memoirs of a Professional Cad*, Sanders explained:

> Perhaps my curious indifference to success will be more understandable if I explain that the driving force of my life has always been laziness; to practice this, in reasonable comfort, I have even been prepared, from time to time, to work. I think I knew instinctively that being a romantic star would demand of me, in terms of time and effort, more than I was inclined to give. I was only interested in getting to the top the easy way, and if I couldn't get to the top the easy way, I would settle for getting *some* of the way the easy way.
> I had become a Hollywood actor earning a handsome salary without exerting myself unduly; and if Fate had been disposed to make me a heartthrob, a pin-up, a Great Lover, I would have acquiesced with my normal graciousness. But I wasn't going to indulge in any Promethean struggle in order to achieve this goal. Quite honestly I didn't care all that much.

Hence, George Sanders can be entered in the Hollywood annals as The Man Who Didn't Come to Lunch. The decision was probably not as capricious as it sounds. Sanders realized that as a character actor he would last longer than as a leading man—certainly, the character player doesn't have to worry about his age. As for the screaming acclaim of multitudes of fans, Sanders said: "I am content to remain unpopular with the lunatic fringe."

Sanders was kept so busy in the early 1940s he doubtless had little time to think about the quality of the vehicles in which he appeared. He batted back and forth playing the Saint and the Falcon; he would be seen over a short period of time playing a jolly-decent Englishman in *Foreign Correspondent,* the arrogant Prussian officer with crew cut and monocle who quickly snuffs out Nelson Eddy in a duel in *Bitter Sweet,* and the would-be dictator of Lichtenberg, adept at throwing people into dungeons, in *Son of Monte Cristo.* Addicted moviegoers of 1940 and 1941 might well have wondered if more than one actor was using the name George

Sanders. He appeared in fourteen films during those two years, and in another eight in 1942. That was the peak of his career in terms of quantity, and although Sanders always liked to give the impression of being indifferent to the films in which he played, he did in fact refuse certain roles and was consequently several times suspended by Twentieth Century-Fox. The year 1942 was a turning point in Sanders's career: aside from finishing his last two Falcon pictures and playing the villain in two Tyrone Power pictures, *Son of Fury* and *The Black Swan,* Sanders essayed his first major screen role, as the Gauguin-like painter in *The Moon and Sixpence.*

In *The Moon and Sixpence* Somerset Maugham had called his painter Charles Strickland, but the model was clearly Gauguin. Sanders performed the part with a quiet, moody single-mindedness that

With Anthony Quinn and Tyrone Power in *The Black Swan*

With Herbert Marshall in *The Moon and Sixpence*

was entirely plausible; his Strickland is a tormented man with "no time to live, only to paint." He leaves his wife after seventeen years of marriage, callously and unemotionally turning away from his middle-class family life and becoming an increasingly shabby Bohemian artist. Eventually he sails to the South Seas and settles in Java, painting native women and finally dying a leper. The film caused some commotion when it was first released due to the paintings of nude women. Maugham's story-telling device was one he used several times—that of having an English gentleman rather like himself, in this case Herbert Marshall, spot the main character in a chance meeting, become interested in him, and follow his career.

The Moon and Sixpence brought Sanders some well-deserved praise, but it also brought a measure of outrage from the female species, who were incensed at the way he treated his women in the picture and at the remarks he made about women in general, such as "The more you beat women, the better they are for it." They started the myth of George Sanders, Woman Hater. In vain he explained that the dialogue was supplied to him by Somerset Maugham as part of the characterization of a brutal man. But the die was cast and Sanders decided to let the impression ride, embroidering on it from time to time at dinner parties and at interviews with newspaper reporters. Typical of the Sanders's line was: "You can treat women like dogs and they will still love you. Personally I always treat dogs with infinite courtesy, and indeed most men treat them better than they do their wives." To a female reporter who asked if Sanders thought a woman should be beautiful before breakfast, he replied: "It would never occur to me to look at a woman before breakfast."

Most of the films Sanders made during the years of the Second World War were routine, topical, and, from this distance, rather ridiculous. He played another Nazi in *This Land is Mine*, an FBI agent posing as a Bund leader in *They Came to Blow Up America*, a propagandizing German broadcaster who is actually a British agent in *Appointment in Berlin*, and a member of the Parisian underground in *Paris After Dark*. His last film on a war subject was *Action in Arabia*, about which he later claimed he could remember nothing, probably because he didn't want to. Sanders's luck picked up in the latter part of 1944, and he appeared in a run of good pictures, the first being *The Lodger*, a turn-of-the-century, fogbound London chiller with Laird Cregar playing Jack the Ripper and Sanders the detective who nails him.

Summer Storm was not a great success with the public but it was a good filming of the Chekov story "The Shooting Party." The central character is a lovely, earthy peasant girl (Linda Darnell) who employs her charms and heartlessly uses men to improve her status. Sanders, as a corrupt judge in a small district of Imperial Russia in 1911, becomes a victim of the girl; he gives up his fiancée and ruins his career for his passion, eventually realizing the girl's worthlessness and killing her. He himself is killed while escaping from the police. As the Russian official Sanders quite obviously drew upon his personal knowledge of Czarist Russia, and gave one of his best performances in a film that deserves wider recognition.

Sanders was perfectly cast in *The Picture of Dorian Gray* as Lord Henry Wooton, Oscar Wilde's satirically witty and challenging cynic, tossing off world-weary epigrams like: "The charm of mar-

With Linda Darnell in *Summer Storm*

riage is that it makes a life of deception absolutely necessary for both parties." Sanders played the part so well he cemented in the public mind the image of himself as a refined cad. The role of Lord Henry is quite an evil one: it is he who plants the fear of aging in the mind of young Dorian Gray and plants the seed of amorality, telling him, "The only way to get rid of a temptation is to yield to it." Gray (Hurd Hatfield) takes the advice to heart and indulges in all kinds of evil with aplomb. By some miracle he remains young and unblemished, while a painting of him ages hideously, reflecting his cruelty and his vile corruption. Wilde took as the inspiration for his plot the Omar Khayyam quattrain:

> I sent my soul through the invisible,
> Some letter of that afterlife to spell,
> And bye and bye my soul returned to me
> and answered,
> I myself am heaven and hell.

Hatfield was excellent as Dorian Gray, yet the part did not launch him as a popular movie actor. Sanders, on the other hand, rose a professional notch with his seemingly effortless delivery of witty and wicked lines.

Sanders was back in the foggy, somber atmosphere of the London of 1903 in *Hangover Square,* but not as a villain. Here he was sympathetic as a Scotland Yard detective and pioneer in the study of criminal insanity. The film marked the last appearance of the remarkable Laird Cregar, playing a brilliant young composer named George Harvey Bone, a kindly man completely absorbed in his music, but with a major quirk in his nature—the striking of discordant chords would bring on fits of aphasia during which he would commit murder and arson. The interplay between Cregar and Sanders was especially touching—the tormented composer realizing something is wrong and appealing for help to the psychiatrist-detective, who gradually, and with gentle understanding, closes in on the tragic case. *Hangover Square* is an excellent film of its kind, and enormously aided by the brilliant musical score of Bernard Herrmann. The film's ending, with Cregar sitting at the piano composing his concerto as his home burns and falls around him, is melodrama taken to the extreme but nonetheless staged with great style. Sadly the death of the composer was followed shortly after by the death of the actor himself. In an effort to reduce his huge bulk from 300 to 200 pounds, the twenty-eight year old Cregar subjected himself to a crash diet course. His appearance had

With Laird Cregar in *Hangover Square*

locked him into the role of villain and he desperately wanted to broaden his scope and play romantic and comic parts. His desperation killed him; his heart was so weakened by the rapid dieting that he died while being operated on for a hernia.

The Strange Affair of Uncle Harry (1945) gave Sanders another chance to be sympathetic but under odd circumstances. Here he was a gentle fellow driven to murder. The scene was a small town in New Hampshire where two sisters and a brother live together, somewhat neurotically, and brood about their past affluence and current lack of wealth. When the brother decides to marry and wisely remove himself, the older sister (Geraldine Fitzgerald) thwarts the marriage plans. When he learns of her vicious plans, the brother decides to poison his sister, but the young sister accidentally takes the poison and dies, and the police pin the murder on the older sister, refusing to believe poor Harry when he pleads that is is the real killer. Hence the "strange affair" of the title—Uncle Harry's committing the perfect crime and not wanting to take credit for it. Aside from playing the interesting role, Sanders profited from selling to Universal the telescope he used in the film—it was one he had built himself, and they paid $500 for it.

Sanders scored again in 1947 with *The Private Affairs of Bel-Ami.* It was not an especially good picture but it allowed him to play a completely caddish Casanova who used women as stepping-stones on the path to social and financial success. The Guy de Maupassant story was set in the Paris of 1880, and the film conveyed a good sense of period and a certain measure of satire. For Sanders it was a field day of callousness to the ladies, limning the

As King Charles II in *Forever Amber*

kind of handsome brute who draws female attention as a flame draws moths. The film focussed the attention of reporters and interviewers on Sanders's actual feelings about women, his most-quoted retort at the time being, "Women are little beasts." It was a stand the women of the world could not allow to pass unchallenged, and Sanders was denounced by women's clubs, and even by the Parents-Teachers Association. Years later he confessed: "I was more or less persuaded into making such wretched observations as publicity for *Bel-Ami*. I doubtless went overboard—I'd developed quite a talent for putting things forcibly. Of course, women long ago coined the phrase 'men are beasts' and they've gotten away with it beautifully."

That George Sanders was not a woman hater is obvious from his marital record, although the record suggests he shares with many other men the predicament of being unable to stay away from women or with them. He was married for the first time in 1940—to Elsie Morie, not long after she had graduated from Hollywood High School. The marriage lasted for seven years, although Sanders neglected to mention it in his autobiography. His most famous marriage was the one with Zsa Zsa Gabor, who had previously been married to Conrad Hilton. By the time they were divorced in 1952, the beautiful Zsa Zsa had developed into a theatrical personality and something of an actress—but more of a character, and clearly a woman whose vivaciousness swamped the languid, leisurely moving Sanders. Reflecting on the five years of the marriage, he recalls that he was "regarded by Zsa Zsa's press agents, dressmakers, the household staff, and sundry visitors and friends with tolerant amusement." Eventually he retreated, his absence apparently barely noticed. He waited a full seven years before trying marriage again, but this time made a wise, and somewhat surprising, choice in Benita Hume, the widow of Ronald Colman. The Colmans had been a notably devoted couple, with Colman's quiet, gentlemanly manner matched with his wife's humor and charm. Sanders married Benita in 1959 and moved to her home in Switzerland, with most of his filming being done in England in the following years. The marriage, seemingly a very good one, ended sadly with Benita's death from cancer in 1967. Sanders's next marriage was a total surprise—in late 1970 he reentered the Gabor family and married Zsa Zsa's sister Magda, but there was talk of annulment within a few months, with a staggering revelation from Sanders that the marriage had never been consummated.

After *The Private Affairs of Bel-Ami*, which was not a box office smash, Sanders slipped into the comfortable and profitable category of supporting player, usually the second or third lead. This served him better both personally and professionally—his status was high enough to draw him top billing only in the less expensive vehicles, but his prestige and popularity were strong enough to get him supporting parts in major productions. He much preferred the latter: "I am not one of those people who would rather act than eat. Quite the reverse. Olivier was born with a desire to act. I was not. My own desire as a boy was to retire. That ambition has never changed." Sanders might have mentioned also his strong liking for the kind of comfort large salaries can provide.

Sanders kept his nose to the celluloid grindstone through 1947 and 1948, playing a heel in *The Ghost and Mrs. Muir*, a foppish and rather lascivious Charles II in *Forever Amber*, the rakish Lord Darlington in *The Fan*—again spouting Oscar Wilde witticisms—and finally in *Lured*, about a sex killer on the loose in London, with Lucille Ball in one of her few noncomedic parts as the lure used by Scotland Yard. Sanders claimed that of all the actresses with whom he worked, Lucille was one of the few he really liked. Among the few of his films he liked was Cecil B. de Mille's *Samson and Delilah*, where he played the Saran of Gaza, a rather jaded monarch with his eye on Hedy Lamarr. Asked why he enjoyed making the picture, Sanders replied: "Because of the big budget. There was no harrowing penny-pinching here. In fact, in some scenes we had 500 extras. Then, too, I didn't have to wear my own clothes. This not only saved me money but also put me at ease. After all, who can make himself feel like a strange character while wearing a suit he had on at a party the night before? I prefer wearing costumes anyway, because with modern clothes you're always conscious of the cut of your garments, whereas if you're wearing a robe dating from several centuries B.C., almost no one can criticize your getup." Sanders went on to explain that he was by nature a frustrated ruler, and enjoyed sitting on thrones, especially if they were comfortable and no real decisions had to be made.

The apex of Sanders's Hollwood career was *All About Eve*, which brought him an Oscar as the best supporting actor of 1950. Brilliantly written and directed by Joseph L. Mankiewicz, the film knowingly probed the psyche and the life-style of the theater and its people, with Sanders as a critic

With Julia Faye and Hedy Lamarr in *Samson and Delilah*

With Anne Baxter, Bette Davis, and Marilyn Monroe in *All About Eve*

described by Bette Davis's actress character as "that venomous fishwife." For the narrative opening, Mankiewicz used Sanders to explain the gist of the story and his own part in it: "My name is Addison de Witt. My native habitat is the theater. In it I toil not, neither do I spin. I am a critic and commentator. I am essential to the theater—as ants to a picnic, as the boll weevil to a cottonfield." The central character of *All About Eve* is an ambitious young actress (Anne Baxter) who worms her way into the affection of her favorite actress (Davis) and with seeming humility advances step by step up the ladder of success. The critic, debonair of manner and Machiavellian by nature, sees through the conniving girl and foils her attempt to break up the marriage of a playwright. In one memorable scene, the critic visits the young actress and unmasks her, threatening to expose her if she proceeds with her plans for the playwright. The critic succeeds in that ploy but not in preventing Eve from rising to the top of her profession. The Mankiewicz film remains the best and the most sophisticated film essay on the theater, a gem among intelligent pieces of film craft, but not one that met with great approval from the public. Sanders believed the picture lacked audience identification. "Our film was about ambitious, wickedly amusing people, and the public wasn't rooting for any of us. Our heroine was an actress passionately in love with success. What she lusted after was an Oscar, and when she got it, this was, to the public, a poor substitute for getting a man."

The winning of an Oscar did not do a great deal for George Sanders's career—it didn't harm it but neither did it advance it. "The truth of the matter is that while Hollywood admires people who win Oscars, it employs people who make money, and to be able to do one does not necessarily mean you can do the other." Sanders followed *All About Eve* with two undistinguished pictures, *I Can Get it for You Wholesale,* and *The Light Touch,* a minor crime story which could badly have used a light touch. In 1952 Sanders went to England for MGM to appear in the first of several historical pictures; in *Ivanhoe,* he was Norman knight Sir Brian de Bois-Guilbert, a brutal fellow redeemed only by his affection for the Jewess Rebecca (Elizabeth Taylor), and finally beaten to a bloody pulp on the jousting field by Ivanhoe (Robert Taylor). This was followed by two stinkers, also made in Europe—*Captain Blackjack,* and *Assignment Paris.*

The winning of an Oscar has not always helped a star's career, and by now Sanders was beginning to wonder if the gold statuette was the jinx to him that it had been to several others. However, things picked up with *Call Me Madam,* the film of Irving Berlin's Broadway musical, and Sanders was offered his first singing role. As the elegant and beautifully uniformed foreign minister of a mythical little European country, Sanders serenaded Ethel Merman with his baritone voice, singing songs like "The Best Thing for You Would Be Me" and "Marrying for Love." The 1953 musical was a moderate success, but most people felt the singing Sanders was out of character and that he was merely mouthing someone else's voice. He also appeared on radio at this time, and on one program with Tallulah Bankhead sang a dramatic Verdi aria which so surprised the studio audience that there was silence when he finished—Tallulah had to step in and lead the applause. Sanders had hidden his singing voice too long.

By his own admission he also lacked ambition; when Ezio Pinza left the cast of *South Pacific,* Sanders made a recording of several of the songs and sent them to Rodgers and Hammerstein, asking to be considered as a replacement. He was invited to New York, auditioned and immediately accepted. Contracts were drawn up and signed—then Sanders went back to California and panicked at the thought of singing every night on Broadway in a long run. The next day he sent a message to Rodgers and Hammerstein telling them that it had become impossible for him to accept their offer.

George Sanders's next venture into filmed history was *King Richard and the Crusaders,* with him as the Lion-Hearted and Rex Harrison as Saladin. The screenplay by John Twist was easier to follow than the Sir Walter Scott novel on which it was based, *The Talisman.* The two actors brought a believable, urbane quality to the outsized historical figures—Harrison making the Saracen a dignified as well as ornate character, and Sanders giving Richard a solid, vainglorious, and plodding character. Sanders made the point that Richard was not a good king: he spent little of his reign in England and he twice bankrupted his own country by financing crusades that proved nothing. Sanders's version of Richard is possibly close to the truth—Richard as a brave and inspiring warrior but a considerable fool, carried through the history books on the basis of a colorful personality.

Like many other movie actors, George Sanders could move beyond his image whenever different kinds of parts presented themselves, but unlike most other movie actors he seldom expended

With Rex Harrison and Laurence Harvey in *King Richard and the Crusaders*

enough energy to seek them. When he said "I drifted into fame" it was a jest firmly wrapped in truth. Such an actor depends largely on luck for getting good parts, and the whole Sanders film list is a record of occasional good parts and many mediocre ones. In 1954 Sanders signed with MGM to do a group of pictures, all of them in costume, the first requiring him to don the robes of a Roman ruler: this was *Jupiter's Darling,* a musical about Hannibal crossing the Alps. Although one of the less successful MGM musicals, the film had a goodly measure of satire and fun. Victor Mature was the beefy warrior who led his elephants to crush the Roman legions, and Esther Williams was the affianced of the ruler, a girl continually putting off her wedding day and obviously looking around for something better—and doing most of her thinking while swimming. But it was Sanders who stole the

With Marge and Gower Champion, Esther Williams, and Norma Varden in *Jupiter's Darling*

film with his amusing characterization of a mother-dominated Caesar. He was deadly earnest in his courting of Esther and, although he wasn't exactly effeminate, there was something about the way he said "Oh, mother!" that suggested Victor Mature didn't have much competition.

Sanders followed his fey Caesar with three more historical pageants, none of them creating much impact with the public. In *Moonfleet* he was Lord Ashwood, an unscrupulous nobleman engaged in smuggling in the Dorsetshire of 1757; in *The Scarlet Coat,* the story of Benedict Arnold, the notorious American traitor of the Revolutionary War, Sanders was a doctor trying to warn the Americans of the impending treachery; and in *The King's Thief* he was again Charles II, but not bothering to put much spirit into it.

By the time he reached his fiftieth birthday in 1956, George Sanders was still making film after film but obviously enjoying it less and less. He was amusing as an egocentric cartoonist who employed Bobe Hope to ghost his work in *That Certain Feeling,* but he was weary in films like *Never Say Goodbye* and *While the City Sleeps.* Whereas in the early days of his career he knew his scripts from top to bottom, now he usually read them a few pages at a time and just prior to the filming of the scenes, claiming that he could only maintain an interest in the screenplay if he didn't know how it would end. Occasionally he would give a performance with some vitality, as in *Death of a Scoundrel,* a modestly budgeted picture, one of the last to come from RKO Radio before that studio was

With Laurence Naismith and Yul Brynner in *Solomon and Sheba*

sold to television. It was the first time in several years that Sanders had been given top billing and it also proved to be the last time. The story concerned an opportunistic European cad who arrives in America and quickly manipulates his way to wealth by romancing influential women. Though denied by the producers, it was clearly based on the nefarious career of Serge Rubinstein, a flamboyant financier who met a violent end at the hands of a partner he had cheated. For Sanders the picture was a tour de force, a summation of years of playing elegantly mannered bounders who lie, cheat, and steal with charming aplomb.

Sanders followed *Death of a Scoundrel* with a string of routine films: *The Seventh Sin, The Whole Truth, From the Earth to the Moon* and *That Kind of Woman.* Things looked up when he was signed to play the villain in *Solomon and Sheba,* with Tyrone Power and Gina Lollobrigida in the title roles. Sanders was Adonijah, the evil older brother of Solomon; seemingly the two sons of King David had nothing in common except parentage. The budget was set at $4,000,000 and the company proceeded to Spain in late 1958, to shoot the interior scenes in Madrid and the many outdoor sequences on location near Zaragoza. Sanders was pleased to be working again with Power. The Hollywood fame of both men had begun with *Lloyds of London* more than twenty years previously, and Sanders had several times played the heavy opposite Power's hero; so it was like old times. The pleasure came to an abrupt and tragic end on November 15th. The two actors were to

With Zsa Zsa Gabor in *Death of a Scoundrel*

film the duel with broadswords in which the wicked brother would be killed by the noble one; they rehearsed the scene in the morning and then took a break. Shortly after he had arrived back in his dressing room to relax, Sanders was told by the assistant director that Power had had a spasm of some kind. "I wandered over to his trailer and opened the door. He was sitting in a chair twisted over on his left side and holding on tightly to his arm. His head was tilted over rigidly as though some crick in his neck prevented him from straightening it. Even though he was wearing makeup his face had a sort of bluish color, but he greeted me with a smile. 'What's up?' I said. 'Oh, it'll go away,' he said, 'I've had it before. It's this damned bursitis.' I suggested to him that he should lie down but he said it felt worse when he tried to stretch out." With that Sanders returned to his own trailer. About an hour later he was told that Power had died. The forty-four-year-old actor had succumbed to a heart attack.

Whether *Solomon and Sheba* would have been a successful picture had Power lived to complete his role is debatable. All of his footage had to be scrapped, and Yul Brynner was brought in to play the role. The end result was a large lumbering epic that failed to draw enough customers to cover its cost. The picture does contain some good battle scenes, thanks to the Spanish Army, which allowed the employment of 3,000 of their troops. Sanders, who has never enjoyed the action sequences of his films, described in his *Memoirs of a Professional Cad* his plight amid the hordes of horses, chariots, and furious men running around with spears and bows and arrows:

> When we were actually joined in battle it was quite terrifying. Even though they were only mock battles, they might almost as well have been in earnest if we consider the amount of damage and the number of casualties involved. No less than twelve horses were killed and countless extras were carted off to the hospital with broken ankles, broken collarbones, or just plain exhaustion and shock. It was nothing short of a miracle that no human lives were lost, and there were times when I seriously doubted my own chances of survival.
>
> I cannot say that I acquitted myself nobly on the field of battle. My sword was made of rubber, my shield of Fiberglass, my breastplate of lightweight papier-mâché. All I had to do was to look heroic and not fall out of my chariot. I was hard put to do either. To look heroic when one is terrified is no easily accomplished feat. If I had fallen backwards out of my chariot I would have been trampled to death by the horses drawing the chariot

behind me. We were galloping at breakneck speed over rough terrain and I had only a small concealed leather strap to hang on to with my left hand while I brandished my broadsword with my right. How those fellows managed to do it for real in days of old, weighted down with the authentic metal armor, is something that is quite beyond my limited powers of comprehension. As it was I ended each day a mass of scratches and bruises just from bumping against the sides and front of the chariot, in spite of the fact that all possible inside surfaces had been lined with sponge rubber by the thoughtful property department in order to give me the maximum possible protection.

> To add to my discomfort I was, of course, suffering from the sort of upset stomach that plagues most foreigners in Spain, and certainly all of those who venture anywhere near Zaragoza where the water is perpetually contaminated.
>
> A combination of abject terror and upset stomach does not, generally speaking, contribute much to the kind of mood that is needed for an actor to envisage a heroic playing attitude.

Sanders survived the making of *Solomon and Sheba* and took up residence with his new bride in Switzerland. He hadn't been there long when producer Andrew Stone contacted him and asked him to appear in *The Last Voyage,* to be shot entirely in Japan. Stone had made an arrangement with a Japanese marine demolition company to allow him to use the old French liner *Ile de France* just prior to their scrapping it. The story called for the sinking of an ocean liner, and Stone's inspired idea was to film such an event in actuality. His film emerged as an exciting piece of entertainment, especially to anyone who had ever sailed on an ocean liner and pondered the thought of it going under. Sanders played the captain, a man obsessed with nautical pride and determined to keep to his schedule even though doing so ran the risk of danger. His constant command "Make speed!" eventually strained the engines of the old liner and she exploded, caught fire, and sank. Stone partially sank the *Ile de France* on a sandbar and, since the ship was to be destroyed anyway, he was able to abuse her at random, giving a graphic account of the excitement and the terror involved in a liner sinking. According to Sanders, the travail in filming the destruction of the ship was secondary to the anguish involved in dealing with the crooked, devious Japanese junkyard tycoons.

The Last Voyage, released in 1960, was Sanders's last first-rate film. He did, in fact, work in some twenty films during the 1960s, but hardly any of them are worth discussion. He freely admitted that his appearance in these films was due to the coercion of his agent and that, once he was involved with them, his main thought was to do the job as quickly as possible and return home. Some of the films were entertaining, although requiring little of Sanders: *The Village of the Damned* was a good science fiction thriller, *A Shot In the Dark* was amusing, and Disney's *In Search of the Castaways* pleased the children; but even Sanders's friends chided him for supporting English comics like Terry-Thomas, Tony Hancock and Charlie Drake in their routine comedies. He just walked through the parts in his tired fashion and picked up his wages, never bothering to see the pictures.

The most ambitious film in which he appeared in the mid-1960s was *The Amorous Adventures of Moll Flanders*, Paramount's blatant attempt to cash in on the appetite for bawdy costume humor

With Kim Novak in *The Amorous Adventures of Moll Flanders*

created by *Tom Jones*. The picture was more specious than spicy, but Sanders cut an amusing figure as a rich banker who marries Moll (Kim Novak) and dies of a heart attack after he finds her in prison—thereby leaving her a lady of wealth. Their nuptial scene was amusing. If nothing else, the sixty-year-old Sanders made a convincing albeit weary roué.

Sanders raised a few eyebrows when he played a transvestite in John Huston's *The Kremlin Letter* in 1971. The spy thriller, in keeping with the times, was more perverse, more crude and earthy, than such pictures had been before, but for all that it did not appeal much to the jaded public. Sanders

as a drag queen with long blonde hair, heavy makeup, and a slit skirt, entertaining in a homosexual bar, was believable in the most bizarre role he ever played but the characterization raised, in the minds of some, questions of taste. For Sanders it was just another job and, as with most of his films, one he was not prepared to discuss.

To be a successful film actor—to last a long time at a difficult trade that is subject to the whims of a changing public—a man must have an image. And that image is largely born of his own character and personality, even of his weaknesses and his insecurities. Sanders admitted: "If I have occasionally given brilliant performances on the screen, the blunt truth is that I invariably play myself. Sometimes playing myself is appropriate to the part and then I receive rave notices and even an Oscar (as I did for *All About Eve*); at other times playing myself is singularly inappropriate to the circumstances of the story and then I am quite rightly panned. Therefore the only credit I can claim for myself is that I have occasionally chosen—or been bribed into playing—the right parts."

George Sanders was unusual among film actors because he was completely honest about his craft; he made no bones about the good luck in drifting into a line of work that was, for him, easy and well-paid—nor did he deny that there was a personal fulfillment in acting out fantasies that he would not have had the courage to perform in reality. Sanders was never afraid to state his opinions, or concerned that those opinions were sometimes painful and offensive. In his *Memoirs of a Professional Cad*, he revealed himself and his fellow actors with a candor that is rare in his trade:

Actors are oddly compounded of fact and fantasy. They are spell-binders who are bound by their own spells.

Sometimes this curious sorcery produces a second man, a sort of sorcerer's apprentice, or marionette, who leads a separate, almost uncontrolled life of his own, and the actor finds himself watching with great astonishment as he is identified as "The Man You Love to Hate" or "The World's Sweetheart" or "The Stingiest Man on Earth," "The Blonde Bombshell" or "The First Lady of the Screen"—although this last has been regarded as an unethical short cut in the more austere circles, since it was admitted to be only a matter of wearing white gloves.

Sometimes this marionette or mask is so intoxicatingly beautiful that the wearer becomes reluctant to reveal his less enlivening aspects to the public, and retires inviolate, securely carapaced from the world by his mask.

In *The Kremlin Letter*

Sometimes he becomes indistinguishable from the parts he plays, as in the case of the late Douglas Fairbanks, who led his life in a state of such uncontained euphoria, glamour, and action as to make his films pale in comparison.

More often the really good actors and actresses are at their best acting. As they spend most of the twenty-four hours at their daily disposal acting, this does not in general detract from their charm.

They are apt not to be particularly practical, because they *want* money, they *need* applause. They may want a wife but need an audience. A lot of times they want an opinion but need the dialogue.

George Sanders's life came to an end on April 25, 1972. It was a sudden and tragic end by suicide. Shocking though it was, his death somehow seemed rather characteristic of the man. He was sixty-five and, although he appeared to be in good physical health, he had quipped about death for a long time. His blasé, cynical gibes were taken as part of his odd brand of humor, but in snuffing out his life he proved himself to have been in earnest. Sanders died from an overdose of Nembutal in his hotel room at Casteldelfels, ten miles south of Barcelona, Spain. He left two notes, the first of which was addressed to "Dear World" and read: "I am leaving because I am bored. I feel I have lived long enough. I am leaving you with your worries in this sweet cesspool—good luck." The second note was written in Spanish, asking its finder to telephone his sister in London and explain what had happened to him. It also pointed out that there was enough cash in his clothing to pay his hotel bill and cover the cost of the funeral.

Lonely, childless, with few material assets, long tired of being an actor and much appalled at the condition of the world, George Sanders clearly saw no reason to continue living. He placed little value on his screen image, probably because he could not share the enjoyment it gave his audiences. Neither could he appreciate the uniqueness of that image—the ultimate cultured cad. Sanders would have yawned or sneered to have heard himself so described. But if a man cannot be replaced, he is indeed unique.

4

VINCENT PRICE

*I*F MOST film actors mine their own personality to manufacture a professional alter ego, Vincent Price is the prime example of these who do not. Prior to *House of Wax* in 1953, he had played a variety of cads, crooks, and weaklings, but since appearing as the mad sculptor in that celebrated horror film Price has worked almost entirely in a celluloid world of weird science fiction, populated by fiends and monsters, demented doctors, perverted scientists, Satan worshipers, torturers, necromancers, and tormented spirits. He has prospered in this milieu of haunted houses, crypts, and dungeons. Asked why, Price smiles a little wickedly and explains, "People love to see a man enjoying his work."

The difference between the private man and his ghoulish screen image is extreme; in fact, there is a distinct dichotomy. Vincent Price is a cultured man and, in a business fraught with emotional imbalance and insecurity, he is remarkably sane. His sanity is anchored in his life-long fascination with art; his career as a popular actor has enabled him to build an impressive collection of paintings, sculpture, and artifacts, as well as a reputation as an art connoisseur. Price has so far delivered more than 300 lectures on art and literature to club and college audiences. His book *I Like What I Know*, published in 1959, is largely an appreciation of art; in 1962 he was chosen by Sears, Roebuck and Co. to assemble their offering of classic and modern paintings, which resulted in Price traveling far afield and buying more than 50,000 items. In addition, Price is a gourmet cook: his book *A Treasury of Great Recipes*, written in collaboration with his wife, has sold a quarter of a million copies. As a member of the U.S. Department of the In-

Vincent Price in *The Raven*

terior's Indian Arts and Crafts Board, Price has brought wide attention to the artistry of the American Indians, and was responsible for Sears's donating five Indian paintings to the White House.

While pursuing his interest in art, lecturing, writing, and raising funds for museums, Price has appeared in a series of horror films generally considered by critics and intellectuals as being cultural rubbish and just about the lowest form of melodrama. One explanation for his appearance in these is the handsome income, but Price offers no apology: "I'm not at all ashamed to be in entertainment pictures. I like to be seen, I love being busy and I believe in being active. I know some people think I've lowered myself as an actor—well, my idea of professional decline is not working. My horror films led to dozens of comedy appearances on television with Jack Benny and Red Skelton, and innumerable talk shows. The constant exposure was more than most actors could dream of."

Price has never looked upon his horror films as anything more than standard escapist fare: "Actually, they are a kind of comedy—they are believed for only a moment and remembered no longer than a boo! I hesitate even to call them horror pictures. To me films that deal with drug addiction, crime, and war are the horror films. Mine are fairy tales. I concentrated on nineteenth-century literature in college and even then I never thought of the Poe stories as horrific but rather as Gothic. These films are Gothic entertainment; their challenge for the actor lies in trying to make the unreal real, whereas in a contemporary crime story the problem lies in making the real unreal enough to be dramatic. My main concern in playing these strange roles is in making them believable, which is not easy. Neither is it easy to scare people in a world where actual slaughter and vicious crimes are common, daily occurrences. Compared to current warfare practices, a good ghoulish movie is comic relief."

Vincent Price is, quite possibly, the least demented of any actor in the film world, and there is nothing in his background that should have led him eventually to specialize in films of fear and fiendishness. Price was born of a nontheatrical, upper middle-class family in St. Louis, Missouri on May 27, 1911. His grandfather became wealthy from the sale of Price's Baking Powder, and his father was the president of a confectionary company. Price, Sr., was able to offer his four children a happy home as well as an affluent one; it was also an environment that encouraged an appreciation of music and the arts and a curiosity about life. As Price readily admits, "I could hardly have been more fortunate in my choice of a family. In the summer of 1927, when I was sixteen, they let me travel to Europe by myself, possibly because my years of constant questioning about the rest of the world had drained them of answers." Price spent

that summer in an ecstacy of discovery—soaking up the atmospheres of the British Museum, The Louvre, and the art galleries of Amsterdam, Brussels, Florence, Venice, Vienna, Nuremburg, and Rome—proving himself to have remarkable interests and appetites for a sixteen-year-old boy. But, he says, "When I got back from Europe, I had only one year left before going to college, and, inspired by that trip, I determined to become an active artist. In that one year I learned a fact that I wasn't about to admit for five years—I had no talent at all. I tried painting, sculpting, and woodcutting, to no avail. But one thing this lack of talent taught me. Appreciation. When you try to do something and can't—and admit you can't—you learn a healthy respect for it and for those who can."

Vincent Price attended Yale University and completed the four years of a straight academic course, majoring in art history and graduating with a B.A. He was an average student with an above average interest in having a good time. The famed Yale Drama School did not appeal to him; he found the atmosphere precious and he believed then, as now, that acting is best learned empirically. He did, however, join and greatly enjoy the Yale Glee Club, which traveled and sang in competition with other clubs, and one summer took its sixty members on a European tour; this gave Price another opportunity to peek at the art houses, "between rehearsals, concerts, and hangovers." His first job after leaving Yale was as a teacher at the Riverside Country Day School, Yonkers, New York, with a secondary job as a bus driver to eke out the meager pay. Discontent set in, due to a strong but vague desire to make a living in the arts, and no idea of how to go about it. Price solved his dilemma by going back to being a student; with the money his father had sent him as a graduation present he decided to enroll at the Courtauld Institute of the University of London and invest two years studying for a master's degree in art.

Price went to London in 1933 as a student but left two years later as a working actor. At the University of London he had the well-timed advantage of attending lectures given by all the great artists, art experts, and museum directors Hitler was kicking out of Germany. "It was a fabulous time. But it was extraordinary to think that these seemingly harmless, erudite men were thought to be such a threat to Hitler. Actually they were because they had been teaching and writing that freedom in art was the true expression of democracy, and that it was the one creative commodity which transcends barriers of race, creed, color, and politics." Price had a chance to visit the country from whence these men were being evicted. In early 1935 he went to Nuremberg; he had chosen for his master's thesis to write on the great Nuremberg-born artist Dürer, who remains Price's artistic hero. Price also spent some time in Vienna, at the School of the Danube, studying Dürer and the whole German Renaissance.

Dedicated as he was to the study of art, Price's attentions were more and more drawn to the theater during his two years in London. While at Courtauld he joined a Gilbert and Sullivan amateur group, making something of a mark with his Captain in *H.M.S. Pinafore*. As a result of this he was persuaded to joint the Gate Theatre, a professional but private theatrical club. This was his entrée into the life of an actor; "My first part was as an American policeman in their play *Chicago,* in which I was also the technical adviser to the English cast of the art of chewing gum. My pay was three pounds a week and I still have a ten-shilling note from the first pay packet." Flushed with success, Price two months later tried out for the part of Prince Albert in *Victoria Regina*. He impressed the producers with his command of the German language and the fact that he read the part with a good German accent. Price was hired. The good notices received by the London company drew the attention of American impresario Gilbert Miller, who was looking for a vehicle for Helen Hayes. Miller bought the rights to *Victoria Regina* and offered Price the same role in the New York production. "Gilbert gave me a salary of $250 a week, once I started with his company, but he didn't give me anything in advance. Most of my London wages had been spent in bookstores and art galleries, and the only way I could get from London to New York was steerage. Gilbert arranged a press reception for me when the boat docked in New York, but they all thought I was in first class, with the result that they missed me and there was no conference. I was accused by Gilbert of pulling a Garbo." No one ever made such an accusation again; Price is the least Garbo-like and one of the most gregarious of actors—he enjoys the limelight and he loves company.

Gilbert Miller's production of *Victoria Regina* opened in New York the day after Christmas, 1935, with Helen Hayes performing what would become one of her most celebrated parts. The play ran for more than 500 performances and her leading man

for the entire run was Vincent Price. As a friend of the greatly esteemed Helen Hayes, he had access to the elite of the New York theater, and the long run enabled him to explore the art galleries of the city and to mingle with people of similar interests. He was offered film contracts during the run of the play but was advised by Helen Hayes, who disliked films, to turn them down and stay with the theater long enough to learn something of the craft of acting. With the close of *Victoria Regina,* Price played in anything that came along—stock companies, soap opera on radio, and, several times, the Orson Welles Mercury Theater. In April of 1938 Price married actress Edith Barrett; their marriage would end in divorce ten years later. Their son, Vincent Barrett Price, has distinguished himself as a poet, an anthropologist, and a teacher at the Westinghouse Learning Institute.

In the summer of 1938 Price made his first visit to Hollywood, invited by Universal to costar with Constance Bennett in a comedy, *Service de Luxe.* The picture was only a mild success but Universal offered Price a contract, an unusual one at the time because it allowed for him to spend half the year working as a stage actor and the other half as a Universal employee. Price returned to New York to appear with Laurette Taylor in *Outward Bound;* after a long and successful run he was recalled by Universal and told that he had been loaned to Warner Brothers to play Sir Walter Raleigh in their expensive treatment of *The Private Lives of Elizabeth and Essex,* with Bette Davis and Errol Flynn in the title roles. "This was a frightening experience. I was still very new to the movie business, a greenhorn, and I walked into an atmosphere on that film that you could cut with a knife. Davis objected to Flynn playing Essex, she had wanted Olivier, and Flynn was at the height of his success and charmingly cavalier—to the extent of not bothering to learn his lines. Every time Errol would blow a line when I was on the set, the director, Michael Curtiz, would point to me and say in his hideous Hungarian accent, 'I get this boy to play part.' I had done Essex on the stage with Mildred Natwick as Elizabeth, and Curtiz used me as a stick to wag in Flynn's face, which did nothing to endear me to Errol. But his part called for him to despise me anyway—Raleigh was a rival suitor for the Queen's favor."

Price's noble bearing as Raleigh inspired Universal to cast him as Clarence in their rather macabre version of *Tower of London,* with Basil Rathbone as Richard III and Boris Karloff as his

With Guy Bellis, James Stephenson, Leo G. Carroll,
Donald Crisp, and Errol Flynn in *The Private Lives
of Elizabeth and Essex*

With Henry Stephenson, Bette Davis, Leo Carroll, and
Errol Flynn in *The Private Lives of Elizabeth and
Essex*

executioner. One of the most memorable sequences in this saga of the murderous monarch is his dispatching of Clarence—Richard gets the unfortunate duke blind drunk and, when he passes out (Price claims he almost really passed out from the nausea of swilling watered-down coke throughout the long rhearsal), Richard and his clubfooted torturer pick him up, stuff him head first into a huge barrel full of wine, and close the lid. The director insisted that the scene be enacted in actuality and not faked. Recalls Price: "It was dreadful. They fixed a hand rail at the bottom of the barrel so that I could dive down and hang on to it. The liquid was water but Basil and Boris had used the barrel to deposit cigarette butts and old bottles; I had to hold on to the rail for a full ten counts, which seemed endless, and then a couple of hefty lads opened this damp tomb and yanked me out by the heels. I got a round of applause from the crew but I was disappointed to find my two costars, who had been very nice to me so far, not on the set. I thought the least they could do was lead the applause. But they appeared a few moments later with a beautifully wrapped gift—a carton of cokes."

Other than this dunking as Clarence, Price did nothing in his contracted two years with Universal that led him to think he had made the Hollywood grade. He was a hunter who got killed while seeking the Inca ruins in a South American jungle in *Green Hell;* he played the title role in *The Invisible Man Returns,* and he was the good brother in *The House of Seven Gables,* with George Sanders as the bad brother who frames him for murder in order to garner their father's hidden wealth. Price singles out *Green Hell* as being the worst of this group: "It's one of the corniest pictures ever made and I'm sure there must be film societies who show this thing just for laughs. It certainly contains the most ridiculous line ever spoken by an actor on the screen: Doug Fairbanks, Jr., played my death scene with me, he being the heroic leader of the expedition, Brandy by name. As I lay dying, struck down by a poisoned arrow, I looked up at him and weakly asked, 'Tell me, Brandy. Is it possible to be in love with two women at the same time and in your heart be faithful to each and yet want to be free of both of them?' I think that line brought down the house wherever it played."

In 1940 Price signed with Twentieth Century-Fox on a seven-year contract, again allowing him time to appear on the stage. His first two roles for them were historical figures; he played Joseph Smith, the founder of the Mormon religion, in *Brigham Young,* and King Charles II in *Hudson's Bay,* with Paul Muni as Pierre Radison, the French-Canadian trapper who first explored Hudson's Bay. Neither film was a great success and Price began to have doubts about his future in films. He returned to Broadway in 1941 and found he was still lucky in the East if not in the West; Price was cast in the play *Angel Street,* which became one of the most successful plays of the war years. Until that time, his image as an actor had been that of a good man, largely because of his identification with Prince Albert. In *Angel Street* Price was a villain, an evil husband; the play ran for a year and he realized that his style and his humor lent itself to the aura of a wickedness and madness. Upon returning to Fox late in 1942 he discussed this with his employers and they agreed. *Angel Street* set the tone of Price's career; beginning with the prosecutor in *The Song of Bernadette,* the man who tried to have the girl committed to an insane asylum, Price started to specialize in roles of cruelty—and to build a solid livelihood on the weaknesses of the human species. Price remembers *The Song of Bernadette* because of the tedious nine-month shooting schedule. "Since it was a great religious picture, Fox approached it on their knees and wasted much money and time on each decision. For example, it took them weeks to decide whether the vision seen by Bernadette should be seen by the audience, and more weeks to decide who should play the lady, supposedly the Virgin Mary, of the vision. Finally they decided on Linda Darnell—I think she was pregnant at the time."

It was during the making of *The Song of Bernadette,* partly to relieve the boredom, that Price opened his own art gallery, going into partnership with another cultured actor, George Macready, also a specialist in screen villainy. Macready had appeared with Price in *Victoria Regina,* playing the part of Albert's brother, Prince Ernest. "We rented a shop in Beverly Hills between a bookstore and a very popular bar, figuring correctly that we'd catch a mixed clientele of erudites and inebriates." The Price-Macready gallery also became a hangout for homesick New York actors and artists, and a social center for the wives of their friends. The gallery lasted two years, neither making nor losing money, but at least providing the owners with a chance to indulge their interests and introduce some painters who profited from the exposure. Price found, as have others, that Hollywood is not a patron of the arts. In his book he says, "I don't suppose there has ever been a community upon which the attention of the world has been more acutely focused, and strangely enough it doesn't stand up in the light. The movie people, who by a flick of a publicity agent could do limitless good for the arts, are listless. A few of them collect for varied reasons—love of it, fashion, investment, snobbery, conversation—but a very few lend real interest and support to the arts. Only a fistful go to exhibitions, buy contemporary local artists' work, lend pictures for public exhibition, or are interested in the basic purpose of the arts—education." Price is aware that his promotion of the arts has made him a somewhat suspect figure among many of his fellow actors, too few of whom have interests beyond their work. "I've seen so many actors stagnate from boredom in Hollywood—doing nothing, in the misguided thought that there's nothing to do."

After *The Song of Bernadette*, Price became a well-employed film actor, playing a variety of parts before being locked into the genre of horror. He played William G. McAdoo in *Wilson*, Fox's huge and overblown tribute to Woodrow Wilson— McAdoo was the Secretary of the Treasury during Wilson's administration as well as his son-in-law.

With Gene Tierney, Clifton Webb, and Dana Andrews in *Laura*

With Jennifer Jones in *The Song of Bernadette*

Price then turned into the elegant weakling Shelby Carpenter, a would-be suitor of *Laura* and a rival of Clifton Webb's for her hand. *Laura* is a film with many virtues, one of them being the rather bitchy exchanges between Price and Webb. In *The Keys of the Kingdom*, Price was a high-ranking churchman of dubious politics and ethics, but

in his following film, *The Eve of St. Mark,* he was allowed one of his few opportunities to present a nice, admirable character—a well-spoken private soldier from Georgia given to oratory while serving on an island in the South Pacific in the Second World War. Based on the play by Maxwell Anderson, the film is fondly remembered by Price although it seems a lost and forgotten picture for most people. His next film was also based on a play: *A Royal Scandal,* taken from the play *The Czarina,* with Tallulah Bankhead as Catherine the Great and Price as the French Ambassador she seduces. The film died in the hands of Otto Preminger, who took it on when Ernst Lubitsch became too ill to direct it, as originally planned. *A Royal Scandal* badly needed the Lubitsch touch.

Leave Her to Heaven gave Gene Tierney her juiciest and most melodramatic role in films, as a jealous and spiteful woman who allows her crippled brother-in-law to drown, aborts her own unborn child, and commits suicide to frame her sister when she learns the sister loves her husband. Price was also juicy in this film, as a lawyer who once loved the heroine and now delights in trying to convict the sister. He was even juicier in *Shock* as a psychiatrist and a murderer, imprisoning a neighbor (Lynn Bari) in his sanitarium after she loses her senses witnessing him killing his wife. By now, 1946, Price had cast his die as a delineator of homicidal dementia. He solidified the impression with *Dragonwyck*, a stylish piece of gothic film written and directed by Joseph L. Mankiewicz. The story was set in New York's Hudson Valley in

As the French Ambassador in *A Royal Scandal*

1840 and revealed a little-known facet of Americana—the almost feudal landlording of vast estates in that area by certain Dutch patroon families, and their fight to keep their tenant farmers in subjugation. Price, as an egotistical landowner named Van Ryn, marries a lovely governess (Gene Tierney)

With Gene Tierney in *Dragonwyck*

and then attempts to do what he had done with his first wife—kill her. The role allowed Price to be suave and subtle in his villainy, and proud in the manner in which he defied the law and met his death. Mankiewicz's *Dragonwyck* did much to establish him as a filmmaker of imagination.

Price's last film for Twentieth Century-Fox under his contract was *Moss Rose,* an English murder mystery in which he was not a villain but a Scotland yard detective. After this, Price became a freelance actor, first going to the RKO studios to appear in *The Long Night,* an American setting of the classic French crime film *Le Jour Se Leve.* Price was a Svengali-like magician who performs a touring act; in a small Ohio town he meets a naive young girl (Barbara Bel Geddes) and captivates her with his charm until he is killed by her jealous boyfriend (Henry Fonda). The film was not a success, possibly because the Gallic qualities of the original did not translate well to the American idiom, especially with director Anatole Litvak slavishly imitating the original.

In *The Web* Price was an industrialist involved with crime, and in *Up in Central Park* he played New York City's "Boss" Tweed, a colorful, corrupt turn-of-the-century politician. This picture was a flop and Price suspects Universal intended it to be because they wanted to dump the expensive Deanna Durbin. "Deanna was a much more lusty and amusing woman than her film image. She wanted to change the image but they wouldn't let her. Then after her box office value dropped and because her contract still specified a large salary, they torpedoed her career. In the case of *Up in Central Park,* they edited out most of the songs, leaving a Sigmund Romberg operetta minus Romberg. Naturally, it died. Deanna later made a settlement with the studio and left Hollywood, never returning."

By the end of the 1940s the Price career was sagging for want of good vehicles. Since he left Fox, his pictures had done little to build his popularity with the public, and it seemed he was heading for the category of supporting player. In the Dick Powell thriller *Rogues' Regiment,* he was a Dutch gunrunner-cum-antiques dealer operating in Indo-China and inevitably rubbed out by his crooked associates; in *The Bribe* he ran a smuggling ring in the Caribbean, until put out of business by Robert Taylor; and in *Bagdad* he was a dastardly pasha leading a band of murdering tribesmen. A bright spot in this period was his appearance as Richelieu in MGM's lavish and rambunctious ver-

As Cardinal Richelieu with Gene Kelly in *The Three Musketeers*

sion of *The Three Musketeers*. But even this part had some built-in restrictions: "As villain of the piece I couldn't be referred to in the script as a Cardinal for fear of offending the Catholic Church —God only knows what I was supposed to be in those red robes. Then MGM sent us all written instructions on how to pronounce the French names: the g in d'Artagnan was said to be hard, and the last syllable of Richelieu was to be sounded as *loo*. It was pointless to argue."

The films in which Price has appeared, whether good or bad, give almost no indication of his personality or his intellect. His film work is something remote from both his social reputation as a man of humor and hospitality, and his avocation as a patron of the arts. His wife, Mary Grant, whom he married in 1949, shares his interest in art and is herself an avid collector—at the time of their

marriage she was a fashion designer at Paramount. Their home in Beverly Hills is a virtual art museum and a satisfaction for Price in the face of his failure to establish an actual art museum in Hollywood. He and Edward G. Robinson, the film colony's premier collector of paintings, opened the Modern Institute of Art in 1948, but it closed two years later for lack of support. The project did, however, result in Price's being named to the board of the Los Angeles County Museum.

In 1950 Price made two films he lists among his favorites, although neither did very well with the public: *Champagne for Caesar,* and *The Baron of Arizona*. The former was a spoof of television game shows with Ronald Colman as an erudite gentleman whose passion in life is acquiring knowledge, and Price as the tycoon of a soap company sponsoring "Masquerade for Money." When Price, in a

With Ronald Colman in *Champagne for Caesar*

floridly comic performance, refuses Colman a job with the company, the omniscient Colman takes revenge by appearing as a contestant on the TV program and building up his prize money week after week until the jackpot reaches $40,000,000, the estimated worth of the soap company. At that plateau he is defeated when asked to state his social security number. In Price's opinion the satire was years ahead of its time.

The Baron of Arizona was a western too offbeat to appeal to western buffs. The film was an elaboration on the historically factual story of James Addison Reavis, a master swindler who was an employee of the Federal Land Office in Santa Fe, New Mexico; he laid claim to some 66,000 square miles in the Southwest on the basis of forged land grants which attempted to prove that his wife was a direct descendant of a nobleman who had been granted the land by the Spanish Crown. Reavis pre-

With Ellen Drew and Reed Hadley in *The Baron of Arizona*

sented his claim and set himself up as a land baron in 1872. In the film Reavis claims the entire state of Arizona and refuses $25,000,000 offered by the government for its purchase. Later, offended by government investigation, he demands a trial to verify his claim and wins the case. Finally, through a sense of shame, he admits to the fraud and is sentenced to six years in jail. The story was not the kind to fascinate an audience expecting wild action, but it provided Price with one of his better roles.

With Donald O'Connor in *Curtain Call at Cactus Creek*

Price's next picture was also a western, *Curtain Call at Cactus Creek,* a Donald O'Connor comedy with Price cavorting as a Shakespearean actor touring the Old West and getting mixed up with a bank robbery. It was the kind of hokum he greatly enjoys doing, freely confessing to being a ham at heart. After this nonsense, Price went to France to play a villain in Errol Flynn's *Adventures of Captain Fabian.* Flynn's own screenplay was a poor one, and the picture did poor business. The real compensation for Price was the three months it allowed him to spend in France: "Errol arrived a month late and since he was the star and the coproducer we could hardly start filming. So there we were, poor things, stranded in Paris with all expenses paid and a tidy salary coming in. Nothing like this had ever happened to us before (or since), so we really had a chance to case Paris, art-wise and pleasure-wise. Mary was the designer of Flynn's costar Micheline Presle's costumes and therefore on salary. We bought a little English car

and cruised around France, returning home with some lovely loot—about twenty drawings, fifty copper molds, enough white faience china for a sit-down dinner for thirty, and two of the most precarious objects ever brought to these shores—a delicate little Greek angel of the fifth century and a monstrously heavy sixteenth-century bronze king from Benin. We didn't know it, but it was the last gasp for the middle-income collector. Five years later the prices of everything began to soar, and all kinds of art and art objects were vacuumed from European shops by the collectors of the world at large."

Vincent Price, no matter what the quality of his films, was never short of work in Hollywood, although by 1952 he must have had doubts about his future and worries about his need for a high income to support his avocation. He followed the Flynn picture by playing a has-been actor, a hammy former matinee idol, in *His Kind of Woman,* with Robert Mitchum and Jane Russell. Then he was a crooked stockbroker in *Las Vegas Story,* with Victor Mature and Jane Russell. Both films were mere grist for the movie mill. In the latter part of 1952 Price gladly accepted an offer from producer Paul Gregory to replace Charles Laughton, who had other commitments, as the Devil in the touring company of *Don Juan in Hell,* the magnificent recitation for quartet from Shaw's *Man and Superman.* Price played to acclaim with Charles Boyer, Sir Cedric Hardwicke, and Agnes Moorehead, and proved, probably with some self-satisfaction, that appearing in absurd films had not sapped his ability to perform classical material. Returning to Hollywood he accepted the lead in a film that would change the course of his career—*House of Wax.*

House of Wax was the first major offering in three-dimensional filming. Warner Brothers pulled from their files the script of a pictures they had made in 1933, *Mystery of the Wax Museum,* and furbished the new version with technicolor, stereophonic sound, gaudy sets, and camerawork that fully utilized the extra dimension—with much furniture and bric-a-brac being hurled at the screaming audiences. *House of Wax* was the most popular of the 3-D films in vogue for a couple of years—until the fans tired of putting on flimsy glasses and became inured to the illusion of objects being propelled from the screen. Warners wisely made the film a genuinely chilling story, not relying on mere devices but using the 3-D technique to add to the aura of horror. Price, as a sculptor who goes mad when his museum burns, revealed a new aspect of

With Frank Lovejoy and Phyllis Kirk in *House of Wax*

his talent—an obvious delight in Grand Guignol storytelling. In time he would become Hollywood's past master in this genre, and one of the few actors who have ever been capable of essaying macabre humor in a richly florid style without being totally ridiculous. But the seeds were sown in *House of Wax* as Price revelled in his waxwork chamber of horrors and stalked young ladies in the foggy streets to kill and glaze them, thereby giving his exhibits a strangely real appearance.

Before the 3-D film appeared on the market, Price played a murderer of common variety in *Dangerous Mission;* but with the success of *House of Wax,* Columbia offered him top billing as *The Mad Magician.* As an inventor of magicians' illusions who longed to be a magician himself, Price turned nasty when his employer closed his show after he

failed his chance to strut his stuff. Frustration turned to revenge, especially since the boss had broken up the inventor's marriage and taken his wife. Price got even by decapitating the ex-boss in his buzz-saw illusion, and later murdering the ex-wife and roasting alive a fellow magician who suspected the murders. He finally ended up himself a victim of his crematorium illusion. Such gory nonsense (invariably filmed in costumed nineteenth-century settings), added to the film's pervasive air of unreality, always finds a market—not a huge market but a solid, reliable minor market.

Price appeared in a variety of pictures in the late 1950s before settling down to horror as a specialty. He was Omar Khayyám in the dreadful *Son of Sinbad:* "The film was simply a write-off for Howard Hughes. He needed a vehicle in which to fulfill his obligations to a swarm of ladies who had been brought to Hollywood over the years as beauty contest winners—and perhaps other reasons—and who were legally entitled to one film appearance. The film with harem scenes was the obvious way out for Mr. Hughes's predicament. Hence, *Son of Sinbad.*" Price, after shedding his robes, reported to Warners to play an operatic impressario in *Serenade,* which presented Mario Lanza as a California vineyard laborer who rises to vocal fame through the loving patronage of Joan Fontaine. Price wagers that it is the film Fontaine would most like to forget: "Lanza, who was, shall we say, not a very gracious man, was at that time dieting—it seems he was always dieting—and apparently living on whiskey and garlic. To put it bluntly, he reeked. Poor Joan had to be almost pried from her dressing room to do the love scenes. I can remember an assistant director knocking on her door and telling her she was wanted on the set. There was a pause, then her voice asking 'now?' "

Price was a newspaper publisher in *While the City Sleeps* and the vicious Egyptian architect strangled to death by Charlton (Moses) Heston in *The Ten Commandments.* He next appeared as The Devil in *The Story of Mankind,* with Ronald Colman as The Spirit of Man. The picture was basically a debate between Price and Colman as to the merits of humankind in the face of possible nuclear annihilation, with dozens of stars appearing in biblical and historical vignettes serving as illustrations for the debate. The film was a disastrous flop—the most star-studded bomb in Hollywood history. Price recalls the filming because of the pleasure of working with Ronald Colman. "He was a marvelous gentleman, quiet and charming and with a delicious humor. We knew during the filming that the picture was heading downwards; the script was bad to begin with and it worsened with daily changes. I remember one puzzled visitor asking Ronnie, 'Is this picture based on a book?' and he replied in that beautiful, soft diction of his, 'Yes, it is. But they are using only the notes on the dust jacket.' "

By 1958 Vincent Price was firmly established as a screen villain, but he was bothered by the lack of good vehicles; the promise of *House of Wax* was wearing thin. To his rescue came *The Fly,* a truly chilling science fiction item about a scientist who accidentally mixes his own atoms with those of a fly and ends up half-man-half-insect. David Hedison was the luckless experimenter and Price played his brother, with Herbert Marshall as the police inspector assigned to solve the mystery of the disappearance of the scientist, whose pretty wife is at first suspected of foul play. The film remains among the best of its kind, due to the generous budget Fox allowed for sets and apparatus, a highly literate script by James Clavell, and the direction of Kurt Neumann. It boosted Price's stock on the horror market, although his immediate recollection of the picture is one of humor: "Herbert Marshall and I had to inspect a spider's web which contained the fly with my brother's head and arms. It struck us as absurd. It took all day to film because we kept breaking up with laughter. Finally, we shot the scene standing back to back, unable to look each other in the face."

His films have never represented Price's total professional activity. His television appearances on all manner of programs number close to a thousand; in 1955 he played the Duke of Buckingham in the New York City Center's production of *Richard III;* and the following year he played on Broadway in *Black-Eyed Susan.* In 1956 he made a number of appearances as an art expert on the very popular TV quiz program "The $64,000 Question:" Eventually, he tied for the grand prize with another art expert, jockey Billy Pearson. This led to his being hired by CBS to coauthor and narrate their documentary "The Revolution of the Eye," filmed in the Museum of Modern Art in New York. Price offered to do a weekly or monthly version of the documentary, arguing that the original had proved effective in stimulating an interest in art in America, but the idea was rejected. On the programme "Person to Person" Edward R. Murrow asked Price what kind of television he would most like to do if he had a choice and Price replied, "A really entertaining educational series—and in prime time, not three o'clock on Sunday afternoon." The reply brought a knowing smile from Murrow but no response from the television industry.

The Fly set the Price course on films of dread, mayhem, and weird fantasy. Except for *The Big Circus* (1959), in which he played a ringmaster, all his films since then have been in this genre. In *The House on Haunted Hill* Price was a millionaire who staged a party in a haunted house, during which he intended to kill his unfaithful wife; in *The Bat* he was a doctor on the run from embezzling bank funds and accused of being a masked killer; and in *The Tingler* he was another doctor, a pathologist who believed fear could cause parasites to crumble the human spine, and finding his own proof. *The Fly* called for a sequel and got it in *The Return of the Fly,* but the returns on the picture were not what Fox had hoped for. In the sequel, Uncle Vincent explained to his nephew how his father had died, but the young man, ignoring the warning, proceeded to fool around with the same experiment and met the same fate. Price was asked by a visitor during the filming why the studio was making *The Return of the Fly.* Price is usually charming and polite, but he felt this particularly dumb question called for an explanation: "So that Fox can make enough money to do the musical version of *The Diary of Anne Frank.*"

Vincent Price abandoned himself to wholesale horror in 1960 when he accepted Roger Corman's invitation to appear in *The Fall of The House of Usher.* The young producer-director had the idea of filming some Edgar Allan Poe in a certain grand style and sold the idea to the newly formed American-International Pictures. The success of *The Fall of The House of Usher* launched Corman, AIP and Price on a winning streak. The imaginative Corman revealed a particular craftsmanship in making this kind of film and in allowing set de-

In *The Fall of the House of Usher*

signer Daniel Haller free scope in inventing plush, rich, and fascinating settings for the stories. In *The House of Usher* Price, as Rodney Usher, employed his acting technique with more scholarship than usual, giving a formal reading of lines that were close to Poe's prose. The story: A young man arrives at a gloomy nineteenth-century New England mansion seeking his fiancée and is warned away by her brother Roger, who feels he must prevent the marriage because the family line is cursed with madness. The young man enters the house on his own accord and finds the girl, apparently dead. Actually she is cataleptic, but she is nonetheless buried in the family crypt by her brother. Some time later she escapes from her coffin, raving mad. She then attacks her brother; in the melee the decaying manion bursts into flame, "and the deep and dank tarn closes sullenly and silently over the fragments of the House of Usher."

While Roger Corman prepared his eagerly awaited next venture into Poe territory, Price appeared as Jules Verne's mad inventor Robur in *Master of the World.* Robur was the man whose ambition it was to bring peace to the world of 1848 by destroying all the weapons employed by the warring nations. His tactics were somewhat warlike—building a huge flying ship and taking off with a load of bombs, sinking an American battleship, bombing British naval yards and wiping out the Austrian army, taking the odd prisoner here and there. The prisoners prove his undoing, blowing up his ship on a Mediteranean island. The hit of the film was Robur's flying ship—a 200 mph Zeppelin-like monstrosity of archaic decor, complete with side porches and sundry comforts.

Corman next presented *The Pit and the Pendulum.* Again much of the credit was due to Daniel Haller and his fantastic sets, especially the one called for by the title—a dark shaft with a huge pendulum attached swishing back and forth and gradually lowering itself and its crescent blade toward the victim strapped to a slab below. The story gave Haller much to work with: a sixteenth-century Spanish castle with torture chambers and dungeons built during the Inquisition. The young hero journeys to this forbidding domicile of Nicholas Medina (Price) to find out the reason for the death of his sister. Unsatisfied with the explanation that she died of fright from accidentally trapping herself in a torture device, the hero stays to poke around for the answers and almost gets sliced to death. It was in reviewing this box office winner that one critic observed, "Price has the odd ability to chew scenery while keeping his tongue in his cheek". The critic was probably moved to make the observation after hearing Price deliver this line, showing off his torture chamber to an unwilling guest: "Ah, yes. Torquemada spent many happy hours here, a few centuries ago."

In 1961 Price accepted an offer to make three films in Rome. He realized that the Italian costume epics for which he was slated would be, as he said, "lead balloons," but the opportunity to spend half a year in the great city was something neither he nor his wife could refuse. The films were (titles translated): *Queen of the Nile,* with Edmund Purdom and Jeanne Crain in Old Egypt and Price as an unscrupulous High Priest; *The Black Buccaneer,* with Ricardo Montalban as the title hero and Price as a white slaving villain; and *The Last Man on Earth,* which starred Price as the sole survivor of a plague. For Price the films were a paid excuse to explore the art treasures of Rome.

On returning to Hollywood Price did a feeble picture called *Confessions of an Opium Eater* in which he was an adventurer caught up in dope dealing and tong wars in turn-of-the-century San Francisco; Next he made his only film appearance as an art critic—playing a cameo role in *Reprieve* as the real-life Carl Carmer, who actually came to the aid of a convict with a talent for painting and brought about his reprieve from prison. Price then resumed his career with American-International, signing a contract with them that would allow his working for other producers. His first film under the new contract was *Tower of London,* a picture with the same title and much the same story as the one he had made in 1939; this time, however, Price played the evil hunchbacked Richard, accentuating his wickedness. Corman directed the film and derived most of the horror sequences from the nightmares of Richard, in which he was haunted by his victims and forewarned of his bloody doom. The end result was not highly regarded, displeasing the history lovers and insufficiently scaring the horror fans.

The next Corman-Price vehicle put the actor back into the affection of horror lovers. This was *Tales of Terror,* a three-part film based on Poe stories. The first part, *Morella,* had Price as an alcoholic recluse who lives with the mummified corpse of his wife, who died while giving birth to a daughter twenty-six years before. When the daughter pays a visit to the gloomy home, the resentful spirit of the mother rises and takes possession of the girl, until Price drops a lighted candle on the

With Peter Lorre in *Tales of Terror*

deathbed and they all go up in flames. The second episode was highly amusing, with Price as an egotistical wine taster and Casanova; titled *The Black Cat,* it was a combination of that Poe tale plus his *Cask of Amontillado.* Peter Lorre played the host whose wife dallies with Price—the price the pair pay for their affair is entombment in Lorre's cellar. The scene between Price and Lorre in a tavern, trying to get the best of one another with their knowledge of wine, is a highlight in camp comedy, with Price outrageously hammy. The third episode was *The Facts In the Case of M. Valdemar,* with Price as the dying Valdemar, kept in a death-forestalling trance by a wicked mesmerist (Basil Rathbone) who refuses to let the wretched man go until his lovely daughter has agreed to marry him. When the daughter finally agrees, driven almost to distraction by her father's agony, Valdemar rises from his bed, turns into a putrified puddle of goo, and envelops the mesmerist.

Roger Corman's film essays with Poe material helped make American-International a major production company. With the horror buffs of the world screaming for more, Corman then turned to *The Raven,* calling in Hollywood's senior ghoul, Boris Karloff, to join Price and Peter Lorre as Poe's three sixteenth-century medical magicians: Dr. Craven (Price), Dr. Bedlo (Karloff), and Dr. Scarabus (Lorre). When Craven finds his friend Scarabus turned into a raven, he reverts him to human form and they both go after Bedlo, resulting in great contests of magic. Richard Matheson's screenplay was a concoction inspired by the Poe poem; Matheson had scripted the previous Corman-Poe projects and hewed fairly close to original story lines, but here he had to invent. Matheson was criticized for the contemporary sound of some of his lines, mostly those spoken by Lorre, as, for example, the one with Lorre peering around a filthy, cobwebbed, vermin-ridden cellar and musing: "Gee, hard place to keep clean, huh?" The line was his, not Matheson's. Explains Price: "Peter was an ad lib genius. He knew every line of the script perfectly but loved to invent his own and sometimes his ad libs were so humorous Corman let them stay in. Peter was a lovable little man but there was a sadness about him, a kind of sad remoteness."

In 1963 Price left Poe and went to United Artists to do a group of three Nathaniel Hawthorne stories, directed by Sidney Salkow, under the title *Twice Told Tales.* In the first tale, *Dr. Heidegger's Experiment,* Price appeared as the inventor of a potion that enables him to resurrect his dead bride; he brings her back, then rejuvenates himself and his best friend only to discover that the bride and the friend were lovers. In the second tale, *Rappaccini's Daughter,* Price was a demented scientist who tries to protect his daughter from the men of the world by injecting juices from poisonous plants into her blood, thereby causing any man who touches her to die. The third episode was a very condensed version of *The House of Seven Gables,* made more horrific than Hawthorne intended, with Price seeking the fortune hidden in the family home and being drawn to his death by a curse from the beyond.

Price did another film for United Artists following the successful Hawthorne venture—*Diary of a Madman,* a rather pedestrian account of the Guy de Maupassant story of a French magistrate who in 1886 killed a murderer in self-defense and was then possessed by the revengeful spirit, that had possessed the murderer. The magistrate unwittingly committed gory crimes until he was awakened from his trance by the sight of a cross. The story was resolved in a manner all too common in horror films —a fire burns the magistrate, his home, and his problems.

Price returned to the American-International fold to do *Comedy of Terrors,* directed by the veteran Jacques Tourneur from an original screenplay by Richard Matheson. The film is memorable for its teaming of Price with Peter Lorre, Boris Karloff, and Basil Rathbone, the only time the four appeared together. They were at that time considered the senior members of the Hollywood spook brigade, with only Rathbone bridling at the label. "Basil didn't like the identification with

horror pictures. He'd had a long and distinguished career and it bothered him to be thought of as a fright actor. But an old actor has to take what he can get and this was all they would offer him. He was a fine old gentleman, rather formal in his manner, but a man who loved nothing better than a good joke. Peter on the other hand couldn't have cared less about his label, and Boris, one of the gentlest men who ever lived, was very grateful for the identification with horror pictures. He spoke warmly about Frankenstein's Monster, realizing it was the thing that prolonged his career. He never deprecated the films in which he appeared."

Comedy of Terrors is amusingly macabre: Price was a lazy, drunken undertaker in a New England town of the 1890s, with Lorre as his incompetent assistant. They worked only when in need of money, and then murdered a few people to create customers. Karloff was Price's disapproving father-in-law and Rathbone flounced around as the Shakespearean-quoting landlord who demanded a year's rent on his funeral parlor, with his tardy tenants making a number of attempts on his life.

Price's next association with Roger Corman was *The Haunted Palace.* The plot: Price, as a practitioner of black magic in a New England community in 1765, is burned to death by the villagers, but before he dies he places a curse on them and their ancestors. More than a hundred years later his great-great-grandson arrives in the village and moves into the old house of his warlock predecessor. The evil spirit then takes possession of his body and, after a number of grisly crimes, the villagers again march on the mansion and burn its master.

Corman and Price returned to Poe in 1964 with *The Masque of the Red Death.* Price was at his florid best as Prince Prospero, a twelfth-century Satan worshipper in an Italian province, resplendent in his brocaded Renaissance costumes and moving amid ornate settings. When the plague approaches his domain, the Prince orders the surrounding houses burned, and then invites a selected group to be his guests in his castle. There he stages a masquerade ball to keep his mind off the pestilence afflicting the land, but one of the guests, an uninvited stranger dressed in red, turns out to be Death.

The success of the Price-Corman-Poe films had been firm and steady: clearly more was called for. Corman now filmed *The Tomb of Ligeia.* It is greatly to his credit that his version is even better than its predecessors. It is one of Price's favorites

In *The Masque of the Red Death*

With Elizabeth Sheppard in *Tomb of Ligeia*

among his own pictures. Like *The Masque of the Red Death, The Tomb of Ligeia* was made in England where American-International's money bought them more quality than the same budgets could garner in the Hollywood of 1965. In this beautifully photographed picture, Price was a man addicted to drugs and haunted by the spirit of his dead wife. When he planned to marry a young girl who resembled the wife, he found the spirit of the dead wife defending her vow that he must never remarry. After completing this film, Roger Corman decided to let it rest as his parting shot in the horror-fantasy genre, and move on to other kinds of film production. The decision was a sad one for Price, who would have preferred to continue the profitable association. Certainly, the Price horror films made thereafter were inferior to those he had done with Corman.

Even without Corman, American-International was reluctant to drop the Poe line, and they assigned Jacques Tourneur to direct Price in *War Gods of the Deep,* filmed in England and released there as *City in the Sea.* Loosely based on a Poe story, it had Price as yet another madman, this one a ruler of an underwater city for more than a hundred years, who captures a seismologist and his girl friend, believing the girl to be the reincarnation of his long-dead wife. Price then went back to being a mad scientist: in *Dr. Goldfoot and the Bikini Machine* he planned to take over the world by manufacturing robots in the form of nubile young ladies and have them seduce all the men who control the world. The film was successful enough to call for a sequel: *Dr. Goldfoot and the Girl Bombs* took the gag a step further. This time

Price built nine delectable robots and equipped them so that they would explode when made love to by the nine military leaders whose departure would pave the way for the crazy doctor's control of the world. Made in Italy, the sequel was itself a bomb, killing the Goldfoot idea, perhaps fortunately. Then, for the first time in a long time, Price stepped out of costume and appeared in modern garb as an illusionist in the German-made *House of a Thousand Dolls.* The film was a routine thriller except for its subject matter—Price and Martha Hyer ran a brothel in Tangiers and used black magic to drug and overpower young women for an international white slavery ring.

Price returned to costumed horror in 1968 with *The Conqueror Worm,* another American-International picture made in England, advisedly so in this case because the story was set in the England of 1645. It called for a large cast of British players to enact a particularly gory tale about a man who sets himself up as a witchhunter and executioner. The film was based upon Ronald Bassett's novel *The Witchfinder General* and released in England with that title. The American title springs from the Poe poem which was used as a prologue to the picture. Price rambled through the film as the bloodthirsty Mathew Hopkins, hiring himself to local magistrates and exacting confessions from witchcraft suspects, brutally torturing them and fiendishly putting them to death in atrocities of fire and butchery. Many of the victims were young women—sexual titillation being a definite adjunct of horror entertainment—and in raping one particular girl and hanging her priest father, Price brings on the wrath of her boy friend, and is himself hacked to pieces. Except for addicts of sanguinary screen mayhem, *The Conqueror Worm* requires a strong stomach from its viewers.

Perhaps as a badly needed respite, Vincent Price next played in a western, *More Dead Than Alive,* as the owner of a traveling carnival, with Clint Walker as his sharpshooter attraction. The action sprang from vengeful outlaws tracking Walker, an ex-gunslinger, and attempting to kill him. Price had a somewhat similar part in his next film, supporting Elvis Presley in *The Chataugua.* In this he was a lecturer on the classics in a touring tent show. Neither film made much impact on the public, and for even more of a change of pace Price returned to Broadway in 1968 to play in the musical comedy *Darling of the Day.* But luck was not with him on this venture—the musical version of the Monty Woolley-Gracie Fields movie of 1943,

Holy Matrimony, closed after a short run, with none of its Jules Styne songs winning popularity. After this Price returned to England to resume his specialty, and appeared in *The Oblong Box.* Again the inspiration was an Edgar Allan Poe story; here Price was a nineteenth-century English nobleman returning from Africa with a demented brother, who had been tortured and disfigured by savages in the jungle. Price first keeps the hideous brother chained up but then decides to bury him alive. Grave robbers spoil the plan and the brother escapes to seek revenge; eventually Price shoots and kills, him but not before the deranged brother savagely bites Price on the hand. Thinking that he is rid of him, Price finds himself taking on the mutilated appearance of the departed brother.

The Oblong Box was directed by Gordon Hessler, who also directed the next two Price terror pieces—*Scream and Scream Again* and *Cry of the Banshee.* In the former he was Dr. Browning, a recluse, occultist, and latter-day Dr. Frankenstein, engaged in gory experimentation to produce superhumans by hacking up mere humans. In graphically depicting surgical transplants on unwilling victims, the film wallowed in blood, with Price, as always, somehow rising above it all, and his elegant malevolence and his velvety voice making banal dialogue sound like wisdom.

Cry of the Banshee returned Price to the evil of medieval England; whereas he had previously played a renegade witchhunter, in this film, as magistrate Lord Edward Whitman, his measures to stamp out the "old religion" were legal. His

In *Cry of the Banshee;* note the intrusive anachronism at the extreme right—a microphone.

merciless mission brings a hex upon his family—the vengeful curse being delivered by a frightful old sorceress played by Elizabeth Bergner, making her first screen appearance in some thirty years. It was a surprisingly odd choice of vehicle for a once distinguished actress's return to films. *Cry of the Banshee* was typical of the increasing sexual sadism in horror films; there was much stripping and torture of women, sacrificial rites with, inevitably, a nude girl butchered on the slab, and one scene of an attractive tavern wench being burned alive under the supervision of the dedicated magistrate. The film, which clearly indicated its limited budget, was not a good one. Critics, stockholders, and horror buffs were justified in reminding American-International that their twenty Price films had reputedly grossed $50,000,000, and that this was no reason for a decline in quality. The hard-nosed film company took heed of the criticism.

In 1971 Price appeared in *Dr. Phibes,* his umpteenth appearance as a mad medical man. Price observes: "If all the mad doctors were extracted from crime, horror, and science fiction, you wouldn't have much left. Think of Dr. Jekyll, Dr. Fu Manchu, Dr. Cyclops, Dr. Caligari, Dr. No, Dr. Strangelove, etc. People are wary of doctors anyway and mystified by the paraphernalia of surgery and medical research. It's always been a rich field for horror stories." In the case of *Dr. Phibes,* Price was even more wide-ranging in his mayhem than in his previous guises, here swearing revenge on the medical team who allowed his wife to die during an operation. He brings upon his victims various plagues, including some which afflicted Pharaoh in the Old Testament—the ravages of rats, bats, beasts, boils, locusts, and hail. The plague of darkness he reserves for himself, injecting himself with embalming fluid and taking his place alongside his dead wife.

By the end of the 1960s it was apparent that the horror film had become a more and more specialized product. Like other kinds of films, it reflected the times, and in a world full of real horror and evil it was not surprising that horror films should have become more gruesome, more vicious and bloody and weird. Price himself believes in the presence of evil and views with genuine horror the crimes inspired by drug-induced hallucinations, of which the Manson case in Los Angeles is a prime example. Price argues with his employers to make their films unreal, as unrelated to reality as possible, and to treat them as a kind of inverted humor. He regards himself as something of a

In *Dr. Phibes*

comedian and he looks back to the humor in the Corman-Poe pictures: "We could use some Peter Lorre ad libs like his reply in *The Raven* to the solemn inquiry, 'Shall we ever see the rare and radiant Lenore?' Out of the raven's beak came Peter's petulant answer: 'How the hell should I know? What am I—a fortune-teller?' "

Vincent Price has frequently been criticized for appearing in films of cultural worthlessness. The criticism is made by those who take his film career more seriously than he does. Whatever the quality and the content of the films, they have enabled Price to maintain his popularity, a high income, and the opportunity to appear in other avenues of the entertainment business. Price reached his sixtieth birthday in 1971, marking more than thirty years in Hollywood, still gainfully employed at a time when most stars of his vintage had dropped from sight. That he has been extraordinarily lucky he cannot deny, but much of his luck has been created by his attitude toward life and work, which is one of unflagging enthusiasm and little conceit: "I'm an old ham. I go nuts when I'm not working and I'll do almost anything. I love acting, even in nonsense. Acting is an expression of joy. I can't stand actors who go around saying how they loathe acting."

Even if Price were an actor who did not enjoy acting, his career in Hollywood would have allowed him to indulge his passion for art. He has decorated his home with an enviable collection of paintings, sculpture, and objets d'art. His home is a twenty-room Spanish mansion in Beverly Hills, sitting in a two-acre garden. Included in his prize collection: a Picasso drawing, a Henry Moore watercolor, Indian bowls, Navajo rugs, African masks, sculpture from the Aztecs and from Poly-nesia, a first-century Roman marble torso, pre-Columbian figures and drawings, Greek figures, a South American statue, a seventeenth-century Mexican gold cross (which hangs on the living room wall next to a huge Spanish chest), a small Goya painting, and, outside on the patio, a twenty-five-foot totem pole which John Barrymore brought from Alaska. Many of the paintings are contemporary American and several are by Indians Price has championed.

The success of Vincent Price is one of Hollywood's best examples of an actor coming to terms with life in a highly commercial artistic system. Other countries have offered various forms of support and encouragement; America has not. The artist in a democracy makes his own way and creates his own luck, and he often does it in the face of brutal indifference. It is a system that has slowly killed some men and quickly deterred others. John Barrymore was a victim and Vincent Price is a survivor. Price, happily devoid of the dark, corrosive introspection of Barrymore, long ago drew a line between what he was capable of doing as an artist and what he needed to make life interesting and enjoyable. Ironically, what he needed in his personal life was contact with the higher reaches of art and what was necessary to reach that plateau was a sacrifice of his integrity as an actor. Obviously the one was much more important to him than the other, and Price has had the good sense—and business acumen—not to take himself too seriously. He has, in fact, shown every indication of enjoying the grotesque nonsense of his professional life. The genial ham of dreadful movies thus supports a cultured gentleman in grand style, and until a better system comes along, the rationale of a Vincent Price will have to do.

5

DAVID NIVEN

WHEN Samuel Goldwyn put David Niven under contract in 1935 at $75 a week, the Goldwyn publicists handed him a questionnaire. One of the questions was: "Who and what was your father?" Niven wrote that his father was killed in action in the Dardanelles in 1915 and that he had been a British Army lieutenant. The head of the publicity department sneered, "A lieutenant? We can't have that." So, says Niven, "He pencilled out the word *lieutenant* and wrote in *general*—which is incredible because from all that I can understand Dad hated the military." Thus David Niven was introduced to the world of deception and illusions called Hollywood.

Niven is unique. No other film actor with a more than thirty-odd-year background as a star originally arrived in Hollywood with no theatrical experience of any kind and no interest in being an actor. The almost always affable and amusing Niven is also unique because he is one of the few remaining specimens of a vanishing breed: the actor who is also an urbane gentleman.

Niven is a natural clown, a slightly comic drifter who has breezed through life and finds himself amazed that he has done so well. To his interviewers he is a delight and a puzzle; he entertains them with a fund of well-worded, flippant anecdotes, but wards off serious questioning with quips. The impression is that he is somewhat embarrassed by his luck and fearful that detailed analysis would reveal him as a fraud. He says, characteristically, "I expect at any moment to have some serious-looking gent walk up to me and say, 'All right, Niven, it's all over, you've been found out.' It really is amazing. Can you imagine being wonderfully overpaid

One of the first photographs of Niven in Hollywood— taken in January of 1935, before he became an actor; in a well-worn English tweed jacket, he visits Arline Judge at Twentieth Century-Fox, where she was making *George White's Scandals.*

for dressing up and playing games? It's like being Peter Pan."

David Niven was born in London on March 1st, 1910 while his Scots father and his French mother were away from their estate at Kirriemuir in the Scottish Highlands. William Graham Niven was wealthy but unwise with his money, and he lost his estate and most of his other assets betting on horses. The family then moved to a modest cottage on the Isle of Wight, and to a life-style far removed from the butler, footmen, and gamekeepers of Kirriemuir.

A year after his father was killed, Niven's mother married again and became Lady Comyn-Platt of Carewell Manor, Berkshire. "My stepfather didn't like me at all and the feeling was mutual, so I was shoved off to boarding school at the age of six. I was at two schools, each a grisly experience. These were the days of the great bullies in English public schools, the days, too, of shell-shocked masters with a sad, sadistic streak. When, at the age of seven, I couldn't master a Latin conjugation, I was stuck out of a fourth-floor classroom window and the window was closed down on my back while I was soundly thrashed. I didn't do too well. For example, in mathematics I got eight marks out of a possible 300. I was expelled from the first school, Heatherdown, after two years for thieving a cauliflower from the garden of a nearby girls' school. We had each been given a little plot of ground in our own school garden and we were supposed to compete for prizes as little gardeners. My plot was an abysmal mess of puny weeds and I thought a great big white cauliflower would at least win me some attention. It did. I was dismissed from the school and ordered home, but his Lordship vowed that he would not have me home and I was sent to a reform school in Southsea where, on a clear day, I could look across the Solent and see the Isle of Wight. I was a lonely, insecure boy."

Lonely, insecure boys quite often grow up to be actors, but no such thought was in the mind of young Niven. In his prayers he asked God to let him grow up to be an Admiral. The nautical aspiration stayed with him, and at the age of thirteen he applied for admission to the Royal Naval College, Dartmouth. "I flunked the oral examination. Standing before a panel of old salts I was asked to name the three greatest British admirals. I readily replied, 'Drake, Nelson and Jellicoe.' I assume that Jellicoe was not held in high regard because they sputtered, cast dark glances at each other, and dismissed me. I was not accepted. I later learned that one of the other applicants answered the same question with a cheery 'Drake, Nelson and excuse me, sir, but I didn't quite catch your name.' He got in."

In 1927 Niven applied for admission to the Royal Military College at Sandhurst. There his poor scholastic record was obscured by his being the son of a deceased Army officer, and he was accepted. Eighteen months later he emerged as a second lieutenant and was assigned to the Highland Light Infantry. Niven served four years, much of that time in Malta, which struck him as a pretty dull place in which to be stuck, little more than a hot version of Siberia.

Lack of zeal marked Niven's early military career. In Malta, he and another young officer rebelled at having to wear their heavy steel helmets during drill practice in the hot sun, so they sent to a toy shop in London for papier-mâché versions. "All went well until a sudden rainburst and there we stood with these things hanging on our heads like uncooked pizza." On another occasion, at a full-dress parade in London, Niven chose to ignore the order, "Officers, draw your swords." The previous day, fooling around with his sword, Niven had broken it, leaving about six inches beyond the hilt. "I prayed to God the Adjutant wouldn't notice but he did. He spotted me and repeated the order. I drew out my midget sword. The Adjutant glared and said, 'Stick an olive on that, Niven. I'll send for a martini.'"

During his stay in Malta, Niven met vacationing Barbara Hutton, then seventeen, and after some good times together she invited him to visit her should he ever find himself in New York. "Being the kind of Briton who was quite willing to sponge on rich Americans, I took her at her word. I got a month's leave and got on a small boat to America which took eleven days to get there. Anyway, we were down in Florida having fun when I realized I'd overstayed my leave. I sent a wire to my Colonel saying, AM WHALE HUNTING OFF THE COAST OF FLORIDA. REQUEST THREE WEEKS EXTRA LEAVE. Back came a wire from him: NO WHALES WITHIN 2,000 MILES OF FLORIDA. TAKE FOUR WEEKS."

After this exposure to high life, Niven found going back to the Army rather tedious and decided to quit, a decision hastened by yet another of his debonair reactions to military protocol. At the end of a lecture given by a distinguished general to the officers of his regiment, Niven responded to the query, "Are there any questions?" with "Yes, sir. I wonder if you could tell me the time? I have a train to catch." The general saw no humor in this and ordered Niven put under close arrest. "One of my colleagues was assigned to guard me but he was an affable chap and proceeded to commiserate by producing a bottle of whiskey. The drunker we got the more he was convinced I should try to escape, which I did. It seemed to me later that the best way to avoid getting into even deeper trouble was to resign. This was easy in those days—they were trying to get rid of people and all I had to do to get out was ask."

Although he had the taste and temperament for a member of international café society, Niven lacked one essential thing: money. The very unequipped ex-second lieutenant now had to plan a course of action. "I emigrated to Canada. This is where we find our fortune. I didn't. I was then a real sponger; I stayed with a fine Canadian admiral named Kingsmill at his home on a little island in the Rideau Lakes. His daughter had married a cousin of mine. This cousin had given me a round trip ticket to Canada in exchange for my car, which wasn't quite paid for. I liked Canada very much, so I cashed in the second half of the ticket and went to Ottawa. The first thing I did there was to get deathly ill with tonsilitis. An enchanting couple, I'll never forget them—Mr. and Mrs. Peter Bate—came to my rescue and gave me a little room at the top of their house. I recall the address quite clearly—32 Range Road. It was Christmas Eve, 1933, and I was lying in bed when I had a hemorrhage. I woke up drowning in blood; it was pouring out. The couple had gone out to visit friends and I was alone. They came back just in time to save me; five minutes more and I would have been dead."

David Niven was a flop as a Canadian immigrant. In half a year he was unable to land himself a decent job—nothing beyond casual labor—and in desperation he took to minor crime. He plagiarized a book called *Fox Hunting in Canada,* writing from it a series of articles for a British magazine, and thereby earned an illicit $150. With this he headed for New York, where his sauve British manners enabled him to acquire a position as a liquor salesman with the Twenty One Club Selected Stores Limited. "I was to get $40 a week plus ten percent of everything I sold. I never got beyond the $40 a week and the manager of the Twenty One Club let me go, after expressing the opinion that my idea of selling liquor was a little too social."

After failing to make the grade in salesmanship Niven was hired to promote an indoor horse racing scheme in Atlantic City. When the scheme went awry, he was obliged to skip to Bermuda, where lack of employment opportunities persuaded him to take the next ship out. It happened to be going to Havana. Niven confesses to having spent most of his time in the Cuban capital in the celebrated bar Sloppy Joe's. The Hollywood publicists would later build these few days into the romantic legend that Niven was a gunnery officer fighting with the Batista revolutionary forces. "What actually happened was that one night in Sloppy Joe's, after a few drinks, I got into a conversation with some mysterious gentlemen who, I gather, were rebels, and I let it be known that I was an expert with machine guns, which was true, and that my services were available. The next morning I was called upon but not by Batista's men. I was summarily escorted to the British Embassy, where the Ambassador was quite unpleasant to me. After telling me I was a stupid fool, he gave me twenty-four hours to leave Cuba. The next ship scheduled to leave was a freighter called *President Pierce* and it was headed for Los Angeles. I had a friend there so I decided to visit him—what else does a British gentleman with no money do?"

In the year or so since leaving the British Army all that David Niven had been able to prove to himself was that he had a talent for socializing and that he could get by on strength of personality. It was Elsa Maxwell who first put the idea of acting into his head. "At a party in New York she told me I should be a movie actor. I thought the idea absurd but I later thought to myself, 'Well, by God, if all else fails, at least I can take up acting.' " All else did fail.

Niven's introduction to the film world was bizarre. Invited to dinner on board H.M.S. *Norfolk,* he borrowed a dinner jacket. As the evening progressed he became drunk and was put to bed by the ship's officers.

"In the morning the Captain came in and said, 'Well, Niven, we're transferring you to H.M.S. *Bounty.*' I thought he'd gone starkers. Then he opened a porthole and told me to look out. I saw a fully rigged, eighteenth-century warship. They rowed me over and there was Charles Laughton as Bligh and Clark Gable as Christian. I later found out this had been a gag thought up by my friends in Los Angeles and the Captain of the *Norfolk.* Anyway, I sailed back to the California coast on the *Bounty.*"

His friends found him lodgings with Mrs. George Belzer, who had four beautiful young daughters, each of whom was, or soon would be, working in films. Their names: Sally Blane, Loretta Young, Georgiana Young and Polly Ann Young. "They were the happiest and kindest people to live with but it was excruciating for me because I fell in love with all the daughters and couldn't afford to take any of them out. It was agonizing to see their young men turning up in expensive cars to whisk them away. I was both jealous and almost paternally concerned about the girls."

Through director Edmund Goulding, Niven was given a screen test and after several months of waiting he received a call from a studio for a possible bit in a picture. But he had another caller, a gentleman from the United States Immigration Service, who advised him that he was in the country on an expired visitor's visa and that he must leave immediately. In typical Niven fashion, he asked "Where shall I go—Catalina?" Where he actually went was Mexicali, a dingy town just over the border from Calexico, California. "I got myself a cheap room and then set about writing home for references, affidavits, etc., to comply with the Immigration Department regulations for reentry. I next went looking for a job. I suggested to the owner of The Owl Bar that since I was an authority on wines and spirits he might like to hire me in the capacity of an advisor. He hired me in the capacity of a bartender. I was in Mexicali for five months and it was a miserable period of my life."

Once back in Los Angeles Niven joined the Screen Extras Guild and picked up work at $3.50 a day. Being an officer and a gentleman with a gift of gab, he was frequently invited to parties, and so was able to live a champagne life on a beer income. Early in 1935 Niven met Errol Flynn, who had just arrived from England and was under contract to Warners. "Errol was an enchanting creature; I had more fun with him than all the others put together. For a while we shared a little house together at Malibu which we called Cirrhosis-by-the-Sea. It was never-ending fun although you had to be careful what you said to him. If you said, 'Look, Errol. Betty's coming tonight so please don't mention Sally,' he'd be poised at the door waiting to say to her, 'David said I wasn't to mention Sally.' "

Niven's opinion of Flynn as a film actor is typical of the way he wraps a truth in a jest: "I think Errol was a good film actor. Just how much talent is required for that is open to question. Personally, I think if you keep your eyes and ears open it doesn't require a hell of a lot of talent. But Errol did have talent. Unfortunately he allowed the serious side of his nature to be defeated by the trivial."

David Niven appeared in some two dozen movies as an extra, often in westerns as a barfly or stage-coach passenger and at least once as a Mexican bandit. The income was pitifully inadequate for his needs as a would-be playboy. At one party, Douglas Fairbanks, Sr. took a shine to Niven and invited him to his club. "He had an idiotic sense of humor. I remember one day sitting with him in the Turkish bath of this club. I was literally faint from hunger, and here lying around in the nude were all these movie tycoons I was trying to see in their offices and couldn't. At one point, Fairbanks said in a loud voice, 'Tell me, Niven, what are you going to do this winter—play polo or bring the yacht around?' Ears pricked up all over the bath and he then introduced me as the British Army's polo champion. I could barely ride a horse in those days. They invited me to appear at the Riviera Country Club as their guest. God, it was a nightmare. In one mad melee I was riding a wild horse that actually reached out in a gallop and bit Darryl Zanuck's backside. At another point, desperately hanging on to the saddle with one hand, I made a swipe at the ball and brought my mallet up between the hind legs of the horse in front of me. The poor beast screamed in agony and pitched off the rider. It was horrible."

It's appropriate that the first film in which Niven had a speaking part was called *Without Regret*. His first line: "Hello, my dear." Having broken the barrier, Niven was now off on a career as a film actor. The Goldwyn studio put him under contract and gave him bits, such as that of a sailor who gets thrown out of a saloon in *Barbary Coast*. As he did with all his actors, Goldwyn rented out Niven to other studios, always at a profit not shared with the actor. Niven appeared in *A Feather in Her Hat* for Columbia, *Rose Marie* for MGM, *Palm Springs* for Paramount, *Thank You, Jeeves* (as Bertie Wooster) for Twentieth Century-Fox, as well as in Goldwyn's own *Splendor* and *Dodsworth*. Niven learned about acting as he went along, and not without embarrassment. "In *Splendor* I was called upon to smoke, which I had never done, and I puffed away in a style that possibly inspired Bette Davis. It cost them about $2,000 in retakes before I looked natural. My coworkers weren't always polite and I blushed easily, something I had to learn to control because a red cheek comes out dark on black-and-white film."

Early in 1936 Niven was advised by Errol Flynn to apply for a part in *The Charge of the Light Brigade*, which Warners was making with Michael Curtiz directing, and which required a lot of British military types. "I was the eighth to be audi-

With Frances Langford and Spring Byington in *Palm Springs Story*

tioned for the part of Captain Randall. I recall it was hot and I was getting irritable with the long wait. Finally, my turn came and I stepped up to do my bit. Curtiz glared at me and said, 'Where's your script?' I told him I knew the lines and had left the script in the makeup tent. Curtiz, who had been an Hungarian cavalry officer and treated actors like puppets, yelled at me, 'Run and get it, and I mean run!' This didn't impress me much and I told him to bloody well run and get it himself. The aides and flunkies froze in horror. Curtiz looked at me for a moment and then said to his crew, 'Dismiss the others, he gets the part.' "

The Charge of the Light Brigade was Niven's first appearance on the screen in a military uniform; it would turn out to be the first of twenty films (of his seventy films) in uniform, mostly British and mostly Army. Goldwyn was now impressed enough with Niven to give him a lead role with Brian Aherne and Merle Oberon in *Beloved Enemy,* a film about the Irish troubles with Niven as a British Army officer in love with Oberon, who in turn was in love with rebel leader Aherne.

Goldwyn lent Niven to Universal for a small part in *We Have Our Moments,* something which Niven considered typical and unlikable about Goldwyn's businesslike manner of using his actors. But the next rental was an agreeable one—to David Selznick for the role of Fritz von Tarlenheim in the Ruritanian romance *The Prisoner of Zenda.* That Niven's attitude to being a move actor was decid-

With Ronald Colman on the set of *The Prisoner of Zenda*

but couldn't. Then Willie brought in the special effects men, first with an onion-soaked handkerchief and then with spray mist designed to open the ducts of any eyes. But with me all it did was make my nose run and I knelt there dripping on poor, limp, wan Merle, who took it for as long as she could and then exploded, 'Really, David, you're impossible!' Wyler finally settled for shooting me from behind, with my back and shoulders doing the emoting. Many people later complimented me for the excellence of my performance in that scene. All I can say is that I've been extraordinarily lucky."

edly puckish is exemplified by an oft-told Hollywood story about his spiking the punch bowl in a banquet scene of *Zenda* and turning the set into a happy frolic of woozy extras:

"It seemed to me that the tepid lemonade they had poured into the punch bowl wasn't doing much for the blasé extras, so I went to Raymond Massey's dressing room and snitched six bottles of gin he had been saving for a party. During the lunch break, I emptied them all in the punch bowl. As the afternoon progressed with take after take, the extras became increasingly boisterous, with a few turning belligerent. I was standing by the director, John Cromwell, and he asked me, 'What the hell is going on?' I said, 'John, you must really have inspired them.' He shook his head in bewilderment and closed down the set."

Niven's ascent in Hollywood was gradual and unspectacular. No one considered him a real actor and it's doubtful he would have had much of a career on film had it not been for his being a personable and amusing young man off the set. Niven was well-liked among his fellow workers, to the point that allowances were made for his lack of dramatic skill. In playing Edgar Linton, the man who marries Cathy (Merle Oberon) in *Wuthering Heights,* Niven was called upon to weep at her deathbed. "I had never cried; as a boy I was told that it was not proper for a boy, let alone a man, to cry, and so the issue had never before appeared before me. But now William Wyler was asking me to break into tears before the cast and crew. I tried

With Merle Oberon in *Wuthering Heights*

Niven did supporting roles in *Dinner at the Ritz, Bluebeard's Eighth Wife, Four Men and a Prayer,* and *Three Blind Mice,* before getting his first real break in films: a costarring role with Errol Flynn in *Dawn Patrol.* This was the film that pushed Niven into the star bracket, and for that very good reason it is his favorite film:

"Making the picture was an exciting experience. We used seventeen planes. Stunt fliers, who handled some of the most dangerous scenes, eventually cracked up all but two of them. Working in *Dawn*

With Melville Cooper, Rodion Rathbone, Errol Flynn, and Peter Willes in *The Dawn Patrol*

Patrol was one of the several things that made me want to join the RAF when the war broke out, but they wouldn't take me; so I went in with the Army. In 1939 I met Pappy Pope in France—he was the almost legendary RAF flier on whom my role was based. Pappy said, 'I saw you in *Dawn Patrol,* and it was all right.' That quiet praise was as good as a decoration."

After *Dawn Patrol* came *Wuthering Heights,* a costarring role with Ginger Rogers in *Bachelor Mother,* a supporting part in the Gary Cooper adventure *The Real Glory,* then the comedy *Eternally Yours* with Loretta Young, and next the film that put him right on top—*Raffles.* Based on the novel *The Amateur Cracksman,* this Goldwyn picture, excellently directed by Sam Wood, allowed Niven full scope as a debonair jewel thief operating in high society and stealing gems and young female hearts with equal felicity. By now Niven had acquired enough skill and aplomb to be able deftly to deliver a line like, "I'd love to dine with you, darling, but these handcuffs are so awkward." The offers would undoubtedly have come in for Niven for more and better pictures after *Raffles,* but this was late in 1939 and Britain was now in the Second World War. Niven lost no time in returning to England to enlist, much to the surprise of Sam Goldwyn, who couldn't understand an actor quitting on a winning streak.

Niven rejoined the British Army, after having been turned down by the RAF, and because of his Sandhurst training he was commissioned a lieutenant. He served the full six years of the war and finished with the rank of lieutenant-colonel. He claims to have done nothing spectacular but the record shows that he served in France, was evacuated at Dunkirk, and was with the Allied armies in the drive through Germany. Niven refuses to discuss his war years except in humorous anecdotes. His favorite: "I was invited to be the commentator at a display of invasion equipment at the Royal Depot in Deal, Kent. Churchill was there and God knows how many brasshats. I had the microphone in my hand and pointed out the various machines and devices in this well-rehearsed arrangement of landing craft. At one point I invited everyone to look upward and said, 'You'll notice that our maneuvre is well-covered by our escort of Spitfires.' As I said that two Messerschmidts flew out of the clouds."

Niven was seconded from the service for two short periods during the war, on both occasions to appear in films considered to be in the national interest. The first, in 1942, was *The First of the Few,* the story of R. J. Mitchell, the man who designed the Spitfire, with Leslie Howard playing

With Olivia de Havilland in *Raffles*

Mitchell and directing the picture. Two years later Niven played the lead in *The Way Ahead,* the role of a militia officer inducted into the regular army in wartime. The film was directed by Major Carol Reed and scripted by Captain Eric Ambler and Private Peter Ustinov. Ustinov never rose beyond the rank of private, due to his distinctly unmilitary temperament and the confusion and doubt he caused in the minds of certain senior officers with whom he came in contact. In the preproduction period of *The Way Ahead,* Ustinov was taken from the company of his fellow privates and put into the company of his fellow filmmakers, all of whom happened to be officers, thus causing a problem of military protocol. Army regulations forbade a private any familiarity with officers, and in order for Ustinov to be able to work with his colleagues an official but a rather comic step was taken—Ustinov was made Lt. Colonel David Niven's batman. This was to raise a few military eyebrows on those occasions when the colonel and the private were seen laughing and drinking together. "Peter was then getting fourteen shillings a day pay and couldn't keep up with his bar bill. So one night he went out and sold one of his paintings for fifty pounds. Years later I came across the painting and its price had increased tenfold."

Niven recalls only one occasion during the war when he was pessimistic about his chances of survival. It was in the spring of 1945, when he and his unit were about to cross the Rhine. Niven was reflecting, as he waited, that for six years he had escaped injury, and that maybe his luck was running out, when a soldier rode up on a cycle and handed him a telegram:

LT. COL. DAVID NIVEN,
ARMY FIELD P.O.
ALLIED EXPEDITIONARY FORCES
DEAR SIR: THIS IS TO INFORM YOU THAT WE HAVE ABSORBED THE LELAND HAYWARD AGENCY OF WHICH YOU WERE A CLIENT. THEREFORE, WE ARE NOW HANDLING YOUR BUSINESS.
YOURS SINCERELY,
MUSIC CORPORATION OF AMERICA

"The thought of death no longer chilled me. I was in safe hands. MCA had never lost a man."

Niven is ever ready to make himself the butt of his anecdotes, and in speaking of his war years he points to an incident that he feels sums the whole thing up to perfection. Early in the war Niven and a group of others were invited by Sir Winston Churchill to dine with him. Churchill, an avid and knowledgeable filmgoer, approached Niven after supper and said, for all to hear: "Young man, I think it was admirable of you to give up your career and come back here to do your duty." Then, while Niven basked in the compliment, Churchill added: "Of course, it would have been deplorable if you hadn't."

The day after being demobilized, Niven started work in London on a large-scale technicolor fantasy called *A Matter of Life and Death* (U.S. title: *Stairway to Heaven*) concerning the special heaven reserved for dead airmen. It was about one airman in particular who was wafted upwards and given the celestial treatment but had to be returned because he hadn't really expired. It was an excellent vehicle for a film actor returning to his trade, but it gave Niven false hope about resuming his former image. As other stars also discovered, this was not to be easy.

Samuel Goldwyn, like many another honorable employer, had assured Niven that his job would be open to him as soon as he returned. He was as good as his word and even negotiated a better contract for the actor. However, Niven would find that Goldwyn still rented his actors to other producers, without much regard for the quality of the picture as long as the price was right. Niven's first three postwar Hollywood films were loan-outs: *The Perfect Marriage,* reuniting him with his old friend Loretta Young; *The Magnificent Doll,* with the doll of the title being Dolly Madison and Niven badly miscast as Aaron Burr; and *The Other Love,* a tepid comedy with Barbara Stanwyck. Niven was now beginning to wonder about his return to film fame. Fortunately, Goldwyn himself came up with a good vehicle, *The Bishop's Wife,* with Niven as the Bishop, Loretta Young as the wife, and Cary Grant as an angel sent down to straighten out the Bishop's affairs.

Niven had left Hollywood a bachelor, but returned as a married man with two London-born sons, David and Jamie. During the war he had met and married Primula Rollo, the daughter of the Hon. William and Lady Kathleen Rollo. She was then serving as an officer in the women's branch of the Royal Air Force. Six weeks after their return to Hollywood in 1946, she fell down a flight of basement stairs at the home of a friend and never regained consciousness. Niven was then a widower for two years until he met Swedish fashion model Hjördis Tersmeden, who added two daughters to his family, Kristina and Fiona.

With Marius Goring in *Stairway to Heaven* (British
title: *A Matter of Life and Death*)

Niven returned to England in 1948—the start
of annual shuttlings back and forth to make British
and American films—to appear in what he hoped
would be a major project for him, *Bonnie Prince
Charlie*. He had known and loved the stories of
Charles Stuart from boyhood, but even his enthusiasm couldn't stop the film from being a turgid
epic. From one of the battle scenes comes a story
Niven is hesitant to tell because it sounds improb-
able. "I was leading a charge down a hillside, my
sword flailing the air, when I tripped and lunged
forward. In doing so, my sword pierced the leg of
a man and pinned him to the ground. The poor
man was squirming on the ground but not making
much fuss. He asked me to pull the sword out. I
gulped and did it. Then he sprang to his feet. I was
about to praise him for his courage and his stamina

In *Bonnie Prince Charlie*

when he pulled up his pant leg and revealed an aluminum limb. He was a veteran and had lost the leg at El Alamein. I know it sounds farfetched —he was the only man with an artificial leg among the 600 extras on that mock battlefield—but I have dozens of witnesses to bear me out."

Goldwyn's *Enchantment* gave Niven some hope that his stock was not starting to slide. Critics praised it as the best thing the actor had done until then. It called for Niven to play a young enamored army officer of the Edwardian era and then the same man, years later, as an elderly general, living in a London mansion during the Second World War, who gives sage advice to a pair of young lovers. Niven was dynamic as the handsome young blade and touching as a sad-hearted old man. As with all Goldwyn pictures, the production was marked by quality and style; nevertheless, Goldwyn again farmed Niven out, something with which he had become increasingly unhappy. Niven was sent to appear in two limp comedies, *A Kiss in the Dark* with Jane Wyman and—worse—*A Kiss for Corliss* with Shirley Temple. "I had much to thank Sam for, he had been my benefactor but I felt the tide running out. I went up to his office and asked to be released from the contract. Somewhat to my surprise he said, 'You're free as soon as you hit the sidewalk.'" The specter of television was then looming over Hollywood and most of the studios were terminating their contracts with the expensive talent, something they would greatly regret in later years when the same actors were able to swing freelance deals for far greater fees than they had been able to earn under contract.

With Evelyn Keyes in *Enchantment*

Free of his Goldwyn ties, Niven still didn't find any signs of upward tendencies in his film fortunes. He began 1950 with a supporting role in Mario Lanza's *The Toast of New Orleans,* then went to England to play Sir Percy Blakeney in *The Elusive Pimpernel,* another costume bomb, and returned to MGM to be an officer again in *Soldiers Three.* Two more British comedies, *Happy Go Lovely* with Vera Ellen and *Appointment with Venus* with Glynis Johns, did little for his stature. His only 1952 release was the dismal *The Lady Says "No",* by which time he was wondering if the public was also saying "no." But two things happened that year that changed his course for the better. First, he appeared with Gloria Swanson in a play called *Nina;* although the play was a flop, Otto Preminger saw it and decided Niven was just right for *The Moon is Blue.* The film was a bit of moral titillation and the first Hollywood film to be released without an official seal of approval from the censors. In lieu of a big salary Niven accepted a piece of the picture, which turned out to be a wise move. His finances were low but the returns on *The Moon is Blue* marked a return to solvency.

Much more important was Niven's decision in 1952 to form a television production company with two other actors whose box office value had waned— Dick Powell and Charles Boyer. Many Hollywood people looked askance at this move, but within a few years the company, Four Star, was among the most productive and profitable studios in the business. Niven admits he, like Boyer, had little to do with its success. Dick Powell was the guiding force, an astute producer and director and a cagey businessman. As long as he lived, Four Star flourished. When he died, the company quickly ran down hill. Despite his seeming flippancy about all things, Niven is not flippant about money: his proceeds from Four Star helped make him an affluent man, the owner of a chateau in Vaud, Switzerland, and a villa at Cap Ferrat on the French Riviera.

The Moon is Blue helped Niven maintain his image as a movie star of some importance, but it brought few offers of worthwhile productions, largely because in the mid-1950s not many worthwhile films were being made anywhere. Niven did three films in England in 1954: two more limp comedies, *The Love Lottery* and *Happy Ever After,* and then a serious drama called *Carrington, V.C.* (The title was changed in the U.S. to *Court Martial* on the assumption that not enough Americans would know, or care, that "V.C." stood for Victoria Cross.) The film was not greatly successful

With Cantinflas in *Around the World in Eighty Days*

but Niven gave a convincing performance as a decorated British army major on trial for questionable conduct.

The King's Thief in 1955 and *The Birds and The Bees* in 1956 did nothing to advance Niven's power at the box office, but he was too busy with his Four Star enterprises to worry much. He was, however, on the verge of an upswing at the movies. Mike Todd was managing after years of struggle to get backing for a colossal filming of *Around the World in Eighty Days*. "I got a call from Mike Todd to come over to his house. I was sitting in my back yard with Humphrey Bogart at the time and since I didn't know anything about Todd I asked Bogie for his advice. He said, 'Watch out for him.' So I went over to Todd and he immediately began questioning me, did I know about Jules Verne and did I know about this book *Around the World in Eighty Days*? I told him honestly that I admired Verne and adored the book—I didn't know he intended filming it. He looked me in the eye and asked, 'How'd you like to play Phileas Fogg?' I was ecstatic and I said 'I'd play him for nothing.' With that Todd said, 'You've got a deal' and dived into his swimming pool. After a stunned moment I dived in the direction of my agent, hoping he could persuade Todd not to hold me to the terms I had just rashly declaimed. I played Fogg for a good price but it was such a marvelous picture I think I might have been tempted to play him for nothing."

Niven followed Phileas with a British mystery, an accomplished screen actor, he was able to delineate sharply Verne's character: an imperious, intrepid, punctilious British gentleman of great means and steadfast conviction with an ability to triumph over all obstacles. Todd spent money lavishly on a cast of dozens of cameo stars in many colorful situations and locations.

Niven followed Phileas with the British mystery, *The Silken Affair*, and three Hollywood comedies of generally little merit: *Oh, Men! Oh, Women!*, *The Little Hut*, and *My Man Godfrey*. Otto Preminger's expensive filming of Francoise Sagan's *Bonjour Tristesse* gave Niven a chance to portray the kind of character he had long been, the gentleman of charm but little substance, but the film was tedious and did little business. The fluctuating chart of Niven pictures next reached a high personal peak with *Separate Tables*.

Separate Tables called for David Niven to play the kind of character he had never played before— a sensitive, deceptive man, the reverse of what he seems. Major Pollock is a bogus major, and Niven

With Deborah Kerr in *Separate Tables*

gave Pollock a sympathetic and detailed reading. Here was a lonely, fainthearted man who had been a lackluster junior officer and who later assumes higher rank and the demeanor of importance in order to cover up his barren life—the most pitiful of frauds, especially when it is revealed he was once apprehended for bothering a woman in a cinema. Ironically, he finds himself only through the compassion of a lonely, mother-dominated, mousy girl, touchingly played by Deborah Kerr. Niven received an Academy Award Oscar for this performance, yet his attitude toward receiving it is typically flippant: "It's nice to win first prize." Niven also shows little interest in discussing his work in *Separate Tables* seriously: "Well, they gave me some good lines and then cut to Deborah while I was saying them."

Despite his proven worth as a dramatic actor, Niven went back to light comedies: *Ask Any Girl* with Shirley MacLaine, *Happy Anniversary* with Mitzi Gaynor, and *Please Don't Eat the Daisies* with Doris Day. In 1961 Niven did two quite dissimilar films about the Second World War, both of them requiring him to get back into British Army uniforms. In Carl Foreman's massive adventure *The Guns of Navarone*, Niven played a corporal, his first time as an enlisted man. It was another knowing military portrait, this picture of a man with grudges and bitterness masked behind an amusing but sardonic front, the kind of man with the intelligence but not the taste for being an officer. In *The Best of Enemies*, Niven was back to being a major, but one who looks upon the job as rather absurd and not to be taken too seriously. The film itself did a good job of lampooning the war in the African desert, as Niven and his group played the game of alternately capturing and being captured by Italian captain Alberto Sordi and his group.

With Charlton Heston in *55 Days at Peking*

With Michael Wilding and Alberto Sordi in *The Best of Enemies*

Niven's best group of films formed a mixed bag: *Guns of Darkness* with Leslie Caron was a drama that met with no interest from the public; the Italian film *The Conquered City* saw Niven as yet another British major in the Second World War— he seems to have worn a uniform almost as long in fantasy as in reality; *Fifty-Five Days at Peking* was a lavish epic in which Niven was Sir Arthur Robertson, the British ambassador to China at the time of the Boxer Rebellion; *The Pink Panther* gave Niven the chance to be, more or less, Raffles-a-quarter-century-later, an adroit safe-cracker and jewel thief. *Bedtime Sory* was much of the same, with Niven as yet another charming but larcenous blue blood. In the amusing *Where the Spies Are* Niven was a doctor reluctantly pressed into espionage. *Lady L*

was a $6,000,000 bomb scripted and directed by Niven's friend Peter Ustinov. *Casino Royale* easily surpassed it by being a $12,000,000 bomb, a horrendous financial disaster from which producer Charles Feldman never recovered: the picture may have had a lot to do with his death two years later. It was an interesting idea to have Niven as the retired Sir James Bond, but Feldman made the mistake of hiring five directors to make the film in segments and dozens of stars to play cameos. The film sank in its own excesses.

David Niven's subsequent films offered him interesting moments but got little public response. *Eye of the Devil* was a thriller costarring Deborah Kerr which seemed quickly to disappear from cir-

With Sophia Loren in *Lady L*

culation; Miss Kerr also played opposite Niven in the comedy *Prudence and the Pill*, the film itself a pill which left a dubious taste in the mouth. It concerned the mix-ups which occur when a mother and daughter confuse their various tablets, with a resultant embarrassment of pregnancies. *The Impossible Years* was a fair comic success, with Niven as a professor who lectures on raising teenagers without problems—at a time when his own pretty daughter herself is a problem. As the father of four children, Niven could only play this one tongue in cheek.

The Extraordinary Seaman was a flop but an interesting one. Director John Frankenheimer had proven himself to be about the worthiest of Hollywood's young filmmakers by producing such intelligent fare as *The Birdman of Alcatraz, The Manchurian Candidate, Seven Days in May,* and *The Train,* but with *The Extraordinary Seaman* he tried to lampoon the Second World War and overreached himself. He also ran into legal difficulties in using excerpts from newsreels, and thereby lost the confidence of MGM in promoting the picture. Niven played a British naval officer, a kind of "Flying Englishman" condemned by his illustrious ancestors to spend eternity aboard his First World War warship until he vindicates the family honor he smudged by falling overboard and drowning during a sea battle. Niven was nonchalant as the dapper officer complete with trim beard, natty white uniform, and whiskey glass at hand, but he skillfully got across the point that this was a man who knew he was a *poseur* and his glorious family tradition a sham. In his book *The Cinema of John Frankenheimer* (Tantivy Press, London), Gerald Pratley says of *The Extraordinary Seaman:* "The film is in its own quiet way the epitaph of an era—the crumbling of a centuries-old western military ideal (a myth further destroyed by the *Pueblo* incident which came after) that sought to dignify war with such old-fashioned virtues as honour, decency, and integrity. The cry 'Don't give up the ship' is as dead as the age of innocence where war is concerned." Whatever the reasons for its failure, the film was a major disappointment for Niven who lost, through no fault of his own, what might have been one of his best screen opportunities.

The year 1969 gave Niven two more British military types, one serious and one crooked. *Before Winter Comes* had Niven as a major assigned to an unimportant post because of what might have been cowardice and what was certainly hesitancy in an action that cost several soldiers their lives. The

In *The Extraordinary Seaman*

incident was not sufficiently grave to cause the major's disgrace, but serious enough to cast doubts in the minds of his superiors. Serious and compassionate, Niven obviously drew here upon his own considerable observation of professional military men. For *The Brain* he had to draw only upon his usual lightweight style of charm and roguishness: here he portrayed a British colonel attached to NATO who masterminds an elaborate scheme to rob NATO of a huge amount of money. *The Brain* did nothing to inspire one's confidence in NATO, and no amount of charm could sugarcoat the character of this particular Niven assignment. Raffles lifting gems from the wealthy is one thing—a ranking officer abusing a supposedly inviolable responsibility is another. Doubtlessly the least-amused were Niven's friends at the Army and Navy Officers' Club in London.

Niven began the 1970s with another film of questionable taste. *The Statue* examines the dilemma of a man whose sculptress wife creates a huge figure that is a perfect likeness of her husband, except for the genitals. The husband assumes that the model for this part of the anatomy is some other man, one who must be intimate with his wife. Just how funny this plot device is depends on

With Virna Lisi in *The Statue*

the individual, but the moral tone of the picture was in keeping with the so-called adult, liberated attitudes of filmmaking that arose in the late 1960s. *The Statue* was not a success, and after its completion Niven turned his attention to things that interested him more, such as skiing; Niven has long been in the habit of devoting several months a year to recreation, and he makes sure that his picture-making does not interfere with the skiing season.

Once past sixty, Niven showed no signs of retir-ing from films or turning in his debonair image. "I shall go on until I am publicly stoned in the streets. I don't mean drunk but stoned with rocks."

It is greatly to David Niven's credit that his name has never been bandied in the gossip columns. His wild oats were sown early and the slightly play-boyish image hides an entirely private personal life. Niven has been astute in his business dealings, cautious with his money, and possibly rather political in the use of his charm and his ability to amuse.

Also to Niven's credit is the sensible manner in which he has raised his children, keeping them from the public eye and giving them no encouragement to follow in his footsteps. "It's really unfair to the kids to be in the movie business. I remember when my two boys were going to school in California—there were two sorts of reactions from their schoolmates: there were those who were impressed by the fact that father was in the movies, and then there was the kind who jeered, 'I saw your Dad last night and does he stink.'

"I had a way of getting around this and I think it's the only wise thing I've ever done. I used to rehearse them before they went to school in the morning with their little buckets of milk. I stood them up and said, 'Now, I'm a horrible, spotty child in your school and I'm going to ask you a question: what does your father do?' Then I gave them their line: 'One, two, three. He's a very, very bad actor but he absolutely loves doing it.' "

6

BASIL RATHBONE

THE lingering image of Basil Rathbone is either that of a cruel, sardonic villain or that of his cool, laconic Sherlock Holmes. Neither has any similarity to Rathbone the man. Basil was a gentleman and a gentle man, he was warmhearted and generous, and as a host he could not have been more gracious. He was a middle-class, old-school-tie Edwardian Englishman, rather formal in speech, dress, and manner, but—as Vincent Price recalls—"a pushover for a laugh."

Philip St. John Basil Rathbone was born on June 13, 1892, in Johannesburg, South Africa of an English father and an Irish mother. His father was a mining engineer who had gone to South Africa a few years previously during the gold and diamond rush and who had done well for himself until the outbreak of the Boer War. Then, Rathbone recalled, "there was a price on my father's head. He was accused by the Boers of being a British spy. Whether he was or not I never knew." In January of 1896, after the failure of the Jamieson raid into the Boer colony of the Transvaal, many British families, the Rathbones among them, thought it wise to leaves Johannesburg. The family made their way by train to Durban, with the father hiding under the seat during the stops when Boer soldiers boarded the train to inspect credentials. Mrs. Rathbone's long skirt formed a curtain for the father to hide behind as he crouched under the seat—and to hurry the inspection she pinched Basil and his sister in order to make them cry. "The desired effect was accomplished—the Boer inspector was heard to say, 'All right, lady, all right—be on your way and may the good Lord protect you.' To the Boers the Bible and the precepts of family life

were a religion they not only professed, but practiced."

The Rathbones were well-entrenched in the business life of England. Various branches of the family were established in shipping, cotton, and insurance. Basil was proud of the fact that his Uncle Herbert was the Lord Mayor of Liverpool for many years, and that his cousin Eleanor Rathbone was the first woman ever to be elected to the British Parliament. Of more interest to Basil the future actor was the fact that another cousin, Sir Frank Benson, was one of the first actors to be knighted. Sir Frank was also the manager of his own theatrical company, and the man who originated the Stratford-on-Avon Festival. Much of Rathbone's own lifelong passion for Shakespeare, and his distinct declamation of Shakespearean lines, grew from Benson's tutorage. "Sir Frank absolutely insisted on Shakespeare being spoken properly and being heard."

In 1906, Rathbone was enrolled in Repton, one of England's renowned public schools, particularly renowned for its accomplishments in the field of sports. Repton's playing fields, like those of Eton, produced a good many distinguished Englishmen. Young Basil was among the school's keenest cricketers and soccer players. For all his long life, Rathbone glowed when he spoke of Bill Greswell, who played for England in the test matches against Australia, and Bunny Austen, who helped England win and retain the Davis Cup for several years. Rathbone was known to his school chums by the nickname "Ratters," and probably nothing Ratters ever did later in the theater or on film made him prouder than he was at Repton when he won his

Rathbone in one of his first Hollywood appearances, as a dancer and jewel thief in *The Masked Bride* (MGM, 1925), with Mae Murray and Francis X. Bushman

"colors" as a prize footballer.

To those who know little of English public school life, the best illustration of its peculiar fervor is James Hilton's novel *Goodbye, Mr. Chips*. Portions of the 1939 film version, with Robert Donat as Chips, were filmed at Repton. When Rathbone saw the film, he confessed: "I wept unashamedly. They build an *esprit de corps* in English schools, a deep sense of pride in the accomplishments of those who come after—as well as those who have gone before. One has a sense of belonging that neither time nor space can erase."

After completing his four years at Repton, Rathbone told his father he wanted to make the theater his profession. He had not been an outstanding student, except for his essays on Shakespeare, and his father asked that he first spend one year in business to give himself time to settle and adjust. The eighteen-year-old agreed, and was placed as a clerk with the Liverpool, London and Globe Insurance Company, which happened to be one of the Rathbone enterprises. At the end of the year he was even more interested in becoming an actor. He wrote to his cousin, Sir Frank Benson, a much older man, asking to see him about a job. From the interview came the offer of one year with Sir Frank's second company, his touring repertory group set up to train young actors. Aside from playing small parts—at a small salary—Rathbone learned about diction, swordplay, dancing, deportment, and makeup. As he put it, "It was an invaluable experience."

Rathbone was promoted in 1913 to Benson's first company, and played juvenile leads in various Shakespearean productions starring Benson. By the outbreak of the First World War, Rathbone was feeling pleased with himself and his progress at his trade. Many years later he admitted that at the time he felt offended by the advent of war and the rift it would cause in his career, as well as feeling revulsion at the idea of being sent to France to fight in the trenches. He was not alone in this sentiment. Rathbone joined the British army as a private and applied for officer's training—he also admitted he felt this would delay his baptism of fire. He was sent to Gailes in Scotland, where he distinguished himself, after a fashion, by organizing a brilliant rugby and soccer team which beat all opposition. At the completion of his training, Rathbone was commissioned a second lieutenant, assigned to the second battalion of the Liverpool Scottish, and soon sent to France. He spent more than two years in the trenches, and by the summer of 1918 he had been promoted and assigned the duties of patrols officer with his regiment. One of Rathbone's exploits brought him a medal for bravery: his unit in need of information about the German units facing them, Rathbone took a volunteer from his men and crawled through no-man's-land and into the German trenches. There he shot and killed an officer, and stripped him of his insignia and his documents. For this Rathbone was awarded the Military Cross.

Rathbone had little difficulty resuming his career after his demobilization in 1919. Apart from his time, his only loss due to the war was his marriage. He had married a young actress in 1914, who gave birth to their son Rodion a year later, but the separation of more than three years caused an estrangement, and shortly after his return to London, Rathbone and his wife agreed to separate. He returned to the stage in the fall of 1919 with the Stratford Festival Company; Sir Frank Benson had left the post of director, but his successors thought highly of Rathbone, and he was given the lead in several plays. Late that year he accepted an offer from Constance Collier to play *Peter Ibbetson*, the success of which launched him into his career as a prominent stage actor.

Basil Rathbone shuttled back and forth across the Atlantic in the 1920s. On his first trip to New York in early 1922 he played in *The Czarina;* a few months later he was back in London in *East of Suez,* which ran a year at His Majesty's Theatre.

Then it was New York again for a play that would bring him wide approval, Ferenc Molnar's *The Swan*. It was during the run of this play that Rathbone met and fell in love with writer Ouida Bergere. It proved to be one of the most solid marriages in a profession riddled with marital woe. For the remaining forty-four years of his life, Rathbone was seldom separated from the woman he called "my beloved Ouida."

Rathbone's success in *The Swan* and several other plays kept him in America for almost five years. He had no desire to live anywhere other than London, but fate decreed otherwise. He lived and worked steadily in London from 1929 to 1932, but in the autumn of that year he received a generous and interesting offer from Katherine Cornell to be her leading man in *Romeo and Juliet, The Barretts of Wimpole Street,* and *Candide,* in a touring company of those plays. It was an offer no real actor could deny, and he headed back to America—little realizing that it would be his home for most of his remaining thirty-five years.

As Romeo, Robert Browning, and Shaw's Morrell, Rathbone was an unqualified success. He was experienced enough to give the roles depth and subtlety, yet young enough to be romantic. Over six feet in height, Rathbone was slim and muscular and handsome. As he grew older his slender face became gaunt, but as a young man with black hair, a distinct profile, and elegantly modulated diction, he was an impressive hero—a side of Rathbone moviegoers never saw. But in late 1934 he knew he was playing Romeo for the last time. "I would never dare to appear as a young man again. I knew I must say goodbye to a phase of my professional life; I wasn't afraid of what was to come, it was only that the passing of the years had for the first time in my life become an undeniable reality. I crossed the Rubicon."

By 1934 Rathbone was a forty-two-year-old actor with a solid reputation on the stage but no claim to fame in the movies. This would be the year of his transition. Rathbone had appeared in a few silent films in England and made his first talkie, *The Last of Mrs. Cheney,* in Hollywood in 1929. Between 1930 and 1933 he had parts in eleven films, none of them memorable and none of them leading him to think of himself as anything other than a stage actor picking up a little work in the movies between plays.

The man who turned Basil Rathbone into a film star was David O. Selznick. By 1934, then thirty-two and with seven years of success as a film producer

With Norma Shearer in *The Last of Mrs. Cheney*

behind him, Selznick was anxious to make films of great scope and lasting importance. He was particularly keen on the idea of translating classics of literature to the screen, and for his first venture in that direction he chose *David Copperfield*, proceeding with it in spite of the finger of doubt wagged

With Elizabeth Allan, Freddie Bartholomew, and Violet Kembe-Cooper in *David Copperfield*

at him by his boss, MGM tycoon Louis B. Mayer, who also happened to be his father-in-law. Selznick was adamant in his plan and Mayer acceded, suggesting his young contractee Jackie Cooper for the title role. Selznick thought it absurd to use an American boy in the part, and he sent director George Cukor to England to find a suitable young actor. Cukor was lucky, and soon signed a beautiful lad named Freddie Bartholomew. Selznick was delighted with the boy—it was an inspired find—and he set about casting *Copperfield* with the finest talent available. He chose Lionel Barrymore as Peggotty, Edna May Oliver as Aunt Betsy, Roland Young as Uriah Heep, and Charles Laughton as Micawber. During the rehearsals Laughton became doubtful about the role of the whimsical, debt-plagued Micawber, and asked to be released, thus creating the problem of a replacement. Selznick then took a long shot and cast W. C. Fields, who had never before played a dramatic role and whose drinking and recalcitrant manner made him even more of a risk. Even in filmmaking, long shots sometimes pay off handsomely, and this one did.

Selznick found the part of Copperfield's mean stepfather hard to cast. He tested several Hollywood actors but none had the icy, ramrod character he felt the role needed. Rathbone, whom he had seen playing with Katherine Cornell, came to mind; suddenly the image of the tall, slim Englishman with the aquiline profile and the chiseled diction appealed to him. He sent for Rathbone, who immediately won the part with his first reading of the lines. Thus, one of the great film villains was born.

Rathbone as Murdstone was every inch the vicious, coldhearted man Dickens had described in his novel, yet it was a role alien to his own gentle nature. Recalled Rathbone: "One morning I had to thrash the living daylights out of poor Freddie. It was a most unpleasant experience. George Cukor directed me to express no emotion whatsoever—merely thrash the boy within an inch of his life. I had a vicious cane with much whip to it, but fortunately for Freddie he was protected by a sheet of foam rubber under his britches and covering his little rump. As Murdstone I tried to make my mind a blank, thrashing Freddie as hard as I could but like a machine. From time to time Cukor would stop me and say, 'Basil, you were thinking of something. Please don't—all right, let's try again.' And so it went on for most of the morning. When it was over I took Freddie in my arms and kissed him."

However cruel Rathbone as Murdstone had been

to Freddie Bartholomew in *David Copperfield,* he was able to make it up to him by playing his loving father in Selznick's *Anna Karenina,* made shortly after. Again Rathbone was an aloof, arrogant figure —more so than Tolstoy outlined in his book. Rathbone objected, but Selznick was not a man to be dissuaded once an image had jelled in his mind. Film censorship of the time probably had some bearing on this: the 1935 Karenin would have to be a man so cold and ruthless as almost to justify his young wife's adultery. Selznick's picture was an excellent film, conveying the glory and pomp of Czarist Russia, with Rathbone as the haughty, ambitious minister of state, an arrogant man who reacts severely to his wife's affair with a handsome young army officer. Garbo was divine as Anna and Fredric March suitably handsome and believable as Vronsky, with young Bartholomew winsome as the boy who has to lose his mother for reasons he can't begin to understand. The part was extremely diffi-

cult for a ten-year-old and he was helped in it by Rathbone, who described one particular incident in his book *In and Out of Character:*

There was a scene in which, after having forbidden Anna ever to see her son again, I had to tell the child that his mother had gone on a long journey, or something of that nature, and that I did not know when he would see her again. Freddie Bartholomew was acting up all over the place and Clarence Brown, our director, suggested I might be able to help the boy since Freddie and I were good friends. I promised to try and Clarence walked off the stage to get himself a cup of tea.

"Freddie, dear boy," I said, "this scene isn't coming off as it should, you know."

"Yes, I know, Uncle Basil. What am I doing, please tell me?" Freddie replied. "you are not listening to what I am telling you, about your mother's going away for a long time. And if you are listening you are not conveying any feelings. You are making a lot of noise and hamming it up," and we both laughed about it.

With Freddie Bartholomew in *Anna Karenina*

"Now, Freddie dear," I continued, "this is one of your very best scenes and you have just got to be good in it for Cissie's sake." Cissie was Freddie's guardian and he simply worshipped her. Then like a flash it came to me. "Freddie, listen to me carefully—in this scene just forget all about my being your stern father Karenin, telling you about your mother going away—when I come in and talk to you just imagine it's me, your Uncle Basil, and I am breaking the news to you that Cissie is dead."

Freddie looked at me, and then turned away from me as his eyes filled with tears. I went quickly to our assistant director and said to him, "Get Clarence as fast as you can. I think Freddie is about ready to make this scene."

Clarence Brown came back at once. The camera was already set up, and all there was to do was turn on the lights. I entered the room and walked over to Freddie's bed. I could tell at once that he was applying the formula. He no longer greeted me as an ogre, but the strain of what he had to do gave his little white face a timidity that was deeply touching. As I talked to him of his mother's going away he was not listening to what I said but translating my words, as it were, into a scene in which Uncle Basil was telling him of Cissie's death. The effect was a heartbreaking scene at the conclusion of which I had to spend a considerable time comforting Freddie and getting him back to normal. Everyone on the set including Clarence Brown praised his performance extravagantly, and in self-defence Freddie had to keep our little secret and admit with us all that he was indeed truly a great actor.

The year 1935 was a stellar year for Basil Rathbone. The two Selznick pictures were released and they played to great success. Rathbone had to discard any plans of returning to the stage, since the film offers now poured in—and at salaries that couldn't be turned down. Late in 1935 he went to Warners to play Captain Levasseur, a French buccaneer who first forms a partnership with Errol Flynn's *Captain Blood* and then fights with him over the favors of young Olivia de Havilland. This film opened up yet another facet of Rathbone's career—the rapier-flashing costume cad.

The duel in which Flynn kills Rathbone in *Captain Blood* was one he always remembered with a shudder: "Errol was a wild man to fence. He was daring and dashing but undisciplined. He looked better than he actually was. The scene was filmed at Laguna Beach and we still hadn't finished it by late afternoon. The extras came up to me during the breaks and tried to talk me into muffing the fight so they could get another day's work out of it, and Michael Curtiz and his assistants were trying to wrap up the scene and clear the location. Curtiz was brilliant with his action sequences but

brutal with his actors. He told me that when Flynn killed me, he wanted me to fall backwards on a big rock at the edge of the water so that the tide would lap over me as it washed back and forth. He then instructed me to keep my eyes open as I lay dead. I did it but it was excruciating. Try dunking yourself in the ocean sometime and not closing your eyes!"

Rathbone continued in costume with his next two historical epics, *The Last Days of Pompeii* and *A Tale of Two Cities*. In the *Pompeii* picture he played Pontius Pilate but not as a villain. Rathbone's Pilate was a Roman aristocrat not without compassion or conscience, a man of high office who condemns Christ as a matter of duty. Not until many years later does he ponder the significance of his part in the killing of the Messiah. The film was a good but conventional toga-and-chariot saga with a touching scene toward the end when the now gray-haired Pilate pauses at Pompeii to visit his friend Marcus (Preston Foster), a former gladiator now a wealthy Roman. The conversation touches upon Christ and, when Marcus tells his son that no such man ever existed, Pilate quietly disagrees and says with obvious sadness, "I crucified him." The role of Pilate fascinated Rathbone, who was a deeply religious man. A decade previously, Rathbone had coauthored a play called *Judas* and played the title part on Broadway. He studied early Christianity, and he believed in life after death. Rathbone claimed he had extrasensory perception and that he had had a number of occult experiences.

For Selznick's *A Tale of Two Cities*, Rathbone turned out one of the most vicious of his villains, the Marquis d'Evremonde, a character created by Dickens to demonstrate the arrogance and cruelty of the French aristocracy of the *ancien regime*. Dickens used the character as a symbol of the conditions that were a cause of the French Revolution, but not necessarily as a representative aristocrat in that grandiose nightmare of history. As played by Rathbone, the Marquis was a supercilious swine who persecuted and starved the peasants. In one scene, his speeding carriage runs over a child in the street; the driver stops the carriage and tells the Marquis what has happened. His only reaction is one of annoyance at the delay: "Drive on!" It comes almost as a relief to the audience when the Marquis is stabbed to death in his bed.

Rathbone was chosen by Irving Thalberg to play Tybalt in his lavish production of *Romeo and Juliet*. It was his only film opportunity to display his affinity for Shakespeare; his interpretation of

With Errol Flynn in *Captain Blood*

With Preston Foster in *The Last Days of Pompeii*

the proud, furious, vengeful Tybalt brought him an Academy Award nomination. Rathbone's skill with a sword was well in evidence, and his duel with John Barrymore is a masterpiece of film editing. Barrymore at this time in his life was incapable of physical dexterity, and Fred Cavens expertly doubled for him, to match Rathbone's speed and style.

Rathbone in the late 1930s was at the peak of his form as a film actor: employment was continuous and profitable, enabling him and his wife to live well and entertain in the grand manner. He was then one of the principal figures in Hollwood's British colony—Sir C. Aubrey Smith, Ronald Colman, Reginald Denny, Herbert Marshall, Nigel Bruce, David Niven, Brian Aherne, and others—most of whom were upper-crust Englishmen, much given to playing cricket, tennis, and golf. Hollywood was, in those years, an outpost of the British Empire on which the sun shone brightly.

The films were plentiful. In *Kind Lady* Rathbone was a Machiavellian butler; in *The Garden of Allah* he was an amorous Italian count making moon-eyes at Marlene Dietrich; and in *Tovarich* he was the coldhearted Bolshevik commissar, Gorotchenko, who hounds Czarist aristocrats Charles Boyer and Claudette Colbert in Paris and forces them to reveal the whereabouts of a Czarist fortune. In 1937 Rathbone returned to England to make *Love From a Stranger,* a macabre story of a gentleman who marries women for their money and then murders them. Rathbone played the part not as a repellent villain but as a neurotic, unbalanced man. His playing was low-key—not always the case with Rathbone, who was often rather florid in his style—and he revealed his intentions primarily with facial expressions. The film was mainly the story of his wooing and wedding of Ann Harding; his best scene came when he persuaded her to sign away her fortune, she thinking she is merely signing a mortgage document.

The years 1938 and 1939 were rewarding ones for Basil Rathbone, with a slew of interesting films. First came the glorious *The Adventures of Robin Hood,* with his arrogantly strutting Sir Guy of Gisbourne, a textbook portrait of the classical villain—cruel, ruthless, and ambitious. As Prince John's first officer for the oppression of the Saxons and the plot to control England in the absence of King Richard, Rathbone looked malevolently handsome in his finery and spat his lines like venom. "I'll have him dangling in a week," he boasts as the prince hands him a warrant for Robin's life. Such misplaced confidence!

Rathbone continued his storybook villainy in *The Adventures of Marco Polo* with Gary Cooper none too convincing as the Venetian explorer. As Ahmed, a minister of state and a plotter against the throne of Kubla Khan, Rathbone kept a cellar full of hungry lions, to which he dropped his unwanted guests through a trap door. Naturally, Basil ends up himself as lion fodder. Next came a far better film and a much more subtle characterization—King Louis XI in *If I Were King,* with Ronald Colman as François Villon. Rathbone's Louis was a devious old man, crafty, eccentric, and weazened. The King is amused by Villon's courage, but uses him to his own advantage and callously plans to discard him when his usefulness is over. Rathbone received his second Academy Award nomination for this colorful characterization.

The mantle of villain had long ago settled on Rathbone, yet he still fought to discard it, and asked to tackle other kinds of roles. In the 1939 *Dawn Patrol* he was the harried squadron commander who sends his pilots into battle knowing they stand little hope of survival. For Rathbone it was a return to the uniform of a First World War officer, and he gave the part authority and compassion. Then came *The Son of Frankenstein,* and his identification with the horror genre, which he would grow secretly to loathe. He was, in fact, the hero of this film; as Baron Wolf Von Frankenstein, the son of the scientist who created the monster, he returns from America to the family estate in Germany intrigued with the idea of reviving the dormat ogre and changing him into a gentle, malleable soul. He fails, of course. Karloff was again the monster in this, the last good picture in the Frankenstein saga. The variations that followed became increasingly shoddy and comic. Rathbone and Karloff were cast by Universal immediately after the completion of *The Son of Frankenstein* in a much better film—*The Tower of London.* This was Shakespeare's *Richard III* devoid of Shakespearean language, with Rathbone giving a black performance as the murderous, egomaniacal monarch. To accommodate Karloff, an additional character was added to the classic tale, that of Mord, a club-footed torturer and executioner at the Tower: he and Richard show a devilish affinity for one another. Spanning the years between the battles of Tewkesbury and Bosworth (1471–85), the film is a minor epic of horror and cruelty, with admirable settings, lighting, and camerawork.

Before assuming the cap and tweeds of Sherlock Holmes, Rathbone had a fling at a variety of pictures. He was an old-school-tie British diplomat on

With Ronald Colman in *If I Were King*

With David Niven and Errol Flynn in *The Dawn Patrol*

With Edgar Norton, Boris Karloff, and Bela Lugosi in *Son of Frankenstein*

the Gold Coast of Africa in *The Sun Never Sets* (the elder brother of Douglas Fairbanks, Jr.), and an escaped convict making his way through the Brazilian swamps in *Rio*. For a complete change of pace he played a music publisher in Bing Crosby's *Rhythm on the River,* looking as out of place as a man using a cricket bat in Yankee Stadium. Not even his fondest fans were willing to buy Basil in a business suit in Tin Pan Alley.

In mid-1939 Rathbone went to Twentieth Century-Fox to play Holmes in *The Hound of the Baskervilles* and its sequel, *The Adventures of Sherlock Holmes.* Thinking that his stab at Holmes was then over and done with, Rathbone went back to seeking variety, but found instead that the curse of typecasting had locked itself in on him. Producers were interested mainly in Basil the Bad. He did another classic costume villain opposite Tyrone Power in *The Mask of Zorro,* as the military aide to the governor of California in the early nineteenth century, when California was still a province of Mexico. Rathbone's aide was a treacherous schemer planning to be a dictator behind the faint-hearted governor. Of course, he didn't reckon on Don Diego (Power), a fop by day and a flashing, black-masked cavalier by night. In this film, finely directed by Rouben Mamoulian, Rathbone was a humorless, twitching man—jabbing at things with his saber and eager for a fight. His duel with Power remains one of the highlights in the art of theatrical fencing, and to anyone with a knowledge of swordplay it was obvious Power's hero would not have lasted a dozen counts in a real fight with Rathbone's villain.

With Tyrone Power in *The Mark of Zorro*

Rathbone was fairly well-behaved in *Paris Calling, International Lady,* and *Crossroads,* but he was a better box office draw as *The Mad Doctor,* as the wife-killer in *The Black Cat,* and as a fanatic surgeon in *Fingers at the Window.*

Basil Rathbone was by far the best swordsman among all the actors who appeared in Hollywood films. He was always the villain in his costume pictures, and lost every duel, but he would joke later, "I could easily have messed up their pictures for them because I could have killed the hero any time I wanted." It was true. Errol Flynn and Tyrone Power would never had stood a chance against Rathbone in an unscripted match. Rathbone had never fenced in competition, but he had taken fencing lessons from the age of eighteen as part of his training as a classical actor. His four principal screen duels were those in *Captain Blood, Romeo and Juliet, The Adventures of Robin Hood,* and *The Mark of Zorro.* For each of these duels he was tutored by Fred Cavens, who also staged these and many other film swordfights, and more often than not appeared in the duels as a double. It was Cavens more than any other man who was responsible for bringing respectability and credibility to swordplay in Hollywood.

Cavens said of Rathbone: "He has excellent form and is the most colorful of all the people I have taught. I doubt if he would do well in competition, but for picture purposes he is better than the best fencer in the world." Cavens also explained that knowledge of fencing is not always a help to an actor: "Film fencers should have perfect grace and form, qualities that are not necessary in competition. I have seen Olympic champions who had such atrocious form they couldn't appear in pictures because audiences would laugh at them. But they would be extremely dangerous in a real duel." In staging his screen duels Cavens devised a style of magnifying the movements of thrust, parry, and lunge in order to give them theatrical excitement. His duels were meticulously staged and he rehearsed his actors as a choreographer would rehearse dancers. And he always insisted that the duel should look like a fight and not a mere display of technique. Basil Rathbone vindicated everything Cavens maintained.

For his article "Swordplay on the Screen" (*Films in Review,* June-July 1965), Rudy Behlmer, a television producer and director by trade and a film historian by avocation, came up with some interesting information on Fred Cavens and his contribution to fencing in films. According to Behlmer's research, Cavens was a graduate of the Belgian Military Institute at the age of eighteen and a professor of fencing three years later. He taught fencing in Europe and America, and came to the attention of Douglas Fairbanks, Sr., in 1924. Fairbanks's own swordplay had been full of flair but none too skillful. He hired Cavens to coach him on *The Black Pirate* and *The Iron Mask,* and improved his skill and appearance greatly. Cavens also coached John Barrymore for *Don Juan* and dozens of others before being assigned to train Rathbone and Errol Flynn for *Captain Blood* in 1935. The stylish duel at a rocky, sandy seashore was perhaps the best screen swordfight up to that time, but Cavens excelled it with his staging of the same actors in *The Adventures of Robin Hood.* Wrote Behlmer:

> That film's final duel took place in Nottingham Castle, where Robin (Flynn) and Sir Guy (Rathbone) covered a considerable area during the course of the action. Director Michael Curtiz loved to use scenery and props to increase the theatricalism and violence of his duels and in *Robin Hood* hero and villain fought their way down a winding staircase, upset a giant candelabra, locked blades over a heavy table, slashed candles, etc. Huge shadows of the two figures on a pillar as they come together in a corps-a-corps were photographed to good effect.
>
> Since the period was late 12th century, broadswords were used, but liberties were taken with the techniques. Actual medieval swords were heavy, hacking weapons and were handled in a primitive fashion. In *Robin Hood* fencing techniques not developed until centuries later (e.g. the lunge, certain parries) were incorporated into the routine. While there usually is fidelity to the proper type of sword in period pictures, liberties are often taken with the way the swords are used. Fencing evolved over many centuries and has many schools and styles, and screen duels are usually a synthesis of them.

In discussing the duel staged by Cavens for *The Mark of Zorro,* Behlmer wrote:

> In addition to being an excellent villain, Rathbone had become a superb opponent in extended screen duels. He looked marvelous in the lengthy and well done Zorro saber duel (he wore high, stiff boots which added to the dramatic line of his lunge). Tyrone Power was doubled in many of the *Zorro* dueling shots by Cavens' son, Albert, who worked closely with his father for many years in training actors to fence, staging routines, doubling, and playing legitimate roles requiring a knowledge of the blade. Before and since his father's death in 1962 Albert has also worked alone in all these capacities.

It was Fred Cavens who was responsible for Rath-

Basil Rathbone as Sir Guy of Gisbourne in *The Adventures of Robin Hood*

bone being given his role in *The Mark of Zorro.* Darryl Zanuck had George Sanders in mind for the part, but Cavens pointed out that Sanders was a languid man by nature and not at all interested in swordplay. Cavens suggested Zanuck use Rathbone if he wanted a truly exciting duel and Zanuck immediately complied. Rathbone was later offered more such sword-wielding roles but he turned them down lest he become typed as a rapier scoundrel. Little did he realize he was on the verge of becoming much more indelibly typed as an intellectual detective.

Basil Rathbone first appeared as Sherlock Holmes in early 1939 when Twentieth Century-Fox released *The Hound of the Baskervilles.* The decision to use him in the role was one of immediate inspiration and once his name was mentioned, no other actor was considered. The decision was arrived at one evening at the home of Darryl F. Zanuck when he was entertaining his friends, director Gregory Ratoff and writer Gene Markey. The subject of Holmes came up and Ratoff said to Zanuck, "Why don't you do a Holmes picture?" Zanuck brightened at the suggestion and then asked, "Yes, but who can we get to do Holmes?" Markey chimed in as if surprised by the question, "Who? Basil Rathbone!"

Rathbone did, in fact, bear a resemblance to the famous painting of Sherlock Holmes by Frederic Dorr, the painting approved of by Sir Arthur Conan Doyle, who patterned his mythical detective on Dr. Joseph Bell, a professor at Edinburgh University, which Doyle attended. Dr. Bell was, according to Doyle, a genius at deductive reasoning. Doyle's first Holmes study was *A Study in Scarlet,* written in 1887 when he was practising medicine. The public response was so favorable that he continued, and over the years he wrote three books and more than fifty short stories involving Holmes and his adventures in solving mysteries. The character of Holmes had such charisma that people believed that he was a living person and that his dwelling at 221–B Baker Street in London really existed.

The Holmes stories were naturals for the movies and as early as 1903 filmmakers were tampering with his image and his adventures. Many Holmes stories were filmed in America, England, and Germany throughout the years of the silent screen. English stage actor William Gillette made a career as Holmes, playing him first in 1899. He wrote the play *Sherlock Holmes* and appeared in the 1916 filming of it. Other actors who appeared in films as Holmes were John Barrymore, Clive Brook, Raymond Massey and Reginald Denny, with most of their work done in England. The subject of Holmes had not been touched in Hollywood for some years when Zanuck decided to proceed with Rathbone.

The Hound of the Baskervilles is the most faithful of the Rathbone versions. It was adapted from the Doyle story of the same title and set in the proper Victorian period. Top billing went to Richard Greene as Sir Henry Baskerville, a man marked for death in his castle on the Devonshire moors. Holmes uncovers the plot and locates the master of the ferocious hounds trained to stalk and kill their victims in the chill and foggy nights on the moor. Nigel Bruce was the happy choice for Holmes's friend and chronicler, Dr. John Watson. The success of the film called for an encore.

The Adventures of Sherlock Holmes was roughly based on the Gillette play. The arch criminal Professor Moriarty appeared in the guise of ominous George Zucco, who schemed to steal the Crown Jewels from the Tower of London, and masked his scheme with an elaborate plot to murder a young lady. Holmes is brought in to protect the girl and

In his disguise as a song and dance man in *The Adventures of Sherlock Holmes*

discovers the real plot. The effectiveness of this and all the other Rathbone Holmes pictures lay in Rathbone's appearance and diction. The tall, saturnine, and emotionless portrayal and the crisp, quick, educated delivery of his lines seemed perfectly to personify Doyle's master sleuth.

The subject of Holmes lay untouched for the next three years, while Rathbone played villains in *The Mark of Zorro* and other, less flamboyant, films. Rathbone himself thought the stories somewhat dated by this time: he doubted if the Victorian settings had much appeal to modern audiences. Universal discussed with Rathbone the idea of modernizing the stories and the actor was sufficiently intrigued with the idea to try it. He was then under contract to Universal, but he might not have proceeded had he foreseen the success of his characterization and the ensuing overidentification of him with Holmes, which almost crippled his career as a serious actor. In all there were twelve Holmes films produced by Universal between 1942 and 1946:

Sherlock Holmes and the Voice of Terror finds

the detective alive and active circa 1942, the deerstalker cap replaced by a fedora and the calabash by a briar pipe. Holmes, along with Watson, is pressed into service by the British government to uncover and halt the people responsible for German propaganda broadcasts originating in England. Holmes not only nails the traitorous broadcasters but foils a Nazi invasion. As a wartime fillip Universal decided to conclude each Holmes picture with a patriotic statement by him. At the end of this one, Watson and Holmes, in the dawn's early light, stand on the white cliffs of Dover and overlook the English Channel. Says Sherlock, "There's an east wind coming, Watson." Dear old Watson grumps, "I don't think so. Looks like another warm day." Holmes gives a little smile and then continues, "Good old Watson, the one fixed point in a changing age. But there's an east wind coming all the same. Such a wind as never blew on England yet. It will be cold and bitter, Watson, and a good many of us may wither before it's done. But it's God's own wind nonetheless. And a greener, better, stronger land will be in the sunshine when the storm is cleared." Maudlin though the words may seem, they were actually written by Doyle for his story *His Last Bow*, on which this film was based. The interesting thing is that they were written before the First World War and were spoken by Holmes as he overlooked the Channel in August, 1914.

Sherlock Holmes and the Secret Weapon: The previous picture had been directed by John Rawlins; this one was directed by Holmes enthusiast Roy William Neill, who went on to direct all the other films in this series. Neill was the guiding force behind the series and, although he was criticized by purists for his distortions, he did remarkably well in maintaining good productions on small budgets. Neill brought in Doyle expert Thomas McKnight as technical director, and together they mined Holmes plots and situations. The source of this film was Doyle's "The Dancing Men," the main device of which was the solution of a cryptogram. Here the cryptogram concealed the names and addresses of four scientists, each entrusted with the production of part of a new bombsight, which had to be kept from Nazi hands. This time Moriarty was played by the icy Lionel Atwill, but no matter who played Moriarty, he never succeeded in outwitting Sherlock.

Sherlock Holmes in Washington: Most of the films in the series were in some way based upon or inspired by Doyle stories. This one wasn't. Here Universal had Holmes in the United States—something that had never occurred to Dolye. The plot involved the disappearance of a courier carrying documents of great importance between London and Washington, with Holmes sent by the War Office to find the courier and the documents before they fall into the wrong hands. The hands in this case belonged to those magnificent villains, George Zucco and Henry Daniell.

Sherlock Holmes Faces Death: With this film Universal pulled back from Holmes's involvement with the Second World War, although the settings remained contemporary. Based upon Doyle's "The Musgrave Ritual," this film finds Holmes assigned to solve the multiple murders of convalescing British officers in Musgrave Manor, which has been turned over to the government as a rest home with Dr. Watson in charge. Strange deaths occur when the clock in the tower strikes thirteen. What else could poor Watson do but send for Holmes?

The Spider Woman: The name of Holmes was dropped from the titles of the remaining films in the series, because by now the pictures were popular enough to bring in the customers merely at the mention of the two names Rathbone and Bruce. *The Spider Woman* has Gale Sondergaard, Hollywood's most elegant villainess, as the diabolic head of a group of killers whose victims are well covered by life insurance policies. The menacing charm of Sondergaard did not work on Sherlock.

The Scarlet Claw is one of the more peculiar pictures in the series, set as it is in Quebec, although a Quebec unrecognizable to natives of that province. The story was not based on a Doyle plot, but it has much in common with *The Hound of*

With Nigel Bruce in *The Scarlet Claw*

the Baskervilles, as phantoms streak across the foggy moors and victims are left with their throats ripped open. Holmes and Watson happen to be attending a conference on international crime in Montreal when they are called upon by a distraught Lord Penrose, played by the gentlemanly Paul Cavanagh, to solve the murder of his wife. His Lordship and most of the other characters in the film look as if they have strayed from Devonshire, but Holmes ends the film with a tribute to Canada, "the link that joins together two great branches of the human family."

The Pearl of Death: Based upon Doyle's "The Adventures of the Six Napoleons," the plot concerns the theft of a gem of great value, called the "pearl of death" because of the toll in human lives it has exacted. Miles Mander played the evil mastermind, a man who steals the gem from the very hand of the curator of the Royal Museum and then sticks it into a plaster cast of Napoleon. There are, however, five other identical casts, and five unsuspecting owners of Bonaparte busts meet a grisly end before Holmes solves the case.

The House of Fear: Based on Doyle's "The Five Orange Pips," this is one of the more dreary films in the series. Seven retired gentlemen, calling themselves The Good Companions, live together in an eerie old Scottish mansion with insurance policies made out to the last surviving member. One by one they are reported as being murdered and mutilated. Replete with stormy nights, clattering window shutters, secret passageways, and mysterious letters containing orange pips, the film bogs down in lugubriousness, and it is not much of a tribute to Holmes that all the victims die before he figures out the solution. But perhaps he realized early in the game that none of the victims were actually murdered and that they were all in league to bilk the insurance company.

The Woman in Green: The film was based on an original screenplay by Bertram Millhauser, who worked on most of the films in this series. He did use one Doyle device: knowing that he is likely to be shot at by Professor Moriarty, Holmes substitutes a bust of Julius Caesar for his own profile in the window of his Baker Street flat. Hilary Brooke played the lady of the title, who, in league with Moriarty on a profitable murder-and-blackmail system, employed hypnosis on her prospective victims. Moriarty was played in this one by Henry Daniell, and, as Rathbone said, "There were other Moriartys but none so delectably dangerous as was that of Henry." The confrontation scene between these two classically trained English actors, each with impeccable diction, was a highlight of the series.

Pursuit to Algiers bears no relationship to any of Doyle's stories. It concerns the young monarch of a Balkan state, a target for assassination, who must be safely transported from London to his homeland. Various villains try to foil the plan but they are in turn foiled by Holmes. Most of the action of the film took place on a ship, and it was the only film in the series to include songs, conveniently introduced by passengers in the ship's lounge. Nigel Bruce sang "Loch Lomond" and revealed a pleasant baritone voice. Feeling pleased with himself, poor Watson is deflated when Holmes explains that musical talent is not necessarily an indication of good character. "The late Professor Moriarty was a virtuoso of the bassoon."

Terror by Night: Scenarist Frank Gruber claimed that his screenplay was inspired by a Doyle story, but which one it was remains more of a mystery than the plot of this film, perhaps the least interesting in the series. The action takes place on a train bound for Scotland, with Holmes assigned to guard an English noblewoman transporting a precious gem. The lady loses both the jewel and her son before Holmes apprehends the criminal.

Dressed to Kill: The last film in the series finds Holmes tackling the problem of locating Bank of England plates stolen and hidden by a thief now in prison. The key to the hiding place lies in the tunes played by three tiny music boxes made by the

With Patricia Morison in *Dressed to Kill*

With Joan Fontaine in *Frenchman's Creek*

thief. Naturally, Holmes taps the code and then taps the criminals. Interestingly, the leader of the criminal band is lovely Patricia Morrison, here elegantly cold-blooded.

With the completion of this fourteenth Sherlock Holmes picture, Rathbone refused to do any more. In addition to the films, he and Nigel Bruce also did some 200 radio broadcasts as Holmes and Watson during the same period. By that time, Rathbone was sick of the part. He turned down the offer of a seven-year radio contract to continue as Holmes, to the consternation of Nigel Bruce, whose work prospects were slim without Watson— by then his alter ego. But nothing could persuade Rathbone to continue as Sherlock Holmes. He found the identification unbearable, especially because film producers, because of the identification, were unwilling to offer him other work.

While doing the Holmes pictures at Universal

Rathbone made only a few other films. In 1944 he appeared in *Above Suspicion, Frenchman's Creek,* and *Bathing Beauty,* none of them memorable. In *Frenchman's Creek* Rathbone was the repulsive Lord Rockingham, a lecherous old blade stabbed to death by Joan Fontaine as he assaults her. Even for an actor who specialized in villains, it was a low level of cad.

It was during the war years in Hollywood that Basil and Ouida Rathbone built their reputation as gracious party hosts. Their parties were lavish and highly esteemed, although in later years Rathbone would cringe when referred to as one of the great Hollywood "party-givers" and a prominent socialite. He would say with some bite, "I can't think of a more abominable word than socialite." In truth, his party-giving reputation grew from his desire to help the war effort. In 1939 Rathbone, British as the Union Jack, volunteered his services to the Crown, but was turned down on account of age. He was, however, approached by the British consul in Los Angeles and asked if he would serve as the official British host for dignitaries and officers arriving in the area. This he and his wife were pleased and well qualified to do. Rathbone also served during the war years as the chairman of the British War Relief, and as one of the mainstays in the organizing and maintenance of the Hollywood Canteen. Rathbone had served well in the First World War, and he served well in the Second.

By late 1946 the subject of Sherlock Holmes was a painful one for Basil Rathbone. He grew sick of being greeted on the streets with "Hi, Sherlock, how's Watson?" and of hearing impersonations of himself intoning, "Elementary, my dear Watson." It was years before he was willing to discuss Holmes dispassionately. In a radio interview in 1958 he talked about the durability of the Doyle stories: "I don't think his stories have lived because they were the best mystery stories, I don't think they are. What makes the stories live are the wonderful characterizations Sir Arthur invented. Holmes is a much more important man than just a detective, a mere analyser of crimes. He is a very remarkable human being. Watson was one of the most lovable characters of all time, and Moriarty was the most shrewd and vicious villain ever written. Doyle made them real people."

Rathbone confessed that after years of playing Holmes he began to dislike the man. "I once said to my wife that the thing I would dread more than anything else in the world would be to find myself seated next to Holmes at a dinner party, because he'd frighten the daylights out of me. I think playing him so much gave me a kind of inferiority complex. I was jealous of his mastery of everything. Couldn't he fail. just once and prove himself a human being like the rest of us? How could such a completely sufficient man know loneliness or love or sorrow? I was disturbed that people might think I was like Holmes."

Rathbone was a man with the courage of his convictions. He left Hollywood in 1946, selling his home in Beverly Hills and moving to New York to resume his career in the theater, which was always his first professional love. It was eight years before he returned to make a film. In 1946 he was fifty-four, an age when most men are willing to settle for less. Instead Rathbone tackled the serious theater and proved himself equal to the task. In 1947 he landed the prize role of Dr. Sloper in Jed

Harris's excellent production of Henry James's *The Heiress,* playing the part in New York and on tour for two years. From that he went to another remarkable play, Archibald MacLeish's *J.B.,* first in the role of Mr. Zuss, a florid, dignified, imposing man, and then as the gaunt, sardonic Nickles. He was brilliant in both parts.

As the years rolled by Rathbone appeared in fewer stage plays—in fact, as the years rolled by there were fewer plays for any actors to appear in. But he was seldom idle. There were guest appearances on radio and television programs, a few commercials, and a number of fine recordings of Poe, Hawthorne, and Doyle for the Caedman Company in New York. He also devised his own one-man stage show, *An Evening with Basil Rathbone,* and toured with it whenever he wasn't busy doing something else.

The film that brought Rathbone back to Hollywood, in 1954, was the Bob Hope comedy *Casanova's Big Night.* It was a matter of employment; now in his mid-sixties, Rathbone had to take what he could get. Occasionally he was lucky and landed a good part in a good film, but always as a villain. By now his always thin face was even more drawn, giving him a cold and haughty look that belied his true nature. In *My Three Angels* he played André Trochard, the hardhearted businessman who visits his softhearted cousin on Devil's Island to find out if the cousin is running the family store at a profit. He isn't, but before Rathbone can do anything about it he is wafted into the next world by the services of helpful convicts Humphrey Bogart, Peter Ustinov, and Aldo Ray.

An obvious outlet for Rathbone's talents in his

With Vincent Price in *Tales of Terror*

last years was horror films. He allowed himself to become known as a chilling menace, although he secretly resented being called a "horror" actor. He played leads in pictures like *The Black Sleep* and *Queen of Blood,* and joined forces with Vincent Price, Boris Karloff, and Peter Lorre in two of Roger Corman's better gothic pieces, *Tales of Terror* and *Comedy of Terror.* The former was a group of three Poe stories, with Rathbone in the last one, *The Facts in the Case of M. Valdemar,* as an evil hypnotist. In *Comedy of Terrors* Rathbone romped as a slightly demented old Shakespearean actor and the landlord of undertakers Price and Lorre, who do their best to do him in.

Rathbone returned to the rapier in Danny Kaye's *The Court Jester,* perhaps the best of all Kaye's pictures. Written and directed by Norman Panama and Melvin Frank, it was a marvelous spoof on chivalry and a beautiful burlesque on swashbuckling. Rathbone strode on as Sir Ravenhurst (a latter-day Sir Guy of Gisbourne), a minister of King Cecil Parker traitorously plotting against him. Ravenhurst meets an unlikely end in a duel with Kaye, a flunky of the Robin Hood type hero. The hero forces the flunky to drink a potion in order to turn his cowardice into bravery so he can infiltrate the palace. Under the spell of the potion Kaye becomes a brilliant swordsman, but a snap of the fingers turns him back into his cringing self. Another snap of the fingers reverts him to hero, and so on. Sir Ravenhurst is unaware of the potion, but keeps snapping his fingers to tell Kaye how easily he will dispose of him—"Like that!" Ralph Faulkner was the fencing instructor for this ludicrous and brilliant piece of swordplay, and he doubled Rathbone in some of the shots, not because Rathbone had lost his skill but because of the need for acute timing in the

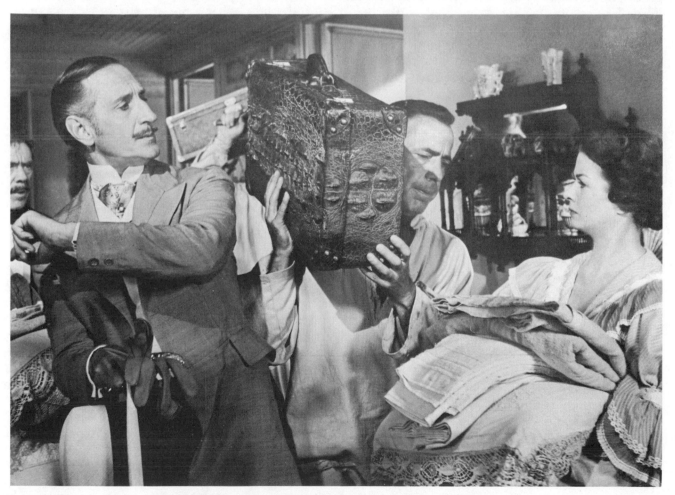

With Leo G. Carroll, Humphrey Bogart, and Joan Bennett in *We're No Angels*

comic portions of the duel. Rathbone was amazed at Kaye's ability with the sword. "He had never fenced before but after a couple of weeks of instruction Danny could completely outfight me. Even granting the difference in our ages, his reflexes were incredibly fast, and nothing had to be shown or explained to him a second time. His mind worked like a camera."

Most of the dozen or so films Rathbone made in this last stage of his Hollywood career were comedy or horror films of little merit. He was simply an old actor picking up work whenever he could. One film, however, stands out: John Ford's *The Last Hurrah,* a highly commendable exploration of American politics, but not a film that found wide favor with the public. Spencer Tracy starred as Frank Skeffington, a wily politician patterned on the notorious mayor of Boston, James M. Curley, who tried to sue the producers but lost the case. Ford surrounded the aging Tracy with a splendid group of movie old-timers: Pat O'Brien, Wallace Ford, James Gleason, Frank McHugh, Ed Brophy, Donald Crisp, Ricardo Cortez, John Carradine, and Rathbone, who appeared as a Boston blue-blooded banker named Norman Case. Rathbone's banker was a man of authority, dignity, and occasional anger, and the archenemy of Tracy's boss mayor. Altogether, it was an outstanding film populated by actors as wily and knowing as the politicians they portrayed. It was Rathbone's last true peak; he returned to the stage and television for four years, and reappeared in Hollywood in 1962 to do the two horror films for Corman. After that, the only offers that came his way were from producers of cheap exploitation films in which he appeared as an evil old menace. He bitterly resented this identification with the horror genre, but it was a matter of this or nothing. Rathbone and his wife always liked to live well, and even in a New York apartment their style was still grand. He appeared in such dreck as *The Ghost in the Invisible Bikini, Dr. Rock and Mr. Roll, Gill Woman,* and last and definitely least, *Hillbillies in a Haunted House,* sharing with Lon Chaney and John Carradine the dubious distinction of being a "guest star."

Basil Rathbone was every inch the English gentleman. In some forty years of living in the United States his elegant diction never varied, and he never renounced his British citizenship. One of his favorite poems, one he always recited at his readings, was Rupert Brooke's "The Soldier," and when he spoke these lines he was sincerely stating his own sentiments:

> If I should die, think only this of me,
> That there's some corner of a foreign field
> That is forever England.

Certainly, there is a corner of America that remains forever Rathbone.

Rathbone was a strong and active contender for a national theater in the United States; he campaigned, unsuccessfully, for the American government to subsidize the stage. He also believed that pay TV should be established by law. Rathbone lamented what he considered a decline in the standards of formal theatrical education, especially in the area of diction. He told me: "I was invited by Lee Strasberg to visit his Actors' Studio and review some of his talent. He had one young man perform and they asked me 'What do you think of what you've just heard?' I said I couldn't say because I didn't understand a word of what the young mumbler had mouthed. Strasberg then informed me, 'That's not important—it's his inner thinking that matters.' Well, I can't see that the inner thinking means much if he can't be heard. I don't know of anything more irritating than not to be able to understand an actor."

Rathbone was also distressed by much that happened in the arts in his last years, especially the commercialization and the tendency to pander to the young, both as customers and as performers: "I see great danger in making young actors stars before they are ready. Once you are a star you are most often treated with deference by your director —you are supposed to know a great many things you do not know, and nobody's going to teach you. Early stardom is a detriment to development. I was on the stage fourteen years before I felt on top of my material rather than it being on top of me."

Rathbone regretted, perhaps like most men who could look back seventy years to the beginning of the century, the speed with which science and technology had advanced civilization, particularly because of the effect it had on family life: "Children have been thrown more and more together and upon their own resources, in a life of their own that has set them apart from their elders. I hear 'Youth' continuously spoken of as if it were a tribal organization precariously attached to some outworn and outmoded traditions that have become no more than antiquated slogans of a dead past. The pace of our lives has so increased that youth is unavoidably caught up in its vortex. The young dreamer soon becomes a neurotic for want of mature companionship and understanding. The young artist seeks out his own people and often finds himself hiding with them behind false values he is not ready to evaluate. Modern art and modern music revolt against a past they feel they cannot compete with, and so ineffectually compete with each other in sheer desperation, and with often distorted and hideous results. Much of our modern literature protests with an angry and frequently ignorant tongue against a life it fails to understand, and consequently falls into an abusive pattern of crude violence and sheer lewdness that it miserably mistakes for reality."

Basil Rathbone died from a heart attack in his New York home on July 21, 1967, just a few weeks past his seventy-fifth birthday. Always a wiry, energetic man, he was active at the end. His last work was a tour with his *Evening with Basil Rathbone,* a two-hour reading of great poems and prose, with the last half devoted entirely to Shakespeare, the writer he admired more than any other. Rathbone's last appearance in California was in April of 1967, when he performed his *Evening* at the Beverly Hills High School auditorium. The audience was a small one, less than 200 people in a hall that could contain many hundreds more. But a reading by an old actor could only be expected to draw his friends and admirers, especially in a community as blasé about celebrities as Beverly Hills. One member of that affectionate audience was English writer and film producer John Cutts, who later wrote an article on Rathbone for the magazine *Films and Filming.* Cutts ended his account:

Suddenly it was all over. Rathbone thanked us for being a receptive audience and we, in turn, showed our appreciation with a burst of applause that must have been heard in far-off Pasadena. My thoughts awhirl, I wandered backstage to find the actor signing autographs from a table set up before a long line of well-wishers. When the crowd had cleared a little, I pushed my way forward to say hello. Stuck for something to say, I held out my hand and spluttered, "It's good to know Sir Guy of Gisbourne lives." Rathbone threw back his head and laughed. Then, placing his hands on my shoulders, he said, "I can see you and I are going to be the best of friends." Later, when driving home, I thought of the perfect answer—"The best of friends, you say? But then, I like to think we always were, sir. Me in my front row seat, and you up there on the big screen." But at the time all I could manage was a half-grin and a simple "thank you."

7

ERROL FLYNN

AND then, of course, there was Errol Flynn. He was a misfit. Flynn would have been at home in the Regency period or as a cavalier fighting for King Charles I. What does such a man do in the twentieth century? How does he reconcile his love of freedom and adventure with socialism, trade unionism, computers, and red tape? If he's lucky, and if he lives in a time when there is a market for romanticism, he becomes a film actor. Flynn was very, very lucky. As a celluloid hero he was able to captain pirate ships, lead cavalry charges, save England, and win the American West. He was Don Juan, Robin Hood, the Earl of Essex, General Custer, Captain Blood, and Gentleman Jim Corbett. No other actor was ever so beautifully heroic.

The image of Errol Flynn that one remembers, colored and exaggerated by nostalgia, is that of the handsome swashbuckler. But there was another side to this man, a sad side. Inside the rollicking rascal was a serious man screaming to get out. Ann Sheridan, who played in three of his films, said that he camouflaged himself. "In all the years I knew him, I never knew what really lay underneath, and I doubt if many people did."

The Flynn everyone enjoyed was an amusing and witty man who romped through his adventure movies with ingratiating ease. Off screen he caroused with friends, sailed his yacht, and excelled as an athlete. He also drank excessively, took drugs, and allowed himself to become a kind of comic phallic figure. Few people took him seriously until 1957 when he appeared in *The Sun Also Rises*. The critics said he was good as Mike Campbell, the bankrupt, charming, gentleman-drifter. Actually Flynn was playing himself.

One scene in *The Sun Also Rises* is particularly touching and revealing. It takes place in a hotel room in Pamplona after several riotous days of fun have come to an end. Jake Barnes (Tyrone Power) comes to see Campbell and finds him sitting on the edge of his bed with a bottle and a glass in his hands. Barnes asks him how he feels and Campbell replies with a flourish: "Never better." They talk; Barnes declines a drink and leaves after a while. As he goes through the door, Campbell raises his glass and says, "Bung ho, old boy." Barnes looks back with concern and quietly replies, "Bung ho." The camera then moves closer to Campbell as the smile leaves his handsome but puffy, bleary face. What we see is a lonely, spiritually desolate man. *That* was Errol Flynn, age forty-eight and two years from the end of his life.

Despite his Irish name and a heavy helping of blarney, Flynn was a Tasmanian, born of Australian parents in Hobart on June 20, 1909. His mother, Marelle Young, was the daughter of a sea captain, reputedly descended from Midshipman Young of H.M.S. *Bounty* fame. One of the family heirlooms was Fletcher Christian's sword and playing with it as a child doubtless whetted Flynn's imagination. His father, Professor Theodore Thomas Flynn, was a distinguished marine biologist on the faculty of the University of Tasmania. He was also the Commissioner of Tasmanian Fisheries and, when seen around the harbor and waterways of Hobart, he often had his young son in tow. Flynn grew up with a considerable knowledge of marine life and lore, and he claimed that the ocean was the only real love of his life.

Attached as he was to his father, Flynn had little rapport with his attractive, flirtatious mother. He

Flynn in one of his first studio portraits, taken in
Hollywood in early 1935

suspected that she was not faithful. Whatever the reason, there was lifelong friction between them. A psychologist might put his finger on this as the key to Flynn's failure to maintain a long relationship with any woman, even though he was drawn to them as a moth to a flame.

By the time Flynn was in his early teens his father had achieved prominence in the field of marine biology and was offered lecture tours and invited to appear at various universities. The family moved to England, and Errol was enrolled in South West London College. At the age of fifteen he was expelled. His father put him in another school, and from that he was also expelled. The family then proceeded to Sydney, Australia, and the boy was sent to one of that city's most famous schools, The Northshore. As a schoolboy he was rebellious and not at all inclined to take after his academic father. He did, however, excel in swimming and boxing.

When Professor Flynn was invited to London to explain some of his scientific discoveries, he took his wife and their baby daughter, Rosemary, but it was decided to leave Errol in Sydney. Not long after his seventeenth birthday the Northshore School ousted young Flynn, and from then on he was on his own. His first job was as an office boy, licking stamps, but it wasn't long before he was fired for tampering with the petty cash box in order to bet on horses.

After roughing it in Sydney for a while, Flynn struck out for New Guinea. This was in 1926, and for the next five years he made several trips back and forth between Australia and New Guinea. Flynn's first job in New Guinea was as a government cadet, which would have trained him as a district officer, a kind of constable. But the affliction of vacillating interest that had plagued him throughout school now hurt his efforts to make a living. He was soon dropped from the government service as incompetent—it being remarked that his main interest seemed to be the pursuit of pleasure. Next came a short period working on a plantation as an overseer; this he left to go into partnership with a friend running a small schooner called the *Maski,* which carried passengers and freight.

It was while running the *Maski* that Flynn first came into contact with motion picture cameras. On one trip he was hired to take a group of film-makers up the Sepik River to shoot background footage for a documentary. Some of the shots included the young Flynn.

Flynn's interest at this time was making money.

Running a schooner in those waters was not lucrative enough, so he sold his interest to his friend and headed for the goldfields of New Ginea. He staked a claim at Edey Creek, but he soon found mining harder and less profitable than he had imagined. Flynn next entered into the illicit business of recruiting native labor for indentured service, a euphemism for slave trading.

In the film that made him a star, *Captain Blood,* there is an early scene in which young Dr. Peter Blood is on trial for his life. It was observed that Flynn played the part well. He had had personal experience. At the age of twenty Flynn had been on trial in New Guinea charged with murder. While recruiting natives, Flynn had been attacked and had killed a man; he claimed self-defense and was acquitted. The fledging movie star was then to bring to the screen experiences beyond those of most actors.

After the trial, Flynn returned to Sydney, buying his ticket with money won in a poker game. There he was treated for his first bout of gonorrhea. Now broke, he sought means of employment and briefly picked up a job in a bottling plant sniffing empty bottles to identify the previous contents.

Flynn's life in these early years was a bizarre series of ups and downs, although many of his so-called adventures doubtless later became embroidered in the telling. At one moment he was a lowly sniffer of bottles and the next he was offered $5,000 for the stake he had made in the goldfields of New Guinea. Apparently his claim lay between two more valuable pieces of terrain the owners wanted to unite, and Flynn's worthless grounds thereby acquired value.

He celebrated his financial windfall with a prolonged spree, and he awoke one morning to find himself with a gigantic hangover and little cash left. But he as acquired, though with no recollection of doing so, the title to a boat. Named the *Arop,* she was an ancient (built in 1881), forty-four-foot long, narrow-beamed cutter. Although at first puzzled by what to do with his new possession, Flynn and three friends decided to sail her to New Guinea —a rash decision in view of the lack of seamanship of the crew, the age of the vessel, and the difficulty of the waters.

The voyage of the *Arop* took place in 1930 and Flynn celebrated his twenty-first birthday en route. The trip stretched out over 3,000 miles up the east coast of Australia, along the treacherous Great Barrier Reef, and north to Port Moresby. This seven-month voyage was the subject of Flynn's first book, *Beam Ends* (1937), a well-written and amusing effort from a man who was genuinely interested in being a writer.

He identified his three companions on the trip as a Cambridge-educated Englishman, Trelawney Adams, nicknamed "Dook" because of his gentlemanly demeanor, and a pair of young Australians referred to by their first names only, Rex and Charlie. That such a boat with such a crew could negotiate such a journey caused Flynn in later years to shake his head. At the beginning of *Beam Ends* he wrote, "Doubtless there is a providence for the purpose of protecting youth from its own folly. I can think of no other reason why I am now able to write the story of our voyage."

In New Guinea Flynn sold the *Arop* and used the money to buy a tobacco farm. He now began to ponder the aimlessness of his life. He thought in terms of being a writer or a lawyer. Years later he would find himself continuously involved with the law, but almost always as a defendant.

As a young tobacco farmer, with natives to do all the work, Flynn filled in his lonely hours with study. He also wrote a number of articles on New Guinea life and sold them to the Sydney *Bulletin* for small fees. As a reporter Flynn had a keen eye. Now twenty-two years old, he also revealed a knack for storytelling. One of his reports from New Guinea concerns a *pourri-pourri*, a native tribal gathering:

> The result of that pourri-pourri seance in Port Moresby (*Bulletin*, November 10th, 1931), at which medicine men enjoying great prestige among the surrounding tribes failed to bring a dead dog to life, should have been a moral victory for the Government. But the Papuan sorcerer is an astute opportunist. The chief pourri-pourri expert suddenly remembered that the medical officer, invited to satisfy himself that the dog was dead, had touched it with his stethoscope. That, of course, cleared up the mystery of the dog's refusal to come to life. Every reasonable native knew at once that the medical officer had applied a powerful counter pourri-pourri. It is unfortunately true that the magicians were given presents of rice and flour—a not unusual instance of official stupidity. If these natives did not return to their village and exhibit the rice and flour as proof that the Government was much impressed with their prowess, then they're not the pourri-pourri men I take them for. They ought to be able to live on their reputation in ease and luxury for the rest of their lives.

The following is Flynn's column in The Sydney *Bulletin* of January 27th, 1932:

> Killing a turtle in New Guinea is a horribly messy business. I once came upon several natives about to dispatch a six hundred pound specimen. The turtle was lying on its back on the beach, helplessly flapping, and my cook-boy, Mai-Iki, squatted near by, kindling a fire in its stomach. Bellowing loudly I rushed to the rescue, scattered the fire, and, in honest rage, was about to inflict grievous bodily harm on Mai-Iki.
>
> Deciding, however, that he knew no better, I sent a boy for my revolver, and, while awaiting him, discoursed to the assembly on the evil of cruelty to animals. To my annoyance Mai-Iki wanted to debate the matter. "Master," he said earnestly, "this fella he no savvy die quick time. S'pose you shoot 'im he no die." "No?" I said, "you watch," and pumped three rounds from a .32 into its head. To my chagrin the turtle showed no sign of having noticed anything unusual, and he did not even interrupt the slow pendulum-like movement of his head from side to side. Rather staggered by such unconcern I fired three more rounds, but with the same result. The thing seemed slightly bored with the proceedings and certainly displayed no resentment. "Bringim akis!" (bring an axe) I shouted desperately. "Cut off head belong 'im." This was done, and the turtle, I thought, was out of its dreadful agony. But when, to my amazement, the headless body continued to breathe through the severed windpipe, as though losing a head was an everyday occurrence, I threw in the towel. "All right," I told Mai-Iki, "go ahead and kill it any way you like." He remade the fire around the edge and removed the stomach shell, leaving the inside exposed. It was such an uncanny sight to see the heart still pumping and everything else apparently working to schedule that I repaired to the house for a drink. Even when I returned several hours later the turtle wasn't quite dead.

Most of Flynn's articles for the Sydney *Bulletin* were written at a time when he was an overseer at a copra plantation at Laloki, a job he took immediately after his venture as a tobacco farmer failed. He spent almost five years in New Guinea and gained a considerable knowledge of the strange, primitive island. Flynn was a highly intelligent man with a talent for observation and recall, and it made him a fascinating conversationalist. Even in his last years, when he was seldom sober, Flynn could still regale listeners with his early adventures and his recollection of life in New Guinea. He was often accused of leg-pulling, but these long-forgotten Australian newspaper articles, and the information contained in his three books, are evidence that Flynn had first-hand contact with his material. They also prove that Flynn did have ability as a writer and might have become one had he not gained fame as a movie star. As a star with a reputation for high living and playboy capers,

Flynn drew so many snickers whenever he spoke of his love of writing that he eventually gave up the ambition. Yet even in surrendering this side of his talent he couldn't help but play along with his gamey image; to a group of newspaper men he said, "I'm giving up one of the things I most love in life." They all assumed he was referring to sex. He joined in their laughter but, as was often the case with Flynn, his laughter hid his regrets.

Aside from his light labors as an overseer and his part-time journalism, Flynn spent his time in Laloki increasing his knowledge by reading books of great literature and law, and books on the study of languages. This application to education was halted by the arrival in early 1932 of an offer from an Australian film producer, Charles Chauvel, who had seen the footage shot of Flynn on the Sepik River. He asked Flynn if he would play the part of Fletcher Christian in a film to be called *In the Wake of the Bounty*. Flynn later recalled this as a total of three weeks work for a salary of two pounds a week.

In Sydney Flynn made one personal appearance at a showing of the completed film, but nothing came of this exposure to acting, and he was soon out of funds. This seems to have been a low point in Flynn's career: he even tells of stealing jewels from a girl friend. Years later, as a star, Flynn tried to locate the girl, but never could. As it turned out, the jewels were in turn stolen from him.

Flynn worked for a while on a sheep farm. He could well joke that he had been almost everywhere and done almost everything. This particular job came to an end when Flynn was found in the bedroom of the farmer's daughter. That was something else that Flynn could joke about; there was always a daughter or another man's wife, always a willing female.

He turned to New Guinea—to the goldfields and to the nefarious business of recruiting native labor for the mines. Flynn knew he could make money at this and he did, but when he left New Guinea this time he never returned. With the money accumulated from this venture Flynn took off for Manila, Hong Kong, and Macao. It was in Macao that he had his first experience with narcotics, and tried opium. Later in Hollywood he would try other narcotics. It was his philosophy to take a stab at everything.

Next was a short-lived adventure. Broke again, Flynn enrolled in the Royal Hong Kong Volunteers, a group gathered for training in case of attack from the Japanese. He was sent to Shanghai, but he

Flynn in his first film role, as Fletcher Christian in *In the Wake of the Bounty,* made in Australia in 1932

deserted the service when they handed him a shovel instead of a gun and assigned him to digging trenches.

By now, Flynn was a weary adventurer, tired of squandering his time and his energies in pursuit of nothing in particular. He headed for England. Throughout all the strange fluctuations of his fortune, Flynn had always written long letters to his father, his contact with reality. In a letter written in Colombo, Ceylon, in March of 1933, Errol told Professor Flynn that he had made a decision. He wrote: "I think I am going to try to make a career of acting when I arrive in London. I feel that is what I want to do and where I may make my fortune."

Errol Flynn went about becoming an actor in much the same way he had tackled other enterprises—with a bold front and the air of a man who knows his stuff. He invented a list of credits in films and plays; the only genuine item on the list was *In the Wake of the Bounty,* of which no one in England had heard. A copy of the film which rests in the archives of the Australian Film Institute reveals a poor production and a wooden young Flynn barely recognizable as the animated figure he later became. Had the film been seen in England in the summer of 1933, it could have done little to land Errol a job with the British film studios. The only opportunity that came his way at this time was an opening in a repertory company in Northampton. When the sports-minded manager, badly in need of a Star for his cricket team, was informed by Flynn that he was an Australian champion, he was hired. Actually Flynn had never been interested in cricket, but, as always, he bluffed magnificently.

After eighteen months with the Northampton Repertory, Flynn again tried to break into films and by sheer persistence managed to get an interview with Irving Asher, the managing director of Warner Brothers' studio at Teddington. Asher was struck by the looks and personality of the twenty-five year old Aussie and took a chance on him. He gave Flynn a lead in a low-budget mystery called *Murder at Monte Carlo,* and during production he signed Flynn to a contract, recommending to the home office that the actor be sent to California when the picture was finished. The brass in Burbank took him at his word, and Flynn arrived at the studio in January of 1935, where his sense of achievement began to deflate somewhat when his employers showed little interest in rushing him into stardom.

In his first half-year with Warners Flynn appeared in just two minor pictures, in a non-speaking bit in *The Case of the Curious Bride,* and in a small role in *Don't Bet on Blondes.* But stardom was just around the corner and it would sweep Flynn up faster and higher than even he could have hoped. Warners had planned to make *Captain Blood* with Robert Donat, due to the great success of Donat's *The Count of Monte Cristo.* Costume

films had been out of favor for some while but the signs pointed—in the drab mid-1930s—to a renewed appetite for historical romance. When Donat decided not to go through with the deal, Warners was stuck for a handsome, heroic-looking young actor. Several were tested, but when Flynn stepped up in costume and with sword in hand, the search was over.

On the ship that took him from Southampton to New York, Flynn had met and become attracted to film star Lili Damita. The French actress was four years his senior and had starred in a number of Hollywood and European films. Later, in Hollywood, Flynn courted her, and they were married in June of 1935, just before *Captain Blood* went into production. Flynn would never admit it, due to his bitterness over Damita and the huge alimony he had to pay her as long as he lived, but she doubtless had much to do with his fast climb. She was a friend of director Michael Curtiz and of the wives of the Warner brothers. Flynn later claimed that he didn't really want to marry Damita but that the fiery actress bullied and threatened him into the nuptials. If this is true, it proves Flynn was willing to pay a price for success.

With *Captain Blood* Flynn took off like a rocket. To the public he seemed like a picture from a storybook come to life, almost too handsome and dashing to be true. Flynn was as pleased about it as his fans. The adventurer had struck it rich. He bought himself a ketch, sailed, fished, hunted, played stunning tennis, swam like a fish, dived, and drank. What he didn't do was play the role of

With Olivia de Havilland in *Captain Blood*

attentive, loving husband—his years with Damita were full of spats and spite. She was not above hitting him over the head with bottles and throwing at him anything she could lift. When interviewed by the press, she would generally play down her problems, but on once occasion she admitted that Flynn was not very demonstrative and that, amusing and charming though as he was, there was a perverse streak in him. In a magazine article, Lily said, "He loves to annoy people in childish ways. He knows their weak points and plays on them. He is a liar, too. You never know when he is telling the truth. He lies for the fun of it."

The Warners publicity department found themselves with the peculiar problem of having to play down the background (and the foreground) of an actor instead of, as they usually did, inventing one. Most of the publicists thought he was lying when he related his many adventures. Flynn lied, or went along with their lie, that he was an Irishman; probably he was easier to market in America as Irish than Aussie. With his parents living in Belfast, it was an easy lie to support. The publicity men assigned to Flynn's pictures found him a pleasant companion but a difficult interviewee, much given to warding off serious questions with quips. More serious work lay in covering his indiscretions (drinking, brawling, and loving) and dealing with letters that arrived from Australia, New Guinea, and the South Seas informing Warners that their star owed them money. To his parents Flynn was a painful pride; his mother loved the reflected publicity, but occasionally hit the wrong note when interviewed by the press—once when asked what Errol was like as a child she said, "He was a nasty little boy." His greatly esteemed father, by now one of the world's foremost marine biologists, hardly knew what to make of his loving colorful son. After Errol died, he admitted, "There was all sorts of publicity, a lot of it bad. But Errol didn't mind. He thought all publicity was good publicity. Sometimes we protested but it was no good. He would laugh it off."

Flynn's first seven years in Hollywood were his best; most of his films were expensive features which brought Warners a good return on their investment. *Captain Blood,* based on the Rafael Sabatini novel, set the image of Flynn as an athletic, dashing hero and, try as he did, he was never able to break the image. The historically dubious but nonetheless magnificently staged *The Charge of the Light Brigade* suggested that Flynn was fully capable of having led the real thing. He then played a

In *The Charge of the Light Brigade*

doctor in modern dress in *Green Light;* went back to historical romance for *The Prince and the Pauper;* did a soap opera opposite Kay Francis in *Another Dawn;* took a crack at comedy in *The Perfect Specimen;* and then met the ultimate Flynn vehicle, *The Adventures of Robin Hood.*

Flynn's *Robin Hood* is, perhaps, the finest film of its kind. It was done with total assurance, the script was literate, the direction swift, the musical score by Erich Wolfgang Korngold bouyant, and the costumes and sets perfect. But the secret of the success of this film lay in casting: Flynn was Robin as every boy imagined him to be—a superman of Sherwood Forest, swinging from the trees, flashing a broadsword with deadly ease, and foiling the attempts of Prince John and his henchmen to take over England in the absence of Richard the Lionhearted. And who could have been a more exquisite Maid Marian than Olivia de Havilland, or a more arrogant villain than Basil Rathbone? What better Prince John than Claude Rains? Or Little John than Alan Hale? This version of *Robin Hood* remains a textbook on this kind of filmmaking.

Robin Hood was the third pairing of Flynn and

With Phyllis Barry in *The Prince and the Pauper*

wanted to find out if he was as tough as he pretended to be on the screen—they usually found out he could handle himself well enough—and by women anxious to discover whether he was really sexy and amorous. Just how great a lover he was is open to question; he garnered a reputation as a ladies' man but evidence suggests he allowed the impression to build to foster publicity, and that he was in fact not a seeker of female company except for sexual gratification. Like many Australians Flynn tended to think of women in the "kitchen and bedroom" context.

Among Flynn's early Hollywood friends was Patric Knowles. The two had met casually at Teddington, the Warner Brothers studio in England, just prior to Flynn's departure for America. When Warners made *The Charge of the Light Brigade* they found they needed an actor to play the part of Flynn's younger brother. Two years his junior and vaguely resembling Flynn, Knowles was suggested and accepted. Later he would appear in three other pictures with him.

"Errol Flynn lived life as if it were a game, a game he enjoyed playing. But he was an impatient

Olivia de Havilland, and they would make another five films together. They were a perfect match, and the public was right in sensing that their feeling for each other went beyond their work. Flynn had fallen in love with the nineteen-year-old Olivia when he worked with her in *Captain Blood*. Had he not been married to Lili Damita he would have proposed to Olivia and quite possibly been accepted. Flynn was not, however, prepared to risk his newly found fame by seeking a divorce from the woman who had been partly responsible for putting him where he was. Olivia kept Flynn at a distance; how she managed to do this is her secret, but there was never an affair between the two of them. Eventually she tired of being the heroine in Flynn epics and asked Warners to stop casting her in them. Continually suspended for refusing roles, she took her case to court and caused her contract to be broken. Many years later she admitted that most of her films with Flynn were excellent vehicles, especially *Robin Hood*.

Things came easily to Errol Flynn in his early years in Hollywood, including trouble and controversy. He was forever bothered by men who

In *Robin Hood*

player, not to win, but to move on to the next bout. And he had the luck of the Irish," says Knowles. Knowles, who would serve as a flying instructor during the Second World War, gave Flynn his first flying lessons in late 1937 while they were in Chico, California, making *Robin Hood.* He recalls it took Flynn only four hours of dual instruction before he was ready to fly solo, and on his first flight he was doing acrobatics. Warners had cautioned Knowles about flying with the star of their picture, and they finally sent him a telegram threatening him with legal action if he persisted in encouraging Flynn to fly.

Knowles showed the telegram to Flynn. "Tear it up, old boy, and forget about it." The two actors then flipped coins to see who would take the plane up first. Flynn won, says Knowles. "He fooled all over the sky—hammer stalls, tight turns and wing overs. After only four hours dual he was a veritable Rickenbacker. He didn't say a word as he climbed out of the cockpit and I got in. He simply leered at me with a let's-see-what-you-can-do look. Well, I did everything but fly through the hangar doors. Then to finish off I climbed to a thousand feet and did two loops, landing at the end of the second one. I was grinning smugly when I got out but then I saw two men, the production manager from the studio and a stranger. The stranger was a man from the Civil Aeronautics Authority who took away my license pending a hearing, and the studio manager told me they were going to lodge a complaint with the Screen Actors Guild. Later, in the car, on the way back to the hotel, I asked Flynn where he was during all the excitement. 'Why, in the car having forty winks, old son. I started to learn my lines for tomorrow and just dozed off.' My license was later reinstated by the CAA and the Guild fined me one hundred dollars. But Flynn wasn't affected at all; that's what I mean when I say he had the luck of the Irish."

It was thought that Patric Knowles was being used by Warner Brothers as something of a threat to Flynn, to keep the wildly prankish Errol in line. Knowles was extensively tested for Flynn's part in *The Prince and the Pauper* but, as Knowles says, "Errol knew he had no worries about my taking over from him, and the whole thing became a gag between us. I visited him at Warners late in 1957 when he was doing the Barrymore role in *Too Much, Too Soon* and we talked of the old days. As I was leaving he put his arm around my shoulder and said with a grin, 'Let me know, old son, when

you want to take over. I'm getting too old for this sort of thing.' It was funny but sad; I remember him when he wasn't too old for anything."

Flynn was anxious not to be typecast. He followed *Robin Hood* with a comedy, *Four's A Crowd,* a drama, *The Sisters,* and an excellent picture about aviation in the First World War, *The Dawn Patrol,* an almost exact remake of the 1930 film, using some of the same footage. The part called for him to be a devil-may-care pilot whose character becomes somber when he is taken out of the air and put behind a desk as the squadron commander. For the first time, the critics thought Flynn might have real ability as an actor. Warners, however, were not interested in the plaudits of critics, only the plunk of coins on the counter. Flynn next appeared in the Wild West, cleaning up *Dodge City,* his refined British accent explained away as belonging to an Irish soldier of fortune with a background as a British army officer in India. So the public would have little time to forget what Flynn looked like in doublet and hose, Warners next cast him as the Earl of Essex opposite Bette Davis in *The Private Lives of Elizabeth and Essex.* Miss Davis was indignant that the part of Essex should go to an actor of no real dramatic range; perhaps she was right, but Flynn certainly looked good, and fortuitously he might well have come close to the real Essex—impetuous, naive, ambitious, and a pawn in the hands of court plotters.

Elizabeth and Essex was not the great success Warners was counting on. Ever economy-minded, they planned a vehicle that would use many of the same sets, costumes, and actors. But first they gave him another slam-bang western, *Virginia City,* no longer bothering to explain his accent; they let it go that he was a southern gentleman and a Confederate officer, and as such had every right to sound cultured. Warners' decision to do *The Sea Hawk* was among its wisest. Flynn, now thirty-one, was in prime form. As an English privateer in the service of Good Queen Bess, he ably commanded a crew of lusty lads and delayed the building of the Spanish Armada. He fenced beautifully and wooed heroine Brenda Marshall with reserved gallantry. Like *Robin Hood, The Sea Hawk* is a near-perfect example of the genre, thanks largely to fine, expensive sets, beautiful settings, and the masterly direction of Michael Curtiz. There was, however, little love between Curtiz and Flynn. The director regarded the actor as not much more than a beautiful puppet, and Flynn objected to Curtiz as a man who would cheerfully sacrifice human flesh and

In *The Sea Hawk*

blood in order to get good footage.

Flynn's marriage to Lili Damita was pitted with quarrels and separations and by 1941 it ground to a halt. The following year he agreed to an alimony settlement he would later regret: $1,500 a month, tax-free, plus a half interest in all his property. Desperate to get out of the marriage, he put his signature to the document. Not surprisingly Damita never remarried until after Flynn's death.

Flynn was embarrassed about his movie heroism once the Second World War got underway, especially as certain of his friends, like Patric Knowles and David Niven, left to join the colors. He tried to join every branch of the armed forces but was turned down for medical reasons. This was a further embarrassment because it forced him to reveal his health problems. He admitted to recurrent malaria, a hangover from his days in New Guinea. Warners thought it best to conceal his bout with tuberculosis. He also began showing signs of heart trouble, brought on by his strenuous athletic activities. Flynn looked to be in marvelous shape but the appearance hid the truth. According to David Niven: "I think Errol suffered because he didn't go off to war with the rest of us. It bothered him but he didn't show it, in fact he rarely betrayed his seriousness, he hardly ever unburdened himself. It would have been better for him if he could have instead of living behind a facade. Errol was a many-sided creature."

Like all Hollywood personalities Flynn was asked to appear in shows for the servicemen. At first he was reluctant to do this; he acidly said to one reporter, "What do you think I should do, step up and show them my x-rays and explain why Fearless Flynn isn't in uniform?" Eventually he did take part in these entertainments and found that he went over well with the troops, mostly by lampooning himself as a hero and lover. He would open his act with a line like, "There were huge crowds to see me off at the airport—mostly my lawyers."

Flynn's screen heroism continued with *Santa Fe Trail*, which looked at J.E.B. Stuart and his pre-Civil War adventures foiling John Brown. Next came *Footsteps in the Dark*, a very lightweight comedy to vary the image (to little avail), and a serious picture about medical achievement in naval aviation, *Dive Bomber*. The Flynn career needed another landmark at this juncture and received it in the form of *They Died With Their Boots On*, a handsome telling of the saga of the controversial George Armstrong Custer, ending with his defeat at the Little Big Horn. The film was greatly popular as an exciting adventure yarn but it greatly romanticized Custer. Flynn made a good Custer, probably because there were parallels between the soldier and the actor—both were bigger than life, both cavalier by nature, loving their fame and treating life as a game. Like many such men, they didn't live to become elderly. Custer died at thirty-seven, and it is said that if the Indians hadn't cut him down, one of his own men might have done the job. Flynn barely made it to the age of fifty: Alexis Smith once asked him after he collapsed during the making of a scene, "Don't you want to live to be an old man?" and Flynn replied, "No, I like this half of life best."

In November of 1942 Errol Flynn was summarily brought into line by a court order. He was arrested and brought to trial on two charges of statutory rape. He was acquitted but the image was tarnished. The highly publicized trial, front page news for months, was considered a kind of *divertissement* from the war. At the end of the trial the judge said to the jury, who had deliberated four hours in reaching a verdict, "I have enjoyed this case, and I think you have." Flynn, on the other hand, didn't enjoy it and paled visibly during the five weeks of the trial. Had he been found guilty he would have faced imprisonment. Not that he intended to submit himself to that indignity—he much later admitted he had arranged with a private aviator to skip the country in case of conviction.

Flynn believed, with some justification, that he had been made a Hollywood scapegoat by Los Angeles City Hall in order to discipline the film colony. The legal manipulations of film actors and executives in Los Angeles, the bribes and pay-offs

With Arthur Kennedy in *They Died with Their Boots On*

and hush-ups, make up an as yet untold story. The Flynn case raised legal eyebrows because neither of the two girls in the case had brought charges of their own accord. They were under eighteen, the legal age of consent in California, at the time they had intercourse with Flynn, but months elapsed before a subpoena was served. Both girls had dubious backgrounds, and it was on those backgrounds that Flynn's ace lawyer, the late Jerry Geisler, was able to base his case. The case of a meek and slightly built waitress named Betty Hansen was dropped for lack of evidence. She accused Flynn of seducing her at the home of Flynn's playboy friend, the Australian sportsman Fredie McEvoy (who also died at an early age, swept overboard from his yacht in a storm at sea). When Geisler asked Miss Hansen if she had resisted Flynn's advances she made the classic reply, "I didn't have no objections."

The case of the very attractive dancer, Peggy Satterlee, was stronger. Flynn's intimacy with her was alleged to have occurred on his ketch, the *Sirocco*, while she was his guest. The case might have gone against Flynn had Geisler not brought evidence that the girl had previously lied about her age in order to get a driver's license, and that she had had an abortion resulting from an affair with another man. Geisler dealt his death blow when he revealed a quirk of Miss Satterlee's: she apparently enjoyed visiting morgues and looking at the bodies. She and a boyfriend had even played hide-and-seek in such a setting.

Flynn's acquittal was greeted with cheers. He emerged from the courtroom beaming like a schoolboy. But the damage to his self-respect was colossal, and he admitted many years later to sitting in the dark in his bedroom after the trial with a loaded gun in his hands. It seemed to his friends and coworkers that the trial had made little difference to the breezy Flynn; it would be some time before they noticed that his drinking had increased and that he was dabbling with narcotics.

Errol Flynn appeared in five films that dealt with the Second World War, hardly enough to justify the widespread joke that he had won the war single-handedly. Two of these pictures—*Desperate Journey* and *Northern Pursuit*—were adventure yarns, not to be taken seriously, but the other three were films of some merit and restrained in their heroics. *Edge of Darkness* was a somber film directed by Lewis Milestone, who had done *All Quiet on the Western Front. Uncertain Glory* had Flynn as a criminal who escapes the guillotine during a bomb-

In *Gentleman Jim Corbett*

In *Objective Burma*

ing in Paris. His best war film was *Objective Burma,* and yet it was the one that brought him the most ridicule. Flynn's performance as a parachute captain leading a mission behind the lines was serious and controlled, but when the film was shown in London it caused a commotion. Flynn was taunted as the man who saved Burma, and in newspaper cartoon he was shown with one foot resting on the grave of a British soldier and one hand waving an American flag. He laughed when it was shown to him but he bitterly resented it.

Flynn's best film during the war years was not a war film. *Gentleman Jim* was the story of James J. Corbett, the first heavyweight champion of the world under the present Marquis of Queensberry rules. Flynn was an excellent boxer and he performed beautifully with nimble footwork and stylist feints, jabs, and hooks. It was one of the few films of which he was proud, understandably so considering he did the film with no double. The film was completed before his rape trial but held up by Warners pending public reaction to the trial. When it was clear the affair had not damaged but in fact increased his appeal, they rushed the picture into wide release. One of the many facts disclosed in the trial was that Flynn had made love to one of the girls while wearing his socks. One wag suggested to Warners that in view of this lapse in love etiquette they change the title to just *Jim*.

Flynn's second marriage grew out of the rape trial. Each day in walking through the courthouse he noticed a pretty redhead serving behind the cigar counter. Her name was Nora Eddington; she was the eighteen-year-old daughter of the secretary of the Los Angeles County Sheriff. Flynn wisely awaited his acquittal before making a move. Within a year she was Mrs. Flynn and during their six-year marriage she gave him two daughters. He already had a son, Sean, by his marriage to Lili Damita.

Flynn lived for sixteen years after the rape trial. As time went by, he would look back and realize what a turning point it had been in his life. By 1942 all of his finest films had been made; those that followed were of varying quality, a few interesting but many mediocre. Lack of discipline was the fatal flaw in his character; he had rebelled against his mother, his teachers, his employers, his wives, and even himself. The hedonistic Flynn gradually smothered the serious Flynn. He resented the reporters and the comedians who fed off his image, yet he did nothing to change their impression of him as a superficial celebrity dedicated to fun, sport, girls, and drink. Yet according to his second wife, Nora, Flynn was considerably embarrassed by his fame and avoided crowded places. "He was shy and he didn't know how to accept a compliment. He was worried by autograph seekers; he would get red in the face and stammer. But he did appreciate what his fame allowed him to have; he was grateful about that to the point of being naive."

It was during his second marriage that Flynn became hooked on narcotics. Recalls Nora: "He said he had no intention of being an addict—I believe that. It's just that he was a born adventurer, he had to try everything, every challenge had to be tackled. He enjoyed the sensations he got from drugs but I don't think there was any doubt in his mind that he could stop any time he wanted. But he didn't; he went on and on, and that's what killed him." Flynn was impossible to contain, and while on drugs he was sometimes dangerous. Nora filed for divorce after six years, to the chagrin of Flynn, who said he would commit himself to a sanitarium if she stayed. There is little reason to think that he would have; his unhappiness was not just marital. At the age of forty Flynn was bothered by periods of ill health, declining fame, career frustrations, and the apparent need to maintain his rakish image. Only his wives would ever know that behind the mask of the laughing cavalier was a scared and lonely boy.

Flynn's great escape was the ocean. If Flynn was anything, he was a sailor, and a very good one. One of the first things he did in Hollywood when he came into money was to buy a ketch, the *Sirocco*. But the *Sirocco* came in for some earthy publicity during the rape trial, and it wasn't long after the trial that he put the boat up for sale and looked for another. He took his time and eventually decided on a 120-foot two-masted schooner which could be sailed or motor-driven. He named his new prize *Zaca*, the Samoan word for peace, probably hoping he would find it with her. He planned to sail her to the South Seas but never got around to making the trip; instead the *Zaca* sailed the Mexican coast and the Caribbean, making her home in Port Antonio, Jamaica, and some years later in a harbor in Majorca. It was on these sea voyages that Flynn indulged his other great interest—writing.

Flynn's second book, *Showdown*, published in 1946 by Sheridan House, was a novel about the adventures of a young Irishman in the South Seas, having to do mainly with his running a small schooner in New Guinea waters. The book made little impression upon either the critics or the public. The plot and the characters were rather tedious and trite, but the book had value because of Flynn's knowledge of New Guinea life, about which he wrote with some flair. His main character he called Shamus O'Thames, but he was clearly a young man named Flynn, garnished with shadows of other characters the author must have known. When he wrote about Shamus working his passage as a stoker on a tramp steamer, Flynn must have been mining his own experiences: "Day after day he shoveled fine coal dust, which, when dampened by water, is the hardest kind of coal to shovel, in a temperature of 120 degrees Fahrenheit." Shamus's adventures in New Guinea were again clearly autobiographical:

At Rabaul he jumped ship and, with a few pounds in his pockets, set out to satisfy his appetite for the South Seas in an attempt to swallow all of Melanesia at a sitting. Six years had passed since then. He had stoked on tramp steamers from the Bismarck Archipelago to the New Hebrides. He had bought wood carvings in Iwa to sell to government recruits at Port Moresby, had joined a gold-hunting party on Woodlark, and netted ten pounds for his share of their scant find before natives drove them off; he had handled the broad wooden clubs and carved and painted ebony shields of the Trobriands and learned there how to use the gall of a certain fish to poison arrowheads. He had solved the mysterious question of the "bush telegraph" by teaching himself to read the signals pounded on drums, which can send a message to distant natives in New Guinea almost as fast as if by modern telegraph. On Goodenough Island he had learned, at the cost of a month's lameness, how natives discourage those who would track them by placing tiny foot spears in their trails. Along the Gulf of Papua he had avoided losing his head to the Kuku Kuku only by lying almost motionless in a spot in the jungle for two days. He had learned from natives how to spend incredibly long minutes submerged and how to kill fish, not with a fishing line, but under water. Along the Fly River he had seen a native commit suicide by climbing to the top of a cocoanut tree and fling himself, head downwards, to the ground. At Wedau, he had watched nursing women fish by leaning over a stream and milking their breasts into the water, then quietly scooping up with a hand net the little fish that rose to the cloudy bait.

The Flynn film career after the Second World War continued with a variety of pictures—a western (*San Antonio*), a comedy (*Never Say Goodbye*), a dark melodrama (*Cry Wolf*), and an old-fashioned love story, (*Escape Me Never*). None of them gave him the professional lift he needed. Under the

With S. Z. Sakall in *Never Say Goodbye*

terms of his second seven-year contract with Warner Brothers, negotiated just before the rape trial, he had received greater command over the choice of material. Flynn had previously complained of having had little say in the production of his films, but there is scant evidence of good judgment on his part in choosing better pictures.

Try as he had to escape the image of costume cavalier, Flynn now agreed with Warners that they should attempt to recapture the past and produce an expensive swashbuckling vehicle. The result was *Adventures of Don Juan*, sprinkled with pretty ladies, plenty of swordplay, and a script tailored to the Flynn image. Vincent Sherman was assigned to direct the film; not having worked with the actor before, he was warned by other directors to be prepared for problems with drink, tardiness, and much waiting around during production. He recalls: "At the beginning of the picture he told me he knew I had heard things about his drinking, and he wanted to assure me that he wouldn't drink on this picture. He said he'd give me all the cooperation he could in making *Don Juan* a great film. I found him charming and sincere, and I think he was serious. Then we began to shoot after weeks of rehearsals and preparations of various kinds. The first ten days he was marvelous, he was never late and he knew his lines. One day he called me into his dressing room; he had a bunch of clippings on the table. He said, 'Have you seen these?' He had just opened in New York in his previous picture (*Escape Me Never*) and the critics were very unkind to him. In essence they said that if Flynn wasn't on a horse and shooting in a Western or a costume picture he was pathetic as an actor. I read these things and it was embarrassing to do so in front of him. He sort of made fun of them, kidding, but inside I could see he was terribly hurt by these reviews. He was covering up. Two days after that he came on the set completely drunk, and for the rest of the time he was drinking on the picture."

Flynn's casual approach to his work increased the budget of *Adventures of Don Juan* by at least half a million dollars. It remains, however, one of his better performances, possibly because he understood the character of the part, knowing, like Don Juan himself, that the reputation of Great Lover is something of a joke and a bit of a bore. Flynn had a talent for comedy which was seldom given scope, but this Don Juan was plainly a triumph of tongue in cheek. Vincent Sherman finished the film with warm feelings for Flynn despite the problems he had given him. "It was hard not to like

In *Adventures of Don Juan*

With Viveca Lindfors in *Adventures of Don Juan*

Errol. He was a man of great humor and charm, and he had real merits as an actor—yet he made fun of the whole business of acting. Few actors have ever been able to wear costumes and handle a sword as he did, with such style and conviction, and yet if you pointed that out to him he was insulted. He didn't really appreciate himself."

Despite their differences, Flynn and Warner Brothers set out on a third contract. With this one, signed in 1947, Flynn demanded even greater latitude. He wanted, and got, the right to make films for studios other than Warners.

In his first film away from Warner Brothers, Flynn was loaned to MGM to costar with Greer Garson in *That Forsyte Woman,* and she remembers him with affection. "He presented out of his artistic and creative imagination, with no assistance from anybody else, a believable and most interesting portrait of Soames Forsyte, so completely different from anything else he had done that it made one realize what potential he had as an actor. It's a tragedy he didn't live longer. There was a great deal more to Errol than people supposed; more than this rather two-dimensional figure, swashbuckling, rascally, and a great man with the ladies. I'm sure he never bothered any woman who didn't want to be bothered, because he was a gentlemanly soul and a great charmer, much more cultured and erudite than people supposed. He had a very light-hearted wit, but most of all he was a romantic."

In his next film, a feeble western called *Montana,* Flynn merely walked through with obvious dis-

With Janet Leigh and Greer Garson in *That Forsyte Woman*

interest. The failure of *Don Juan* to do tremendous business at the box office caused Warners to pull back on their budgets for future Flynn vehicles. His next for them was another western, *Rocky Mountain,* better than the previous one. Flynn gladly accepted MGM's offer for him to play Mahbub Ali, the Red Beard in *Kim,* especially since it took him to India—he was ever ready to take off for faraway places. Then he went to France to film his own screenplay, *The Adventures of Captain Fabian,* as a coproducer with William Marshall. It was a poor picture and the partnership soon fell apart. He returned to Warners in early 1952 to make an adventure yarn, *Mara Maru,* a fair effort which met little response from the public. Warners, like the other studios at this time, were trying to get rid of their stars; television had thrown the industry in a panic and the moguls acted none too wisely, cutting their overhead costs and selling their old films to TV, thus creating their own stiffest competition. Flynn and Jack L. Warner talked over their problems and Flynn's contract was dissolved. Flynn claimed he was fired but Warner denies it.

To bolster a sagging career Flynn next played in three costume pictures, one after the other—despite his distaste for this kind of vehicle. Free to choose his material, he now did precisely what his previous employers had done—capitalized on his swashbuckling image. He did *Against All Flags,* a pirate picture, for Universal, then went to England to make *The Master of Ballantrae,* released through Warners as his last commitment to them. He now decided to stay in Europe, partly because his popularity was greater there than in America, but also because he was financially pinched. He once said, "My problem lies in reconciling by net income with my gross habits." It was typical of Flynn to speak his truths as jests. By 1952 he had begun to lapse on his alimony payments and fall behind in his income tax. By now he also had a third wife to support, actress-dancer Patrice Wymore, and by setting up his own film company in Rome he hoped to cure all his ills. His first Italian film was *Crossed Swords;* although beautifully color-photographed by Jack Cardiff, it was a palid imitation of *Don Juan.* The European returns covered its costs but it played to poor houses in America. Seemingly, the great good luck that had carried Flynn through most of his life was no longer in evidence. For him, life did not begin at forty.

Errol Flynn was well aware he would never live to be elderly. He was often heard to quip that dying is easy, living is the hard part. Director Raoul

In *The Master of Ballantrae*

Walsh, who was to be one of Flynn's pallbearers, recalls that in 1950 the actor was told by a doctor he had only a year or two left. Flynn called Walsh to his home and asked for his advice. Walsh said, "I told him to give up drinking. He started playing tennis and swimming again. Then I went to Europe, and when I got back I found he had been drinking heavily."

Flynn's appearance began to change when he reached his forties. There was a slight and gradual coarsening of the face and a deadening of expression in the eyes due to alcohol and drugs. He was unable to perform as athletically as before. But perhaps the biggest change was mental. Flynn continued to put up a brave front, but there were signs of despondency and bitterness. By his own standards he considered himself something of a failure. His popularity, even as a swashbuckler, was waning, and he had failed in his attempts to be taken seriously as an actor.

Even when he did give a good performance, as in *That Forsyte Woman,* the film was met with only a fair reception. He had worked long and hard to write a novel, *Showdown,* but that, too, failed to make much impression. The collapse of his second

In *William Tell*

marriage hurt him. He confessed to a friend that although he was hopelessly and helplessly polygamous, he genuinely admired those who were happily monogamous. Flynn began taking failure in his stride and assumed that everyone would, one way or another, take advantage of him.

Despite having made three costume pictures in a row, none of them greatly successful, Flynn still considered it wise to try another. This would be his own production, into which he would pour all the cash he could muster; it was to be a vehicle of quality, one Flynn hoped would bring him esteem as well as cash. He budgeted *William Tell* at $860,000, about half of this his and the rest from Italian backers. After the company had completed enough footage for three reels of the picture, approximately half an hour of running time, the backers informed Flynn the company had exhausted all the money at hand and needed more immediately.

Flynn now found himself in the direst financial straits. Production on *William Tell* was halted and never resumed, and various members of the cast and crew sued him for back salaries. The United States government brought charges against him claiming $840,000 in back taxes, and his lawyers reminded him that he was badly behind in his alimony payments.

This predicament was largely the fault of Flynn's business manager in Hollywood. The man had just died, but before dying he had admitted to misappropriating funds, and to losing Flynn's money at gambling. To appease his many creditors, Flynn began disposing of some of his properties—his house in Hollywood, his cars, and a few of his valuable paintings. Two things to which he clung and refused to surrender were his estate in Jamaica and his yacht, the *Zaca*. Flynn was cagey about money, and years after his death it was discovered his business investments in England had accumulated a value close to a million dollars; he also had a bank account in Switzerland, and he went to the further precaution of carrying gold bars on the *Zaca*. But in late 1953 Flynn was hard put for cash.

The *William Tell* fiasco brought to an end one of Flynn's closest friendships. Bruce Cabot, in the years prior to his entering the military in 1942, had been among the handful of hard-drinking, hard-playing buddies with whom Flynn most preferred to spend his leisure time. They were all sportsmen, bettors on horses, and occasional brawlers. Cabot had appeared with Flynn in only one film, as the heavy in *Dodge City*. The fact that he didn't work with Flynn in other films he attributes to the good judgment of Warner Brothers, who wouldn't trust the two of them on the same set again.

When Cabot returned from the war he noticed a marked change in Flynn, which he thinks was due partly to his coming under the influence of John Barrymore and his coterie. Flynn admired Barrymore enormously, and Cabot claims he took on some of the mannerisms of the older actor. Some of Barrymore's illustrious friends were drug addicts, and this is how, in Cabot's opinion, Flynn became hooked. Flynn, mostly for fun, had tried almost all the narcotics—opium, marijuana, cocaine and morphine. Says Cabot, "Eventually it was the heroin that got him. And even then he lived ten years longer than most who took what he took."

With the collapse of the *William Tell* project, Bruce Cabot, who had been hired as the villain, sued Flynn for his salary on the picture, claiming he had received nothing. Flynn, now in deep financial trouble, resented Cabot's action and the two never met again. Recalls Cabot: "Flynn's business judgment by then was very bad. The drugs had reached him to a point where he was his old self for only a few hours a day. His analytical powers were gone, and he picked people badly. Errol used to be a shrewd businessman. But in 1953 he wasn't thinking as clearly as in 1943. In those days he'd have fought a bear with a short switch. He used to read his contracts for loopholes to sting Warner Brothers for more money."

Cabot looks back on the incident as part of a much larger tragedy—the gradual decline of Flynn through drugs. "Dope is just like termites. It destroyed him the way termites destroy a house, and it was a pitiful thing to see. You couldn't put your finger on it but you could see it happening. His associations changed. He didn't take the care he used to take with his appearance or his performances. Dope destroys the fiber of a man, the character, the reliability, the self-respect. With Errol it was the saddest case I've ever seen."

Flynn's home for most of the period between 1952 and 1956 was his yacht, sailed and moored in the Mediterranean. His drinking was heavy and continuous; had he not been a lover of swimming and sailing, exercise and fresh air, the drinking would have killed him. After the collapse of *William Tell* Flynn assumed his film career was over. He was rescued from his drifting by the veteran British producer Herbert Wilcox, who offered to help Flynn straighten out his financial affairs if he would costar with Wilcox's wife, Anna Neagle, in a film to be called *Lilacs in the Spring* (retitled in America *Let's Make Up*). Flynn jumped at the chance and was delighted to find it gave him an opportunity to do a little dancing and singing. It's quite possible Flynn would have been a good entertainer had he not been locked into the heroic mold. The Wilcox film did good but not spectacular business in England, and almost none in America. Flynn then went back to swashbuckling as the Black Prince in *The Warriors*, his last foray into historical romance. He began asking himself what he was doing in armor, trying to wield a broadsword at this time in his life. Many people asked the same question. Not knowing what to do, Flynn accepted another offer from Wilcox, to costar again with Neagle, this time in a filming of the Ivor Novello operetta *King's Rhapsody*. The results were horrendous, with British exhibitors making remarks about both Flynn and Neagle being box office poison.

Flynn's next venture was a cheaply produced TV series, a weekly half-hour show called "The Errol Flynn Theatre." About twenty programs were made and sold for syndication. Flynn hosted each program and played in several of the stories, but the whole enterprise was lackluster and brought little profit to the backers.

Flynn went back to drifting on the Mediterranean, later confessing there were times when he dived into the ocean with the intention of never coming up. He was, however, on the verge of an upward swing. Universal offered him the lead in *Istanbul*, which he accepted, thinking he could cruise the *Zaca* to the Turkish capital. This Istanbul happened to be on the back lot of Universal's studio in Los Angeles, a place Flynn had vowed he would never set foot in again. But his name was on the contract and he followed through. The picture was no winner but it did, so to speak, put him back in the ring. Spots of luck began to come his way: in New York he appeared on the TV show "The $64,000 Question" and picked up a large sum with his knowledge of the sea and ships. This windfall made the title of his next film apropos— *The Big Boodle*, a minor murder mystery filmed in Havana, Cuba. Some of the critics commented that this new Flynn, thickened in body and with his thick and world-weary expression, seemed to have more authority as an actor, more credibility, than he had with his former image.

The big break now came. Darryl F. Zanuck decided to take a chance on Flynn—against considerable negative advice—as Mike Campbell in his filming of Hemingway's *The Sun Also Rises.*

Flynn himself was dubious and Patrice Wymore tells of having to talk him into doing the part. It meant accepting fourth billing, behind Tyrone Power, Ava Gardner and Mel Ferrer—it would be the first time Flynn had played a supporting role since *Captain Blood.* The result was a touching and amusing characterization that won him the best notices of the film. There was some talk of him being nominated for an Oscar, which didn't materialize, and much talk about his "comeback."

As his career picked up, his marriage to Patrice ran down. He quipped, "I don't marry them, they marry me." He never announced any formal separation but just drifted away from his wife and their daughter Arnella. When Wymore said, "I wish I could hate him but I can't," she might well have been speaking for all the people Flynn had slighted over the years with his offhand behaviour.

With Tyrone Power in *The Sun Also Rises*

With Dorothy Malone in *Too Much Too Soon*

Few people could hold a grudge against him, so defeated were they by his charm.

With *The Sun Also Rises*, the Flynn tide turned and he felt he had a new lease on life. But it was already late in the day. Warner Brothers called the prodigal son home and offered him the role of John Barrymore in *Too Much, Too Soon*, based on the confessional book Diana Barrymore had written with Gerold Frank. It was a part Flynn was eager to accept; Barrymore had long been an idol of his —he had known The Great Profile and caroused with him. Commenting on Barrymore while making the picture, Flynn said, "We have some things in common; we both owned boats and we made a lot of headlines. He was unlucky in his emotional life and destroyed himself. Perhaps I have had a little better luck." The comparison was deeper than that, whether Flynn realized it or not. Sadly, Flynn seemed to tread exactly the same path as his idol, except that it took Barrymore sixty years to burn himself out and Flynn only fifty.

While making *Too Much, Too Soon* he met the fifteen-year-old girl who would be his companion for the remaining two years of his life. Beverly Aadland was playing a bit part in *Marjorie Morningstar* at Warners when the eagle-eyed Flynn noticed her. She had been a model and dancer for several years and looked older—not that Flynn cared about her age. Beverly was a bright, lively girl and, as Flynn said, "She amuses me." The two were almost inseparable from then on; he said he would marry her, but it seems doubtful in view of his knowledge of his health and the fact that he was still married.

The demand for Flynn's services increased, but he made an odd choice; he elected to accept an offer to do a stage play. The offer came from his old friend, millionaire Huntington Hartford, a patron of the arts who had written an adaptation of *Jane Eyre* for his actress wife Marjorie Steele. By the time Hartford was ready to stage it his marriage had dissolved; rather than scrap the play he decided to retitle it *The Master of Thornfield* and stage it with Flynn as Mr. Rochester. Hartford overlooked the fact that Flynn's effectiveness on the screen was largely the result of editing, and required short takes done over and over. He soon saw that his actor was incapable of memorizing a long text, and the debut of the play in Detroit was a shambles, with a team of prompters calling the lines to Flynn from several positions. After a week in Detroit and another in Cincinnati, Flynn skipped out. Hartford filed suit against him for unprofessional behavior and Actor's Equity talked of suspending him, but nothing ever came of it. Flynn had a perfect and timely exit excuse—an offer from Darryl F. Zanuck to proceed to Africa to star in *The Roots of Heaven*.

The Roots of Heaven, directed by John Huston from the Romain Gary novel, should have been a major film. Instead it was an interesting miss, and one of the most difficult films ever made. The cast and crew were transported to French Equatorial Africa and spent months on location in the extreme heat, doped to the point of stupor with drugs to ward off tropical diseases. Many of the company became seriously ill, with Eddie Albert delirious for weeks. Only Flynn seemed untouched by it all,

probably because the two bottles of vodka he consumed daily made him an unpalatable subject for the mosquitoes and sundry bugs. Once again he played a debauched drunkard, but now a far less attractive one than his Mike Campbell or John Barrymore. The interest in his comeback rapidly abated.

Flynn made one more film. In the summer of 1958 he went to Cuba and filmed a story of his own invention called *Cuban Rebel Girls*. A cheap, shabby production which never got wide bookings, it quickly—and mercifully—sank from sight. Several closeups of Flynn in this travesty were painful to see; he looked, as Jack Warner said, like one of the living dead. His reason for going to Cuba was his fascination with Fidel Castro. He admired Castro as a crusading revolutionary—this was before any hint of Castro's leanings toward Communism. Flynn's admiration was of the Byronic kind, and possibly he saw himself in Cuba as a kind of peripheral revolutionary. He did, in fact, follow Castro on some of his campaigns and wrote a number of magazine articles, which were never published. The whole thing smacked of Flynn's yearning for the past; in 1937 he had gone to Spain to take a look at the Civil War and write as a correspondent for the Hearst press. A series of his articles were printed, but they revealed only the romantic, idealistic side of his nature and no real insight into political reality. He made headlines from Spain with a report of his being killed in action. As Mark Twain would have said, the report was greatly exaggerated. Flynn had merely been knocked out by a flying piece of brick while watching a shelling. Both the Hearst press and Warner Brothers agreed to recall him when the Spanish Government made noises about a certain Hollywood star using a tragic cause for self-aggrandizement. Flynn's Cuban adventures received almost no press coverage, but he did turn up on Jack Paar's TV show wearing a Cuban flag around his shoulders and limping from a wound received on the right shin. By this time in his life nobody took anything he did seriously, and Flynn was beyond caring. A newspaper reporter noticed that he had a question mark as an insignia on his shirt pocket and asked him why. "It means why," explained Errol. "Why is anything? Why is our life? Why yours? Why mine?"

Flynn had contracted some time before he went to Cuba to write his autobiography. He got a generous advance on the gamble that such a colorful character with a talent for writing might come

With Juliette Greco in *The Roots of Heaven*

up with a best seller. They had not reckoned with Flynn's tardiness, nor did they know it was now difficult for him to concentrate on anything for a length of time. Eventually they assigned Earl Conrad, a veteran author and newspaperman, to help Flynn. Late in 1958 Flynn invited Conrad to stay with him on his estate near Port Antonio, Jamaica. They spent ten weeks together; Flynn had sketched out a few chapters on his early years, but Conrad had to reshape them. He hired two court stenographers for several hours a day and prodded Flynn to relate his adventures. The writer returned to New York with some 200,000 words of notes and put together what became known as *My Wicked, Wicked Ways*. It sounded so much like Flynn that few people suspected the hand of another man. The book did, indeed, become a best seller but Flynn never lived to see it.

Looking back on his association with Errol Flynn, Earl Conrad muses, "He was a macrocosm. That is to say he was a convoluted, contradictory enlargement of other men; and through examining him and what had happened to him, you could get insights into the nature of other men, rather like a scientist looking with a microscope at some devilish microbe. It helped me to understand the complicated nature of living as it pertains to all of us. Flynn was a collection of disparate personalities, and he had had too much of everything. Eventually he became a ripped-out-at-the-seams caricature of himself, trying to keep up an image he really didn't want. I noticed he kept no photos of himself and he seemed to avoid looking in mirrors. He told me he would rather have written a few good books than made all his films. Everyone in the world thought they knew Flynn but they didn't—he was isolated by his fame, probably because he was an isolated human being to begin with."

Errol Flynn toward the end of his life found himself with almost no close friends, partly because he moved about the world so much, partly because he became bored with people, and largely because he exhausted those around him. "I found that after four or five hours with Errol," says Earl Conrad, "I had to get away from him and be by myself. He was a man on fire; there was so much action and excitement in him. He once told me, 'If I have any genius, it's a genius for living.' Being with him was like a constant party, a whirlpool. From the time he got up until the time he went to bed everything had to be a scene, a happening; he couldn't stand anything dull."

In the last chapter of *My Wicked, Wicked Ways* Flynn made many revealing comments on himself and the contradictions of his nature, such as, "I want faith, and I am faithless," and "I want to be loved, yet I myself may be incapable of really loving." Conrad admits that it was necessary almost to psychoanalyze Flynn to reach these confessions, and that he did in fact put the actor through a number of psychiatric questionnaires. Flynn realized he was a paradox, and that the only thing he could do about it was to laugh and make light of it.

In the opinion of Earl Conrad, Flynn was a man with suicidal tendencies who enjoyed flirting with death. "He seemed to be an expert on drugs. He told me there were six different ways of killing oneself and that an overdose of morphine was the easiest. One of the things he did for a kick was skin diving, going down eighty and ninety feet. One day he came rushing up to me after he had just come out of the water and he said, 'My God, what an escape I've just had. My air tank gave out when I was ninety feet down and I don't know how I got up.' He was elated with the exertion, with the excitement of having survived a hassle with death. That gave him a great kick; he lived on that for the rest of the day. That was typical of Flynn."

Flynn stayed in Jamaica after Conrad left. He intended to retire from acting within a year or so and live in the new house he was building on his estate. In the summer of 1959 he went to Hollywood to appear in a TV film, "The Golden Shanty." The half-hour playlet was filmed in three days and directed by Arthur Hiller. Flynn looked like a much older man—a sick older man. He had trouble remembering his lines, even in reading them off cue cards. For all that, says Hiller, "He was still a humorous, likable man with a mischievous air about him. But it was painful to look at him now and remember what a graceful athlete he had been only a few years before."

In the first week of October 1959, Flynn made his last appearance before the cameras. He was a guest on "The Red Skelton Show," playing a gentleman tramp in a comedy sketch. A few days later he and Beverly took off for Vancouver, British Columbia, where he intended to discuss the sale of his yacht, the *Zaca*, to a Canadian businessman. A price of $100,000 was agreed upon, with a contract to be drawn up later. Flynn spent several days in Vancouver being entertained by his hosts; on October 14, while being driven to the airport, he complained of great pain in his back. He asked to see a doctor; his hosts immediately drove him to the apartment of a doctor they knew, Dr. Grant A. Gould. Dr. Gould administered a pain-killing drug and Flynn soon felt better, although stiff in the back. His mood perked up and he began telling stories about famous Hollywood personalities and giving impressions of them, among them John Barrymore, Bette Davis and W. C. Fields. After a while he asked the doctor if he could go to the bedroom and lie down for a while. Because of the stiff back Dr. Gould advised Flynn to lie flat on the floor. Beverly covered him with a blanket, and his last words were, "See you in an hour." She rejoined the others but decided to look in on Flynn about thirty minutes later. She found him lifeless and a blue gray color. Dr. Gould shot adrenalin straight into Flynn's heart but neither this nor mouth-to-mouth resuscitation had any effect. Flynn was rushed to a hospital and given oxygen, but he failed to respond and a short time after reaching the hospital he was pronounced dead.

The autopsy performed on Errol Flynn showed he had died of a massive heart attack. The coroner expressed some surprise at the condition of the body, saying it was that of an aged man. The liver and the kidneys were almost gone, evidence of the ravages of alcohol. Flynn had been a chain smoker and a user of many kinds of drugs, and he had suffered on occasion from gonorrhea, malaria and

tuberculosis. That he had reached the age of fifty was in itself rather remarkable.

Much as he hated Hollywood and especially its pretentious cemeteries, Flynn's widow decided to bury him at Forest Lawn. He had expressed a desire to be buried on his estate in Jamaica, but there was no written evidence of this. He received a respectable Episcopal service on October 20, with his ex-boss Jack L. Warner delivering a eulogy and Dennis Morgan, his colleague for many years at Warners, singing "Home is the Sailor." On the way out of the cemetery pallbearer Jack Oakie remarked to pallbearer Raoul Walsh that the casket seemed unusually heavy. Walsh, the director of some of Flynn's best pictures and a fellow-roisterer, then informed Oakie, "There were a couple of cases of vodka in there with him."

In an interview I taped with Flynn about a year before he died, I asked one very deliberate question. I had been one of his boy idolators and I had learned a lot about him over the years. I knew him well enough by now to needle him:

"Errol, you've often been called Huckleberry Flynn, the perennial bad boy. Now, tell me. Do you feel more sinned against than sinning?"

He feigned mock outrage. "Sir, I resent that question, I resent it." Then he laughed and admitted, "No, I contributed. I had a hell of a lot of fun and I loved it—every minute of it."

8

A GALLERY OF ADVENTURERS

No story has epitomized the genre of romantic, costumed adventure better than Anthony Hope's classic novel, *The Prisoner of Zenda*. Filmed four times so far—1913, 1922, 1937, and 1952—the story has a solid plan: men of honor versus men of avarice. The setting: the mythical, picturesque little country of Ruritania, at a time when handsome men wore magnificent uniforms and danced with lovely ladies at court balls. The ingredients: political ambition and royal intrigue, gallantry, swordplay, and love. The perfect formula. In Metro's 1922 version Rupert of Hentzau, an endearing rogue, was played by a young Mexican actor named Ramon Novarro. Barely twenty-three and new to the film world, Novarro donned moustache, beard, and monocle to make himself seem more sophisticated; his Rupert made him a star and he went on to swashbuckle as *Scaramouche* and win the chariot race in *Ben Hur*.

Scaramouche (Metro, 1923) contained what was probably the best fencing filmed to that time. The swordplay in Hollywood's previous costume pictures had consisted of little more than actors clanging swords from side to side, with no semblance of form. The man who introduced style to screen swordplay was Henry J. Uyttenhove, a Belgian fencing master and coach at the Los Angeles Athletic Club. In 1920 Douglas Fairbanks hired Uyttenhove to supervise the fencing in his *The Mark of Zorro,* and retained him for *The Three Muske-* *teers* and *Robin Hood.* Fairbanks was not, despite his verve and his acrobatics, a very good swordsman or a very good pupil—at least not under Uyttenhove. It took a better fencer and a better teacher —Fred Cavens—to contain the buoyant Doug and make his swordplay plausible. But with Ramon Novarro and Lewis Stone as the hero and villain of *Scaramouche,* Uyttenhove had two willing students and, although the duel is rather static by later standards, it was one of the first to employ correct feints, thrusts, parries, and lunges.

Monsieur Beaucaire (Paramount, 1924) was an ideal vehicle for the Italian heartthrob Rudolph Valentino. The Booth Tarkington story—it was both a novel and a play before it became a silent movie—presented the Duc de Charres, the pride of the court of King Louis XIV, a dashing cavalier of royal blood who posed as a barber named Beaucaire in order to avoid a political marriage. Equally adept at swordsmanship and womanizing, Valentino's Beaucaire thrilled his multitude of hysterical fans. But in 1924 neither he nor his fans had much time left to enjoy his fame—he died two years later at the tender age of thirty-one from the highly unromantic effects of a perforated ulcer.

In 1946 Paramount refurbished *Monsieur Beaucaire* as a Bob Hope vehicle, giving the comedian one of his better pictures. They neatly inverted the story line: instead of pretending to be a barber, the dashing duke this time persuaded King Louis's barber to assume his identity in order to avoid yet another political marriage. The duke, seemingly, was not a man much given to weddings. In the film's best scene, Hope engages in a lengthy duel with Joseph Schildkraut, cravenly using his rapier as a stick to beat off the expert opponent, and turning the court into a shambles as he stumbles backward. Duels are not easy to burlesque, but this one succeeded hilariously.

Fredric March was the first of the new stars to shine in Hollywood with the advent of sound films, and about the only one to last. He had spent most of the 1920s as a stage actor, achieving some distinction on Broadway. March quickly took to the screen, winning an Oscar in 1931 for his *Dr. Jekyll and Mr. Hyde*. In the genre of romantic costume pictures he appeared as the Earl of Bothwell in *Mary of Scotland*, as Robert Browning in *The Barretts of Wimpole Street*, and as the adventurous Italian artist in *The Affairs of Cellini*, but he turned down *The Count of Monte Cristo* and *The Prisoner of Zenda*, for fear of becoming typecast. March first strutted in ancient costume in Paramount's *The Sign of the Cross* in 1932, a Cecil B. de Mille epic of the early days of Christianity, with Charles Laughton as Nero and Claudette Colbert as an amorous Poppaea. March was Marcus Superbus, a dashing Roman prefect who scorns Poppaea and falls in love with a lovely Christian maiden (Elissa Landi), thereby dooming himself to the hungry lions but, presumably, finding eternal happiness elsewhere.

Anthony Adverse was Warner Brothers' ambitious 1937 attempt to translate Hervey Allen's massive novel to the screen. The long narrative of romance and intrigue in Napoleonic times was difficult for the producers to compress for the screen, but the results were nonetheless entertaining and profitable. Fredric March made a handsome Anthony, an orphaned love child adopted and raised by a wealthy merchant, then sent abroad to tend to his stepfather's interests. Olivia de Havilland, then nineteen and fresh from her triumph with Errol Flynn in *Captain Blood,* was the enchanting little creature Anthony loved and lost—to Napoleon, no less. The rich musical score by Vienna's Erich Wolfgang Korngold was an enormous aid to the picture, giving it a fluidity and an emotional flavor it might otherwise have lacked.

By far the best of Fredric March's action-costume pictures was *The Buccaneer* (*Paramount,* 1938). Cecil B. de Mille again sliced a saga from the pages of history, here telling the story of Jean Lafitte, the French privateer who helped General Andrew Jackson whip the British Army at the Battle of New Orleans in January of 1815—the only major battle of the otherwise confusing War of 1812 and, by one of the ironies of history, a battle fought two days after the war had been ended by the Treaty of Ghent. March adopted a French accent and swaggered convincingly with Gallic fire and flair. Perhaps he had read Byron's lines:

He left a corsair's name to other times,
Linked with one virtue and a thousand crimes.

De Mille dwelt heavily upon Lafitte's one virtue, his siding with Jackson to save New Orleans, but he didn't touch on many of the thousand crimes. Good as he was as the pirate captain—here dealing with the treacherous Robert Barrat as his faithful lieutenants Anthony Quinn and Akim Tamiroff stand by—March elected to retire from swashbuckling and stick to the field in which he excelled—Americana. Years later he would portray a marvelous Mark Twain in *The Adventures of Mark Twain* and a touching Willy Loman in *Death of a Salesman,* and pick up a second Oscar for his small-town banker in *The Best Years of Our Lives.*

As Mark Antony in *Cleopatra* (**Paramount, 1934**), Henry Wilcoxon looked like a Roman bust come to life. He was one of the very few film actors who looked at ease in Roman garb—and capable of commanding a legion in battle. Born in South Africa in 1905, Wilcoxon went to Hollywood in the early 1930s, after a few years on the stage in England, and had the good fortune to meet **Cecil B. de Mille**, who was so impressed with him that he immediately cast him as Mark Antony, opposite **Claudette Colbert**'s Cleopatra. Wilcoxon was never a good actor and his fling at stardom was brief; he lacked warmth and charm, but he was a ruggedly handsome young man in 1934 and just right for de Mille's lavish account of the legendary lover.

Henry Wilcoxon got his last crack at top billing in a major film in Cecil B. de Mille's *The Crusades* (Paramount, 1935). Here he was King Richard the Lionhearted, engaged in the Holy War when not quarrelling with his fellow crusaders. Based on Harold Lamb's *The Crusades: Iron Men and Saints*, with Lamb as one of the scenarists, the picture was staged with de Mille's customary flair for historical pageantry, although it was somewhat one-dimensional in its portrait of the noble, heroic Richard—some historians feel his time and efforts would have been better spent in England. Wilcoxon, with his manly good looks and his robust manner, again looked highly credible as an historical figure come to life. However, with no conspicu-

ous public following, he afterward dropped to supporting roles, almost always in costume films in which he wore splendid military uniforms. Wilcoxon, a close friend of de Mille, appeared in most of his films and eventually became a de Mille executive—he was the producer of the 1958 remake of *The Buccaneer*. In this scene from *The Crusades*, Wilcoxon, with his arm around his beloved Berengaria (Loretta Young), confronts King Phillip II (C. Henry Gordon) as the Holy Man (C. Aubrey Smith) holds the cross to remind them of their mission. To the right of Wilcoxon is Joseph Schildkraut as Conrad, Marquis of Montferrat, and William Farnum as Duke Hugo of Burgundy.

Robert Donat tried just one role as an adventurer, the memorable *The Count of Monte Cristo* (United Artists, 1934). His health—he was chronically afflicted with asthma—prevented any strenuous athletics, and in time it curtailed his career. He died in 1958, at age fifty-three, after completing his role as the mandarin in *The Inn of the Sixth Happiness*. But at twenty-nine he gave a convincing presentation of Dumas's classic hero Edmond Dantes, a young man framed by three villains and sentenced to a life term on the Mediterranean island of If. After many years, Dantes escapes, taking with him the map to a treasure that makes him a rich man.

He then tracks down and settles the score with the three men who caused him to be incarcerated in the dank dungeons of the Chateau d'If. Here, Donat confronts Sydney Blackmer, in the role of Mondego. With *The Count of Monte Cristo* conspicuously successful, Robert Donat was approached by Warners to play in their proposed *Captain Blood*. Donat refused, perhaps because he knew his health would not provide the energy it would take to play a swashbuckler, and the part was given to an unknown Australian named Errol Flynn.

They seek him here, they seek him there,
Those Frenchies seek him everywhere.
Is he in heaven? Is he in hell?
That damned, elusive Pimpernel.

The Scarlet Pimpernel (United Artists, 1934) was Leslie Howard. No better actor could have been chosen to play Sir Percy Blakeney, the noble hero of Baroness Orczy's famed adventure story of the French Revolution. Howard was perfect as the English aristocrat rescuing his French peers from the sentence of the guillotine—posing as a pacifist and a fop to mask his missions in Paris, puzzling the lovely Lady Blakeney (Merle Oberon), and confusing the wicked French ambassador Chauvelin (Raymond Massey). Howard was not a physical adventurer; his heroes were of the soulful kind and intensely appealing to the ladies. Howard became an actor as a form of therapy after being invalided out of the British Army for shell shock in the First World War, and his talent was quickly discovered. He was a stage actor in London all through the 1920s and took to film in Hollywood in 1930, achieving box office power with pictures like *Berkeley Square, Smilin' Through, Of Human Bondage, The Petrified Forest,* and this one—as the noble Sir Percy.

Leslie Howard, at forty-three, was not really right to play Romeo in Irving Thalberg's *Romeo and Juliet* (MGM, 1936), but his dreamy personality and his velvet diction somewhat overcame the problem of age. Norma Shearer's Juliet was no teenager, either, but they were a beautiful pair of lovers, surrounded by MGM expertise and Hollywood Englishmen like Reginald Denny, Ralph Forbes and, most notably, Basil Rathbone, the rapier-flashing Tybalt, here having his account settled by Romeo. Most of Leslie Howard's film fame came from his Hollywood ventures; his first British film of distinction was the 1938 *Pygmalion,* after which he returned to Hollywood to play Ashley Wilkes in *Gone With the Wind* and the musician lover opposite Ingrid Bergman in *Intermezzo.* But it was Howard's wholehearted war efforts that marked him as a man of substance, aiding the government in propaganda enterprises, making films in the national interest, and finally undertaking a mission to Portugal that cost him his life. In early 1943, shortly after his plane left Lisbon, it was shot down by the Luftwaffe, reputedly because the Germans thought Sir Winston Churchill was aboard.

It might be said that if Robert Clive, the East India Company clerk who rose to become a military commander and wealthy landowner in nineteenth-century India, didn't look like Ronald Colman, then he should have. *Clive of India* (Twentieth Century, 1935) was one of several Hollywood films of the 1930s which extolled the glories of the British Empire, and with Colman, everyone's ideal Englishman, in the title role it played to multitudes of admirers. Ronald Colman was one of the few film stars who was in person very much what he seemed to be on the screen—a gentle, charming, dignified man. He emigrated to the United States in 1920, after having had some stage experience and two years with the British Army in France, and although he spent the remainder of his life in America, he always seemed as if he had just recently arrived from his native Surrey. Colman was also one of the few silent stars to make a happy transition to sound films; it was, in fact, his beautifully precise, softly modulated English diction that assured him his success in talkies—that, plus his intelligent understanding of film acting.

In David O. Selznick's admirable version of *A Tale of Two Cities* (MGM, 1936), Ronald Colman was the perfect Sidney Carton, the philosophical Dickensian gentleman who gallantly gave his life to save another. The Selznick film managed to convey some of the horror of the French Revolution, particularly the guillotining of aristocrats as almost a spectator sport. Here, Colman rides the turmoil on the way to the blade, possibly musing on the far, far better thing he is about to do than he has ever done before.

The Prisoner of Zenda (United Artists, 1937) was just right for Ronald Colman. In Anthony Hope's novel, Rudolf Rassendyl was an English gentleman of culture and courage who, while on vacation in Ruritania, becomes involved in a plot to usurp the throne. When the king is drugged and incapacitated on the night before his coronation, his friends persuade Rassendyl, a distant cousin and an absolute double, to take his place and save the crown. Rassendyl agrees, little realizing he will fall in love with Princess Flavia (the gorgeous Madeleine Carroll) —a love that can never be—and that he will have to protect himself against the sword of Rupert of Hentzau, a black-hearted but good-humored cavalier-plotter who finds him out. Douglas Fairbanks, Jr. played the roguish Rupert and his saber duel with Colman, while not one of the great film encounters with blades, is amusing because of their taunting dialogue. When Rupert realizes the game is up, he bids Rudolf a cheery farewell and dives out the window into the moat, to find mischief elsewhere.

If I Were King (Paramount, 1938) allowed Ronald Colman to besport himself as the beloved rogue of French literature, François Villon. Colman was splendid in a splendid picture—the personification of the vagabond poet who purportedly became the hero of the poor in the Paris of wily old King Louis XI, played with high style by Basil Rathbone. He and Colman were excellent in their scenes together; impressed with the way the audacious Villon has led the revolt against him, the crafty monarch appoints him Grand Constable of France and Brittany, until he feels he has outlived his usefulness. Here Colman draws his sword against arrest as Rathbone cringes and the lovely Frances Dee stands on the stairs and hopes for the best. The best is about to happen—Paris is attacked by the army of Burgundy and Villon leads his forces to victory, driving the Burgundians back. Brian Hooker, in his lyrics to the operetta based on the same story, *The Vagabond King,* summed up the situation:

> Come, all you beggars of Paris town,
> You lousy rabble of low degree,
> We'll spare King Louis to keep his crown,
> And save our city from Burgundy.

While there was nothing in the least swashbuckling about Charles Laughton, he did appear in a number of excellent costume-adventure films, most notably as the severe martinet Captain Bligh in MGM's *Mutiny on the Bounty* in 1935. Clark Gable appeared as the mutinous Fletcher Christian, and the film gave both actors meaty parts by which they will always be remembered. No impersonation of Laughton was ever complete without Bligh's wheezing threat to Christian, "I'll have you hung from the highest yardarm in the British Navy." The rotund Yorkshireman had been in films six years by the time he played Bligh; he had already done Nero in *The Sign of the Cross,* the lusty monarch in *The Private Life of Henry VIII,* and Dumas's dogged policeman, Javert, in *Les Miserables.* Immediately after *Mutiny on the Bounty* he tackled *Rembrandt,* followed by the stuttering emperor Tiberius Claudius Drusus in *I, Claudius,* a film that was never completed.

Charles Laughton was not averse to hamming it up on occasion. In 1945 he was a rascally, puckish, vicious, but somehow rather lovable *Captain Kidd* (United Artists). It took little effort for Laughton to swagger and mug his way through this tale of a pirate who cheated at every turn—even when given a commission by the crown he attempted to keep the booty for himself. Eventually he is nailed—by aristocrat Randolph Scott, of all people. Confronted with the facts by King William III, played with venomous style by the magnificent Henry Daniell, Kidd-Laughton is led away to Execution Dock, as Scott and his lady Barbara Britton look on in haughty disdain. Both critics and fans disapproved of such nonsense, but he paid no attention. He played the part, forgot it, picked up his check, and carried on with the things that interested him much more—his art collection, his stage plays, his readings, the acting classes which he held in his home for youngsters he thought worthy of encouragement. He worked in films until he died in January of 1963, from cancer at the age of sixty-three.

Tyrone Power was the third of his family line to bear the name. He came from generations of Irish actors; his father, Tyrone Power II was born in London in 1869 and emigrated to the United States as a young actor, where he became a matinee idol on the stage, and, later, a character actor in silent films. He was stricken with a heart attack while filming *The Miracle Man* in 1931 and he died in the arms of his young son. Ironically and tragically, it was in precisely the same manner that Tyrone Power died in 1958. Even more ironically and tragically, Tyrone Power IV—the son Power always wanted—was not born until four months after his death. His two daughters came from his marriage to Linda Christian, which ended in divorce. The image of Tyrone Power that lingers from television reruns of his films is that of a greatly attractive young man and a capable but not impressive actor. Power was, in truth, a dedicated actor and in his last years he proved himself on the stage in plays like *Mr. Roberts, The Dark is Light Enough,* and *John Brown's Body.* He did a few excellent films, notably *Nighmare Alley* and *Witness for the Prosecution,* but for most of his career Power was under contract to Twentieth-Century Fox, and both his employers and his fans were well-pleased with his work as a dashing, romantic adventurer.

Tyrone Power's first role in a major film was as Madeleine Carroll's young lover in *Lloyds of London* (1937), Twentieth Century-Fox's highly romanticized account of the early days of the renowned British insurance syndicate. The film was set in the Napoleonic era, and Power appeared as Jonathan Blake, a fictional friend of Horatio Lord Nelson. He dallies with a Lady Elizabeth and is shot by her uncharitable husband (George Sanders in his Hollywood debut). As he lies on his death-bed, Jonathan peers out the window to the street below to watch the funeral cortege of his heroic friend Nelson. Whether the film did much for Lloyds stock in the business world is debatable but it did much for twenty-three-year-old Tyrone Power, handing him the stardom he retained all his life.

Tyrone Power was loaned to MGM in 1938 to appear as Count Fersen (another young lover) in the expensive and spectacular *Marie Antoinette*. Irving Thalberg devised the lavish production as a vehicle for his wife, Norma Shearer, but he died before the filming began. Nonetheless, the end result had the obvious Thalberg stamp; nothing was spared in telling the story of the beautiful, doomed queen and her demise in the vortex of the French Revolution. Power was somewhat lost in the star-studded cast. Here he is presented to the amorous queen as the foppish Joseph Schildkraut takes a good guess as to the outcome of the meeting, and Anita Louise beams almost in disbelief at the incredibly handsome young man.

Tyrone Power was not a great athlete or a particularly good swordsman, but he successfully swashbuckled as a dashing outlaw in *The Mark of Zorro* (Twentieth Century-Fox, 1940) on the basis of his engaging appearance and personality, and his ability to convey heroism through acting. The invidious comparison with Douglas Fairbanks, Sr., and his *Zorro* was obvious: Power was no Fairbanks. But the remark was also true in reverse, and in terms of production, the Power version is vastly superior to the Fairbanks, thanks to the stylish direction of Rouben Mamoulian, who gave the picture elegant images and swift-paced action. His *The Mark of Zorro* is a prime example of the swashbuckling genre. For his leading lady, Fox teamed Power for the third time with the beautiful Linda Darnell. They made a splendid couple, almost a personification of picture-book romances.

Rouben Mamoulian was also the director of Tyrone Power's *Blood and Sand* (Twentieth Century-Fox, 1941). Once again Mamoulian brought elegance to romanticism. In this story of a matador's rise from poverty to adulation in the bull-ring and of his death in conflict with the inevitable bull that cannot be beaten, Mamoulian graphically sketched the bravery, the pride, and the honor of the Spaniard with his almost religious sport. His artistic use of color, of lighting, of groupings, and of movement made *Blood and Sand* a minor masterpiece. Mamoulian also wrested from Power the actor's best performance to that time and one Power himself considered a favorite. Again he was paired with Linda Darnell, but for the last time. Like him, Darnell was locked into a studio contract that gave little freedom in the choice of material. Also like Power, she died at an early age. Darnell was forty-three when she died in a fire in 1966.

Son of Fury (Twentieth Century-Fox, 1942) was based on Edison Marshall's adventure novel *Benjamin Blake,* with Tyrone Power playing the role of that young Englishman of the Regency period. Blake underwent considerable hardships in establishing his birthright as a member of the landed gentry. Cheated and beaten by his vicious, scheming uncle (George Sanders, of course), young Blake takes leave of England and sails to the South Seas, where he falls in love with a native maiden in the form of Gene Tierney. Some time later he returns to England to oust his uncle and claim his just deserts, which he then parcels out to his servants and friends. Having disposed of his material wealth, Mr. Blake goes back to his real wealth—Miss Tierney in Polynesia. *Son of Fury* is an easier picture to watch than discuss.

The Black Swan (Twentieth Century-Fox, 1942) was a pirate picture full of sound and fury. The recipe: buccaneers, booty, blood, booze, broadsides, and beauties. Tyrone Power was the nautical bandit persuaded by gorgeous Maureen O'Hara to mend his ways and fight for the king. George Sanders was treacherous Captain Billy Leech and since he couldn't be persuaded to reform, he had to be killed—by Ty, in a duel, of course. Thomas Mitchell was the steadfast No. One to the hero; most impressive of all was Laird Cregar as Captain Henry Morgan, the buccaneer who changed his ways and became the governor of Jamaica. Cregar, six-foot-three and some three hundred pounds, was only twenty-five when he appeared in *The Black Swan*; his talent and his style quickly made him a popular film figure and he would doubtlessly have had a long and colorful career had he not died three years later.

Captain from Castile (Twentieth Century-Fox, 1947) is Samuel Shellabarger's sprawling novel of Spanish adventures in the New World. The attempt to turn it into a film was largely successful, thanks to veteran director Henry King, who sought out colorful Mexican locations in which to stage his pageant of Cortez and the *conquistadores* and their conquest of the Indians. The film also touched upon the Inquisition in Spain and made the interesting point that Cortez recruited some of his men from its victims, one of them a Castilian nobleman, Pedro de Vargas (Tyrone Power), fleeing from a false charge. Outstanding in the film—it was possibly his best performance—was Cesar Romero, handsomely bearded and costumed, in the role of the great explorer, Cortez. With brilliant art work, plenty of action, and lusty acting, *Captain from Castile* continues to be a first-rate film of its kind.

The Black Rose (Twentieth Century-Fox, 1950), based on Thomas B. Costain's novel of the same name, was the most pedestrian of Tyrone Power's costume pictures. The producers took on more than they could chew in telling the story of a Saxon nobleman who, after being dispossessed of his lands by the Normans, seeks adventures in the China of Kubla Khan. The picture came alive only when Power came into conflict with Bayan, the legendary Mongolian general, played by an orientalized Orson Welles with typical Wellesian flamboyance. In this photograph Power and his chum Jack Hawkins might well be wondering "What the hell can we do next?"

Prince of Foxes (Twentieth Century-Fox, 1949) failed to bring in as many customers as the home office hoped, but it was a delight to the eyes for all those interested in Renaissance Italy. It was filmed in genuine locations, and the machinations of the plot were garnished by resplendent costumes, decor, tapestries, and settings, fretted archways and looming masonry, and the glory of Italian period paintings and murals. The screenplay, based on Samuel Shellabarger's book, was less than successful in presenting its complicated canvas of characters, furtively shifting in the Borgia intrigues of the early sixteenth century. Tyrone Power was Orsini, the Borgia spy who is sent to the Duchy of Citta del Monte to soften it up for conquest by Cesare Borgia (Orson Welles), but who is himself softened up by the warmth and benevolence of the Duchy, especially by that of its Duchess (Wanda Hendrix). *Prince of Foxes* remains a textbook example of the dangers that lie in translating a mammoth historical novel into two hours of film. But it also remains a textbook of tasteful instruction to art directors and set designers.

Tyrone Power died while making *Solomon and Sheba* on location in Spain in 1958, and the film was largely the cause of his death. He was aware of his heart condition; in fact it was shortly before leaving for Spain that he did a film for the American Heart Association in which he warned of the dangers of exertion and said "time is the most precious thing we have." *Solomon and Sheba* was the kind of film that demanded physical effort, a costume epic with much action; Power was the kind of actor who was loathe to let a double do what he felt he could do himself. On the afternoon of November 15, he filmed a scene with George Sanders as the villain, in which the two performed a duel with broadswords. The scene was incomplete when Power asked to stop and went to his dressing room complaining of pains in his arms and chest. An hour or so later he died. He was forty-four. The body was flown to Los Angeles and Power was given burial service at which hundreds of fans and curious people were held in check by police. Because of his military record—he was with the U.S. Marine Corps from 1942 to 1946, and was a reserve major at the time of his death—a squad of marines fired a volley over his grave, lending some dignity to the sad occasion.

Anthony Adverse (Warners, 1937) gave Louis Hayward his first crack at a major picture and Claude Rains his first role in what was to be a long and profitable association with Warner Brothers—where he was cast more often than not as a suave, soft-spoken villain. Hayward was twenty-seven at this time and recently arrived in Hollywood after a few years in England on the stage and in films. Rains, at forty-seven, had already acquired a reputation as a British stage actor, but he was comparatively new to films when he appeared as Don Luis, the vicious nobleman who kills the lover (Hayward) of his young bride (Anita Louise)—but not before the lover has sown the seed that grows to be Anthony Adverse (Fredric March). To make the adultery palatable, Warners made sure Rains was thoroughly unsympathetic—he runs the young man through at the instant his attention is diverted by the sight of the anxious Anita. *Anthony Adverse* aided the film careers of both Hayward and Rains, although the younger man would never receive a fraction of the distinction of Rains.

Louis Hayward's best swashbuckler was *The Man in the Iron Mask* (United Artists, 1939), based very roughly on Dumas's *Twenty Years After*, a story in which d'Artagnan and the three musketeers appear as middle-aged gentlemen. Veteran Warren William appeared as d'Artagnan, with Alan Hale as Porthos, Miles Mander as Aramis, and (not seen in this photograph) Bert Roach as Athos. Hayward played the dual role of royal twins—one a stinker and the other a noble lad who, whisked away to Gascony after birth, grows up as a ward of d'Artagnan. The mean brother grows up to be King Louis XIV, and when he learns of the existence of a look-alike brother, he has the unfortunate boy masked in iron and put away in the Bastille. Naturally, d'Artagnan and the old boys see to it that he doesn't stay there.

Dumas, Sabatini, and Stevenson were the authors (in public domain) from whom Hollywood screenwriters filched most of their plots for swashbucklers. The producer who most worked the Dumas mine was Edward Small; pleased with the success of *The Man in the Iron Mask,* Small put Louis Hayward under contract and used him next in *The Son of Monte Cristo.* Dumas had never given Monte Cristo a son, so Small had his writers attend to the matter. They arranged for Cristo, Jr., to turn up in Lichtenberg and save the duchy from the ambitions of would-be dictator George Sanders, the chief minister of Duchess Joan Bennett. No doubt inspired by the adventures of his supposed father, Junior goes about his business by posing as a foppish banker by day and becoming The Torch (à la Zorro) by night. Poor George doesn't find out until too late—until that dreadful moment he realizes he isn't the best swordsman in Lichtenberg.

Louis Hayward appeared in films other than swashbucklers but as with many film actors, his image led to typecasting and he finally gave in to the pressure. There was, however, a gap of six years between *The Son of Monte Cristo* and his next venture into the form, *The Return of Monte Cristo*, during which time he did service in the war. *The Return of Monte Cristo* was similar to its predecessor but not as good. Much better was *The Black Arrow*, which Edward Small produced for Columbia in 1948. Based on the Robert Louis Stevenson book of the same name, the story is set in fifteenth-century England just after the War of the Roses, with Hayward as a young warrior returning to his estate to find that his father has been murdered in his absence. The culprit turns out to be land-hungry George Macready, as reliable a villain-player as ever lived. The end result is a duel to the death between knights in armor, in this case staged and shot particularly well. Here, Hayward cuts down on the opposition by snuffing out Rhys Williams.

The average action-costume film is closely akin to the western in its structure and its intent, and just as many second-magnitude American stars settle down to playing westerners, Louis Hayward, with his English accent and manner, settled on being a star of minor-league swashbucklers. The films were modestly budgeted and timed to between eighty and ninety minutes; they played as first features in minor markets and seconds in the majors. Hayward appeared in *Pirates of Capri, Captain Pirate, The Lady and the Bandit* (in which he played Dick Turpin), and *The Lady in the Iron Mask*. Typical of them all was this one—*The Fortunes of Captain Blood* (Columbia, 1950). Inspired by the Sabatini novel, it has Blood, a feared seventeenth-century pirate, stalling the attempts of the Spanish king, Charles II, to curtail his free-wheeling command of the seas. Hayward again proved his skill with the blade, both in individual bouts and in fighting off groups in arched alleys. But by 1952 Louis Hayward had had enough of these repetitions, and so had the customers. He sheathed his rapier and then looked for work in the theater and on television. For Louis the swashbuckling game was over.

Cornel Wilde was the only player of sword-flashing heroes to arrive in Hollywood with a substantial background in fencing. Born in New York in 1915, he engaged in competition fencing all through his high school and college years and in 1934 won the National Intercollegiate Fencing Championship in foils. He was also, in 1936, a member of the U.S. Olympic Training Squad in saber; later, as a fledgling actor, he and a partner earned money giving displays of swordsmanship. In 1940 Wilde was selected by Laurence Olivier to play Tybalt in his Broadway production of *Romeo and Juliet,* a choice obviously influenced by Wilde's fencing ability. When the play closed he left for Hollywood and spent the next five years playing bits and supporting roles until Columbia gambled on him as Frederic Chopin in their juicy version of the composer's life, *A Song to Remember.* The picture was an enormous hit, despite the sneers of the purists, and Wilde was launched on his career as a popular picture actor. His first outing as a screen swashbuckler was in *A Thousand and One Nights,* which required him to duel with the scimitar. In this Arabian Nights fantasy Wilde soon learned that film fencing is a choreographed variation on sports fencing, and considerably more dangerous.

The Bandit of Sherwood Forest (Columbia, 1946) allowed Cornel Wilde to romp around the greenwood with bow and arrow as Robert, the son of Robin Hood. The situation faced, and solved, by the son is exactly the same as that faced, and solved, by the father: keeping King John in line. The shifty, ambitious monarch of this version was advised by his chief minister, a Norman baron of evil proportions—played by Henry Daniell of cruel mouth, cold eyes, and acid voice. Few actors matched Daniell in the art of sketching vicious costume villains. London born, he had acted on the stage since 1913; he started his Hollywood career with the introduction of sound, his cultured British diction and his icy manner making him a perfect cad. He was Garbo's would-be suitor in *Camille*; the school supervisor who treated *Jane Eyre* so brutally; and Boris Karloff's fellow conspirator in the plan to use fresh corpses for medical research in *The Body Snatchers*. Henry Daniell worked to the very end of his life—he died in 1963 in his seventieth year while filming *My Fair Lady.* His role in *The Bandit of Sherwood Forest* made small demand on his talent: he had little to do other than make summary decisions like "Take them out and hang them." Daniell was deficient in only one aspect of screen villainy—he loathed swordplay, and all his duels were extensively doubled. Cornel Wilde, on the other hand, here surpassed himself, even continuing to fence with his left arm when wounded in the right.

Forever Amber (Twentieth Century-Fox, 1947) was lavish, colorful, lusty—and a sad disappointment to its producers, so eager to cash in on Kathleen Windsor's spicy novel of the ups and downs of a courtesan in Restoration England. The film needed to have been a little bawdier and much more slyly humorous. Only George Sanders as Charles II seemed really aware of the naughty character of the period. Fox brought Peggy Cummins from England to play Amber and then scrapped the film after months of shooting because they didn't feel she was sexy enough in the part. With a million dollars already invested, the studio then gave the part to their contractee, Linda Darnell, which was another mistake—Amber needed an actress of great intelligence and cunning, as well as beauty. For Cornel Wilde it was another chance to swashbuckle—here as Bruce Carlton, the cavalier who is Amber's one real (though unrequited) love among the many men who troop through her life. But *Forever Amber* is still worth the viewing for its technicolor photography of court, theater, tavern, and bedroom sets, some well-staged swordplay, and some graphic indications of what plague and the Great Fire of London were all about.

At Sword's Point (RKO Radio, 1952) was filmed under the title *Sons of the Musketeers,* which would have given the whole thing away, and would have been hard to explain, with Maureen O'Hara playing Clair, the daughter of Athos—according to this screenplay the old blade never had a son. Under any title, the picture would have been merely routine had it not been for the brilliant swordplay devised by Fred Cavens. With Cornel Wilde as d'Artagnan's son, Cavens had an actor who needed little coaching, and in Maureen O'Hara Cavens found an actress with a real flair for fencing. According to the late Cavens, the red-headed Irish beauty was the best of Hollywood's lady fencers. As for the plot of *At Sword's Point*: the grown-up children of the old musketeers answer the call of their queen to save France from the evil intrigues of certain statesmen. They succeed.

Films dealing with the American Revolution have never been big at the box office—they appeal not much to American audiences and hardly at all to the British. *The Scarlet Coat* (MGM, 1955) told the story of the intrigue behind the defection to the British of General Benedict Arnold, with Cornel Wilde as Major John Bolton, the American counter-spy who was assigned to uncover the plot by which Arnold intended to hand over West Point to the British. Here, Wilde wards off a thrust made by Michael Wilding, playing the part of Major John André, the British officer who negotiated with Arnold. The honorable André paid with his life for his involvement in this sorry episode, but he lives on as a martyr in British history books.

Cornel Wilde's last fling at historical romance was his own production *Lancelot and Guinevere* (Universal, 1963), in which he and his beautiful blonde wife, Jean Wallace, played the title roles. Wilde directed the picture, filming his exteriors in Yugoslavia, where he employed native cavalrymen, and his interiors at Pinewood Studios, London, with a large cast of English players. The finished product was lively, pleasing to the eye, and considerably better than any of the costume pictures in which Wilde had appeared only as an actor. The French accent he affected for Lancelot was a little stiff, but his staging of the battle scenes and his own participation in them was admirable. Mrs. Wilde's version of Guinevere gave a good indication of why Lancelot strayed from the Round Table, and Brian Aherne was a most patrician King Arthur. With *Lancelot and Guinevere*, Cornel Wilde established himself as a filmmaker of some merit; with his beautiful and often brutal *The Naked Prey*, perhaps the best picture ever made in Africa, he revealed even more ability. With his *Beach Red* and his *No Blade of Grass* Wilde settled the matter—the never-acclaimed movie star was now a well-acclaimed movie-maker.

Sir Laurence Olivier is not a man of great physique or athletic skill, but his rich talent as an actor has enabled him to convey heroism and to shine in several films of derring-do. The film that gave him his first chance to swashbuckle was also the film that made him popular—*Fire Over England* (London Films, 1937). By then the thirty-year-old Olivier had been an actor on stage and in films for a dozen years, but this was the year his career took flight, not only as a film figure but, for the first time, as *Hamlet* at the Old Vic. In *Fire Over England* Olivier was a fictional friend of Queen Elizabeth I (Flora Robson) at the time of the formation of the Spanish Armada. He goes to Spain to ferret out Britons in the employ of King Phillip II (Raymond Massey) and returns to England in time to help whip the Spanish navy in the celebrated encounter in the English Channel in 1588. The film was produced with an eye to alerting Britons to the growing threat of Hitler and his burgeoning Nazi war machine, and in that respect it was, of course, a failure. But for Olivier the experience was a delight—he was cast opposite the exquisite Vivian Leigh (as a lady-in-waiting). Their own love affair was much more fiery than the one in the script of *Fire Over England*.

Sir Laurence Olivier's name is not readily associated with Hollywood, yet four of his most popular films were made there in 1939 and 1940: *Wuthering Heights* (Goldwyn), *Rebecca* (Selznick), *Pride and Prejudice* (MGM), and *Lady Hamilton*. The last was produced by Alexander Korda for the very definite purpose of boosting England's heroic image in America and bolstering morale in England itself. Olivier played Admiral Horatio Lord Nelson in a most cool and confident manner. His bride, Vivien Leigh, played the celebrated mistress of the great naval hero. The film was titled *That Hamilton Woman* in the United States; Korda didn't want to give Americans the impression it was the saga of some stuffy British noblewoman. Under both titles the film did great business, especially when Sir Winston Churchill let it be known that it was his favorite film. In this sequence, Nelson spots the French fleet at Trafalgar and tells Captain Hardy (Henry Wilcoxon) to inform his crew that "England expects each man this day to do his duty." It was this officer to whom Nelson said, as he lay dying, "Kismet, Hardy." The observation is more often quoted as "Kiss me, Hardy," thereby putting Horatio in a light that would have puzzled Emma Hamilton.

Henry V (Two Cities, 1944) remains Olivier's crowning achievement as a filmmaker. As the star, the director, and the producer he created a picture that was exciting entertainment, highly artistic, excellent Shakespeare, and a valuable piece of British wartime propaganda. He was able to muster the cream of British film craftsmen and actors —cinematographer Robert Krasker, art director Paul Sherriff (who employed the Bayeux Tapestry, actually an anachronism, and motifs from the Duc de Berri Book of Hours), and composer Sir William Walton, who provided one of the landmarks in screen scoring. Olivier had the inspired idea of opening and closing his film with Elizabethan actors performing *Henry V* in London's Globe Theatre in 1600; and for his amazing re-creation of the Battle of Agincourt he took his cast and crew to Ireland, setting his hordes of archers and his ranks of cavalry in luscious green landscapes. The total result was a film of beauty and value. Prior to filming Olivier had sought advice from Charles Laughton on how to play the title role. Advised Laughton: "Be England!" It was counsel Olivier followed to the letter.

If Olivier's *Hamlet* (Two Cities, 1948) is second to his *Henry V,* it is because the structure of the play doesn't allow for the stunning expansion and thrilling scope of his previous Shakespearean film. But *Hamlet* gave Olivier as an actor even greater range. His *tour de force* in the title role did, in fact, bring him an Oscar as best actor of the year, not that anyone would have been less impressed if it hadn't. Olivier both produced and directed his *Hamlet,* and he was entirely responsible for the changes, the truncations, and the various eliminations of characters in the screenplay. The scholars objected, but for most people it was a lucid and compelling introduction to Shakespeare. Olivier was able, with the aid of striking sets, artistic lighting, and a fine cast, to convey all the poetry and turmoil of the "melancholy Dane." At the conclusion of the film, Olivier staged a brilliant rapier-and-dagger duel with Laertes (Terence Morgan), which was watched with varying degrees of concern by Horatio (Norman Wooland), the king (Basil Sydney), and his mother the queen (Eileen Herlie). In any consideration of film swordplay, this vicious, flashing duel should be given attention.

The Beggar's Opera (Warners, 1953) has the dubious distinction of being Olivier's least successful film. It did poor business in Britain and almost none in North America. Its title, giving the impression it was actually an opera, made marketing difficult but Olivier refused to allow a change to *MacHeath the Highwayman.* Based on John Gay's eighteenth-century drama of the same name, the film had a new score of songs composed by Sir Arthur Bliss and sung by Olivier himself in a modestly pleasing baritone. He roistered engagingly as a lusty wine-women-and-song bandit, and easily won the heart of little Polly Peachum (Dorothy Tutin) , but he didn't win the hearts of many moviegoers. A pity.

Olivier would doubtlessly not have filmed *Richard III* (Lopert, 1956) had it not been for the success of his previous Shakespearean films. He had, of course, played Richard many times to acclaim on the stage—Olivier's primary career interest was in Shakespeare on the stage; his film career he considered quite secondary. To make the story of the evil, hunchbacked monarch more fascinating to the wide moviegoing audience, he made his *Richard III* as colorful, as spectacular, and as sanguine as his budget allowed. For all that, the film did not at all match the popularity of his *Henry V* or his *Hamlet*. The monstrous Richard lacked the great heroism of the one and the philosophical interest of the other. It therefore remains a film of interest to students of Shakespeare, and students of creative acting and imaginative filmmaking. Few death scenes have ever matched the sheer, bloody brutality of that of Olivier's Richard on the field at Bosworth, savagely fallen upon by his enemies and hacked to death.

The Wicked Lady (1946) was the fourth of James Mason's costume pictures for Gainsborough Studios. Halfway through the Second World War it occurred to Gainsborough that audiences were tired of war films and that the escapism of historical romance was an avenue of profit, provided it was sufficiently spiced with sex and sadism. Scoring a hit with his arrogant marquis—a beast to the ladies—in The Man in Grey (1943), Mason intensified his ingratiating loathsomeness as the drunken, brutal Lord Manderstroke in the Victorian melodrama Fanny by Gaslight (1944), and reached the ultimate in swinery as the finger-smashing lover of pianist Ann Todd in The Seventh Veil (1945). His popularity soared. The nearest Mason came to being a Gainsborough swashbuckler was in The Wicked Lady, as Captain Jeremy Jackson, the highwayman lover and partner of wicked Lady Skelton (Margaret Lockwood). Mason and Lockwood, along with Stewart Granger and Phyllis Calvert, helped turn Gainsborough into Britain's most solvent studio—until public taste changed with the realities of the Cold War and the Space Age.

James Mason began his Hollywood career in 1949 but he never quite regained the popularity he had enjoyed as a Gainsborough beast. On the other hand, his prestige as an actor grew and he was never short of work. He excelled himself as Rommel in *The Desert Fox* and as Brutus in *Julius Caesar*. In the costume-caper department Mason cut a mean style as Rupert of Hentzau in the 1952 remake of *The Prisoner of Zenda* and here, as Sir Brack, the suavely villainous Black Knight in *Prince Valiant* (Twentieth Century-Fox, 1954). Based on Hal Foster's comic strip, the handsome spectacle was loaded with heavy armor and light-hearted history. As Prince Valiant, the Viking lad who leaves Scandia and heads for Camelot in search of knighthood, Robert Wagner seemed more like a long-haired Palm Springs tennis player lost on the way back to Beverly Hills.

By the time he appeared as Mark Antony in Gabriel Pascal's lavish movie version of Shaw's *Caesar and Cleopatra* (United Artists, 1946), Stewart Granger had already made his mark as a costume romantic in *The Man in Grey* and *Fanny by Gaslight*. This, however, was Granger's first opportunity to dash around sword in hand and show off his considerable physique. Other opportunities were immediately forthcoming in period melodramas like *Madonna of the Seven Moons* and *Blanche Fury*. The London born Granger (real name: James Stewart) was almost without competition in the tall-handsome-athletic-hero-division in British films after the Second World War. His role in *Caesar and Cleopatra* was merely a supporting one on a screen dominated by Claude Rains as the Roman emperor and Vivien Leigh as the Egyptian minx. The doleful-looking gentleman is the late Cecil Parker.

Whether the great violin virtuoso and composer Nicolo Paganini was as robust as Stewart Granger is doubtful, but in *The Magic Bow* (Universal-International, 1947) Granger gave a lusty and very profitable account of one of history's most fantastic musicians. According to this film, Paganini was not only a great fiddler but a great hand with the ladies and no pushover with a sword. Here he settles an affair of honor with Dennis Price. The gentleman on the extreme right is, again, Cecil Parker. After his Paganini caper, Granger's screen image became increasingly heroic, as he played an Irish rebel leader in *Captain Boycott* and a Swedish soldier of fortune in *Saraband*. Each film was a step in the inevitable direction of Hollywood; Granger went there in 1950 to play the stalwart Allan Quartermain in *King Solomon's Mines,* thus touching off a solid decade of MGM stardom.

MGM's 1952 version of *Scaramouche* contained the longest and most elaborately staged duel ever filmed. It was staged by Jean Heremans and enacted with great flair by Mel Ferrer as a marquis and the finest swordsman in France, and Stewart Granger as Scaramouche, a theatrical clown who studies fencing in order to avenge the death of a friend once slain by the marquis with cavalier disdain. This fantastic set piece, which lasts more than six minutes, takes place in a theater and covers some 300 yards of aisles and corridors, on stage, off stage, and back stage. In terms of reality the duel is ridiculous—no two men could have the stamina to fence so ferociously for so long—but as theatrical entertainment, the complicated performance of Granger and Ferrer is nothing less than marvelous.

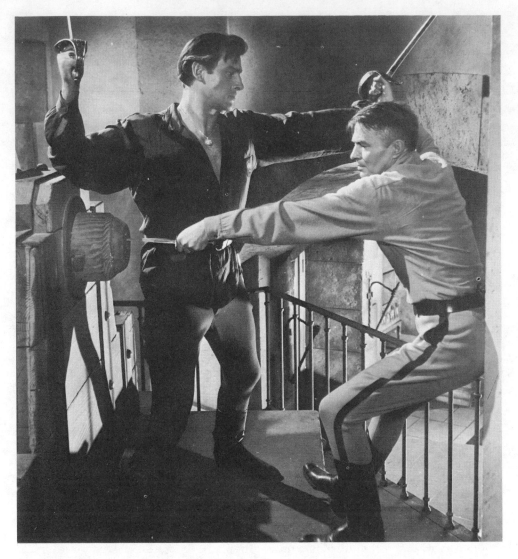

In remaking *The Prisoner of Zenda* in 1952, MGM acquired the rights to David O. Selznick's 1937 script, and recreated it almost shot for shot, even to the extent of using the musical score Alfred Newman wrote for Selznick. The MGM version was handsome and well-cast, but it suffered from an economy wave in the studio at that time. Several crowd scenes were eliminated from the Selznick script, causing Ruritania to seem sparsely populated. Stewart Granger performed his dual role with likable conviction, although he complained he could have done better had director Richard Thorpe not hurried the production and settled for first takes. The end result was good entertainment, but a picture with not quite the style or panache of the Ronald Colman version. In one particular the Granger version was greatly superior to its predecessor—the duel between Granger and James Mason as Rupert of Hentzau. Staged by Jean Heremans, who also doubled for Mason in the long shots, the long exchange with cavalry sabers was a brilliant piece of swordsmanship, excitingly filmed, and a credit to Granger's ability with the blade.

Stewart Granger was a logical choice for *Beau Brummell* (MGM, 1954). Few other actors at that time had the build or the stance or (as some of his fellow players have noted) the natural ego to strut with total conviction in Regency finery. The film used actual locations and admirable decor to tell the story of George Bryan Brummell, the dandy and amateur politician who became a friend and advisor to the Prince of Wales (Peter Ustinov), later King George IV. Brummell's sartorial elegance and his arrogance in selecting the wardrobe of the Prince won him the nickname "Beau." The meeting between the two men occurred when Brummell was cashiered from a cavalry regiment for criticizing the uniforms designed by the Prince. Faced with the confident, conceited Brummell, however, the Prince is sufficiently intrigued to retain him as an advisor.

Moonfleet was filmed by MGM in England in 1955. Directed by the distinguished German veteran Fritz Lang, the picture had much to offer in the way of scenery and settings and the stylishly macabre atmosphere for which Lang was noted. For all that, it did only moderate business at the box office. Set in Dorsetshire in 1757, *Moonfleet* related the exploits of a band of smugglers (mostly of silk and brandy from France) headed by Stewart Granger—a high-living dandy when not engaged in his nefarious trade. Possibly the picture suffered from having a leading man who was neither hero nor villain but a confusing bit of both. Adding to the confusion was the appearance of George Sanders as an aristocratic politician in league with the smugglers but bound by his office to put an end to them.

Swordsman of Siena (MGM, 1963) fell short of being a major contribution to screen swashbuckling. It wasn't big enough, long enough, or well-cast enough, and consequently it was not promoted enough by MGM. But for aficionados the picture, which was filmed entirely in Italy, does contain beautifully colored settings and costumes, and some first-class swordsmanship, again supervised by Jean Heremans. Stewart Granger appeared as Thomas Stanwood, an English sixteenth-century soldier of fortune and mercenary who becomes involved in a plot to free Siena from Spanish occupation. Granger played the part with more veracity and less appeal than in his previous forays into fictional heroism; here he was a man who used his boot if the odds became too rough. By 1963, regrettably, the Sir Galahad concept seemed to be on the way out.

The Spanish Main (RKO Radio, 1945) gave Paul Henreid his chance to play a swashbuckling pirate captain. Henreid, the product of a cultured and affluent family, had studied fencing as part of his dramatic training in Vienna. Yet, although he gave a good account of himself in this rollicking and good-humored picture, he was running counter to his popular image as a smooth, Continental romantic. Here Henreid was the captain of a Dutch merchant ship wrecked off the coast of the Carolinas, where the dastardly Spanish colonial governor (Walter Slezak) orders the crew sold into slavery. But Henreid escapes and when next seen he has become a feared buccaneer of the Spanish Main; by way of revenge he kidnaps the governor's lovely bride (Maureen O'Hara), marries her, and then deserts her. Later, realizing he loves his bride, he pursues her and is captured by the governor, from whom he finally escapes in a rousing climax. RKO, not a studio that specialized in this sort of hokum, was generous in its expenditures, building a pair of full-sized galleons, providing excellent sets and costumes, and staging some brisk battle scenes and swordplay Directed by Frank Borzage with flair and a touch of satire, *The Spanish Main* ranks with the better Hollywood trips through pirate waters.

To play *The Gallant Blade* (Columbia, 1948) Larry Parks went back to the France of 1648, at the end of the Thirty Years War. Parks, as the best swordsman in France (naturally), played the aide to a certain General Cadeau, a civilized gentleman concerned with containing the warlike tendencies of a fellow general, who wished to continue the conflict by attacking Spain. Thanks to Parks, Spain was saved. In the role of General Cadeau, George Macready played one of the few sympathetic roles in his movie career. The beautifully spoken, cultured Macready, an avid art collector, arrived in Hollywood in 1943 after distinguishing himself on the stage, and settled down to become a cold-hearted and frequently depraved villain in dozens of films; he reached his nadir of nastiness in *Paths of Glory*, as the French general who used his men as fodder for his own glory. As for Larry Parks, his fling at stardom came to an end in 1951 when he was blacklisted for his alleged involvement in Communism.

The Pirate (MGM, 1948) was an attempt on the part of Gene Kelly and director Vincente Minnelli to spoof—with song, dance, and comedy—the whole business of swashbuckling. The results were not quite right, partly because Kelly overdid his Fairbanks-Barrymore impersonation. He played an entertainer of the early nineteenth century, stuck in a Caribbean seaport and pretending, out of desperation, to be a notorious pirate. But with his dancing, Judy Garland's singing, some sparkling songs by Cole Porter, stunning sets and costumes, and Minnelli's pacing, the picture had much to offer. Here, Kelly negotiates with Walter Slezak, Vienna's charming contribution to celluloid villainy.

Alexandre Dumas's *The Three Musketeers* is, of course, the primary swashbuckling vehicle. Aside from several European versions, the story was first filmed in Hollywood in 1911, and again in 1913 and 1914. Douglas Fairbanks, Sr., brought off his romping treatment in 1921; Walter Abel played d'Artagnan in the 1935 version and Don Ameche did a musical comedy account in 1939. The most lavish filming of *The Three Musketeers* was MGM's in 1948 with Gene Kelly giving a leaping, vaulting, tumbling interpretation of the young Gascon, obsessed with the idea of becoming a musketeer. Kelly choreographed his own extensive acrobatic routines and worked with Jean Heremans on the swordplay, of which there was plenty. Kelly and his comrades—Van Heflin as Athos, Gig Young as Porthos, and Robert Coote as Aramis—crossed rapiers with the Cardinal's guards in a marvelous five-minute fight "behind the Luxembourg," and Kelly fenced with great style and gusto in one encounter with a guard at the seashore—the man playing the guard was Jean Heremans himself, which explains the brilliance of the duel. The MGM film tended to burlesque the old Dumas classic—a little too much here and there—but the swordplay, Gene Kelly's vigorous and graceful athletics, and the overall spirit of the expensive picture was highly entertaining. Every now and then the supercharged swordsman manaegd to spend a moment with an adoring June Allyson.

The Flame and the Arrow (Warners, 1950) presented Burt Lancaster as a man somewhat akin to William Tell. Complete with bow and arrow and young son, Lancaster led his fellow townsmen in a revolt against the German invaders of a medieval Italian city—but not until he had amply demonstrated his amazing athletic skill in running, leaping, jumping, climbing ropes, and swinging from trees and balconies. Lancaster had been a circus acrobat prior to his Hollywood experience and the ability, developed there, matched with his superb physique and his confident, breezy manner, made him one of the very best film swashbucklers.

The Crimson Pirate (Warners, 1952) allowed Burt Lancaster even greater scope for his gymnastic skills, possibly because he was one of the producers of the picture. The film was stylishly directed by the brilliant Hungarian Robert Siodmak, who tilted the vehicle in the direction of satire. Lancaster appeared as a tremendously athletic pirate who aids a group of South American revolutionaries in their struggle against Spain, but who wipes out his employers in the end when he discovers what a treacherous lot they are. Lancaster could undoubtedly have picked up more roles as a spoof-swashbuckler, but he was intensely ambitious in his desire to prove himself an actor. His next film was *Come Back, Little Sheba,* in which he played a weak, alcoholic husband with a dowdy wife. Thereafter he limited his athletics to westerns and modern adventure stories—to the regret of those who would have enjoyed seeing him play another roistering pirate or rebel leader.

Robert Taylor had been an MGM star for fifteen years by the time he first donned historical costume for *Quo Vadis*. Within his limitations, Taylor was a good film actor, possibly because he was wise enough never to go beyond these limitations. As Marcus Vinicius, the commander of a Roman legion in *Quo Vadis*, Taylor had the advantage of his noble good looks and his masculine, authoritative bearing. In private life, Taylor was a conservative, untheatrical, no-nonsense individual —and this personality came across in his style as an actor, helping to lend credibility to the costume roles to which he was not entirely suited.

Robert Taylor was MGM's choice for *Ivanhoe* in 1952. They filmed it in England, partly to take advantage of sweeping landscapes and genuine settings in real castles, and partly to use accrued funds in the Olde Country which could not legally be removed. The result was wholly impressive. Sir Walter Scott's romantic classic was translated into colorful moving pictures of pomp and ceremony and excitement, with Taylor as the Saxon leader fighting to free King Richard from his Austrian captors and put him back on the throne of England, despite the ambitions of rotten Prince John. As the Prince's principal henchman, Sir Brian de Bois-Guilbert, George Sanders made a noble Norman villain and a vicious adversary of Ivanhoe. Their duel to the death on the jousting field, banging away at each other with axe and spiked ball, is a highlight in the roster of film fights. Here, Taylor surrenders to Sanders in the hope of freeing heroine Elizabeth Taylor from a witchcraft charge, as Norman knights Robert Douglas and Francis de Wolff sneeringly look on. They know, as do we, that the only way Liz is likely to be sprung is for Taylor to rub out Sanders.

MGM filmed *Knights of the Round Table* in England and Ireland in 1953, spending a lot of money producing a splendid account of King Arthur and the romantic adventures in Camelot. Partly based on Malory's *Morte d'Artur,* and with an obvious indebtedness to Tennyson's *Idylls of the King,* the film was mostly concerned with Lancelot—his hopeless love for Guinevere, his devotion to Arthur and his chivalrous cause, and his conflict with Mordred, the evil knight with plans to rule England. The MGM film was one of the first successful attempts to employ Cinemascope to full advantage in depicting subjects of grandeur and great detail. The battle scenes and the tournaments were vividly staged tableaux, and the costumes, the weaponry, and the settings could have been faulted by only the most captious critics. Seen here is the assembly of the *Knights of the Round Table*: in the center is Mel Ferrer as King Arthur, to the right is Robert Taylor as Lancelot, and to the left of the king is Stanley Baker as Mordred. The gentleman in the robes, to the right of the table, is the venerable Felix Aylmer in the guise of Merlin—or vice versa.

Quentin Durward (MGM, 1955) came late in Hollywood's medieval cycle and turned out to be the least popular of Robert Taylor's four costume pictures—a fate it did not deserve. *Quentin Durward* is a film of enormous beauty and, unlike most films of its kind, it has a measure of wit and humor. Taylor played the honest, upright Scottish knight of the title, sent to fifteenth-century France to acquire a bride for his uncle but falling in love with her himself. Since the girl was Kay Kendall, an amusing actress as well as a lovely one, Taylor's weakness was fully justified. His mission also led him into a pit of problems created by the opposing politics of Louis XI (Robert Morley) and Charles the Bold of Burgundy (Alec Clunes). The screenplay was an improvement on Sir Walter Scott's rather dull and pedestrian novel, and the film greatly enhanced by being shot in authentic castles and châteaus in England and France. The script drew shrewd parallels between medieval and contemporary politics; its fifteenth-century heroine lamented the lack of chivalry and yearned for the gallantry of a past era. For devotees of historical romance, *Quentin Durward* is a choice item.

As a man of only medium height and build, and not handsome in the classical sense, Richard Todd was not the likeliest candidate for movie swashbuckling. He was, however, a man of genuine courage, having served with distinction as a British Army parachute officer in the Second World War, and a most personable young man. Todd cut his professional teeth on the stage, then made a firm impression in 1949 as the doomed and very proud Scottish soldier in *The Hasty Heart*. In 1952 Walt Disney chose Todd for his *The Story of Robin Hood,* which was made in England, in order to utilize frozen British funds. Happily Disney also utilized the real Sherwood Forest and a splendid cast of British character actors. The boyish Todd gave a believable interpretation of the legendary outlaw, in no way aping either Fairbanks or Flynn. His success as *Robin Hood* led to him doing two more swashbucklers in Britain for Disney—*Rob Roy* and *The Sword and the Rose*. Amusing as they were, the pictures lacked sufficient impact to register Todd as a star of costumed adventure films and he thereafter returned to vehicles in the modern mode.

1654-35

Mark of the Renegade (Universal-International, 1951) owed something to *The Mark of Zorro* in telling the story of a Mexican hero who foiled the efforts of a villain to wrest the California of 1825 away from Mexico and set up a dictatorship. The film was given an aura of credibility by the presence of two of Hollywood's leading Mexican actors —Ricardo Montalban, then recently arrived after several years of stardom in Mexico, and Gilbert Roland, long a gallant on the Hollywood scene. Both actors are advocates of physical fitness and as antagonists in *Mark of the Renegade* they fenced with conviction. The film was further graced by the dignified Antonio Moreno (central in this photograph), and by the stunning Cyd Charisse (to the right of Moreno) in one of her first starring roles.

Richard Greene is remembered as a Hollywood figure mostly because of his work in a group of costume pictures. His career was never a shining one, but he was a likable player with his good looks and his soft English accent. Greene first appeared in Hollywood in 1938, a mere twenty years old, and did fairly well as a contractee at Twentieth Century-Fox. Returning to Hollywood after serving in England in the Second World War, Greene free-lanced, playing supporting parts until getting the male lead in *Lorna Doone* (Columbia, 1951). This was the first of a string of costume vehicles, most of which were minor league and aimed at the junior market. *Lorna Doone* was based on R. D. Blackmore's classic novel of the same name, and the lady of the title was played by Barbara Hale. Set in England's West Country in 1673, the story was that of an oppressive, powerful family, the Doones, who exacted heavy taxation from the villagers and farmers in their domain until Richard Greene led a revolt against them. After much violence in the form of whippings, hangings, and swordplay, the Doones are put in their place. By one of the convenient ploys so common in fictional history, Lorna Doone was then revealed to be not of Doone blood, thereby making her romance with the rebel leader perfectly acceptable.

The Black Castle (Universal-International, 1952) gave Richard Greene one of his more interesting costume parts. He costarred with Boris Karloff in a gothic yarn about a young English lord who wangles himself an invitation to a certain mysterious manor in order to investigate the disappearance of two friends. The lonely estate was forbidding and storm-swept, and the vast, eerie, old house came complete with torture chamber, alligator pit and a team of menacing bodyguards. Stephen McNally was the evil host who fiendishly enjoyed playing cat and mouse with his guests before killing them; a black patch over his right eye enhanced his wicked manner considerably. Two of McNally's mean colleagues are seen with him here: the Australian-born Michael Pate, and John Hoyt, a distinguished product of the American theater. Since both Pate and Hoyt were actors of some education and culture, they were perfect when cast as villains in costume films. Elegance of speech and manner seem to make a scoundrel even more detestable.

Sword of Sherwood Forest (Columbia, 1961) grew from Richard Greene's "Robin Hood" television series, and employed many of the same cast and crew, locations and facilities. Greene, a much shrewder man than his pleasant good looks suggest, realized his Hollywood career was sliding badly by the mid-1950s. After pictures like *Bandits of Corsica, Captain Scarlet,* and *Shadow of the Eagle,* Greene had had enough of Grade B swashbucklers; he then became involved in a production company and launched himself into a weekly half-hour TV format as Robin Hood. Filmed in England at a modest cost, the project was greatly successful. By the time he cast off his Sherwood green costume, he had completed 165 episodes, and his own share of the profits had made him a wealthy man; Greene then bought himself an estate in Ireland and retired at an early age.

Tony Curtis was not considered much of an actor when he appeared in *The Black Shield of Falworth* (Universal, 1954). The handsome Bronx-born young man with the background almost of a juvenile delinquent was placed under contract by Universal in 1949 and shunted from picture to picture, many of them unsuited to his image. The unschooled actor's biggest drawback was his New York diction—in *The Son of Ali Baba,* he pointed to a distant building and informed heroine Piper Laurie, "Yondah lies da home of my faddah." In *The Black Shield of Falworth* Curtis played a medieval English knight who saved the throne of King Henry IV from the machinations of the Earl of Alban. English actor David Farrar was imported to the Universal back lot to play the evil earl, and here, in the inevitable duel with the hero, he met his match and his maker. Curtis may not have been believable as an Englishman, but he made up for it with enthusiasm. To his credit, he was an eager student of filmmaking, and quickly became one of the few Hollywood actors with a genuine interest in fencing. Curtis showed further evidence of this in *The Purple Mask* and *The Vikings* before going on to reveal himself as an actor to be taken seriously in such films as *The Sweet Smell of Success* and *The Defiant Ones.*

Warner Brothers intended for Errol Flynn the role of C. S. Forester's nautical hero of Napoleonic times, Horatio Hornblower. Flynn, by his pranks and his ill feeling toward his employers, caused many of his projects to be delayed. In 1951, with Flynn no longer a major box office attraction, Warners decided to give the part to Gregory Peck. *Captain Horatio Hornblower* was made in England and directed by the veteran action-epic specialist Raoul Walsh. The results were interesting and entertaining but Peck, so often described as Lincolnesque, was not quite right as the flamboyant hero of Forester's descriptions. On the other hand, who would have been? Actors capable of being impressive in costume heroics have always been in short supply.

Edmond Rostand's *Cyrano de Bergerac* is one of the classics of literature and perhaps the finest characterization of a heroic, rapier-wielding cavalier ever written. But film producers have shied away from it because the hero spouts philosophy, is afraid to woo the girl he adores, and, worst of all, has a hideous nose. Stanley Kramer took a gamble in 1950 and brought *Cyrano de Bergerac* to the screen for Columbia. The endeavor was admirable but the result was disappointing. Kramer's one saving grace was Jose Ferrer, the Puerto Rican born actor with the baritone voice and diction as clear as crystal. Ferrer, who had made his film debut two years earlier playing the Dauphin in Ingrid Bergman's *Joan of Arc,* was a well-schooled stage actor and as such he had studied fencing. His swordplay as Cyrano was superb, particularly in the duel with Valvert in the Theatre de Bourgogne. Valvert was the bumptious duke who paid for insulting Cyrano's nose by being run through by the poet-swordsman. For the role of Valvert Kramer wisely used the man who staged the duel and coached Ferrer—Albert Cavens, the son of Fred Cavens, Hollywood's master fencer.

John Derek's best costume picture was *Rogues of Sherwood Forest* (Columbia, 1950), in which he played the son of Robin Hood, leading his father's veteran Merry Men on yet another campaign to contain the ambitions of King John. If Hollywood historians are to be believed, John must have been the most avaricious swine in the annals of British monarchy: in this account, the miserable king planned to levy back-breaking taxes in order to hire Flemish mercenaries to augment his power. Robin, Jr., rode to the rescue. Here he is seen with two of the old gang—Little John (Alan Hale) and Friar Tuck (Billy House). Sadly, it was Hale's last screen appearance; he died at the age of fifty-eight just before the film was released. Fittingly, his last role was the characterization with which he was most identified— he had played Little John in the Douglas Fairbanks version of 1923 and with Errol Flynn in 1938. The genial Hale was also Flynn's sidekick in a dozen other films. He was continuously employed from the early 1920s, and with his death Hollywood lost one of its most engaging character actors.

Any study of films dealing with historical adventures that failed to list Charlton Heston would be like a treatise on cathedral architecture that overlooked Sir Christopher Wren. Heston, who went on the stage right after graduating from Northwestern University, began his Hollywood career wearing a business suit in *The Dark City* in 1950. His assignments were unspectacular until he played Moses in *The Ten Commandments* (1956). After that, Heston's screen image became grandiose and somewhat grave. In time he played John the Baptist, President Andrew Jackson, General Gordon, and Michelangelo. In 1959, the husky Heston, as *Ben-Hur*, played the Hebrew hero with great dignity and purpose, and won an Oscar for his pains. The pains in playing *Ben-Hur* were real ones: Heston, a serious-minded man, spent the better part of a year on the film, subjecting himself to considerable hardship, especially in learning to drive a chariot at high speed around a frightening course. Heston was doubled in some shots but most of the furious driving was his own.

El Cid (Bronston-Allied Artists, 1961) beggars the idea of epic—a word dulled into meaninglessness by Hollywood's publicity flacks. This picture was a true epic, trying to display in three hours a vast and complicated segment of eleventh-century Spanish history—the story, partly legendary, of the nobleman who helped to bring about the unification of the warring principalities of the Iberian peninsula, by uniting the Christian and Moslem Spaniards to repel a common enemy, the Moors.

Charlton Heston tackled the role with dignity, managing to convey the simplicity of a man of destiny, a man who was described by historians as one who "would humble a king and give aid to a leper." *El Cid* is particularly interesting because of its locations; actual Spanish castles were used and a great deal of time was obviously spent on researching costumes and sets. The whole thing was beautifully color photographed by Robert Krasker.

The War Lord (Universal, 1965) took Charlton Heston back to the eleventh century—not to Spain but to Normandy. While not as impressive as Heston's previous expeditions into ancient history, the film does have much to recommend it in the way of sets and costumes, and in its expression of the life-style of the period. Heston, as proud as *El Cid* but not as benevolent, played the Duke of Normandy's war lord, sent to oversee a village on a bleak shore of the North Sea—a village frequently harassed by a band of Frisian marauders led by dear old Henry Wilcoxon. The plot becomes complicated when Heston falls in love with a village maiden (Rosemary Forsyth) and claims her on the night of her wedding to a vigorous, and justifiably irked, young villager (James Farentino). Heston's passion, the chink in his armor, sets off a medieval maelstrom of clanking swords and swishing arrows, all handsomely recorded on color film.

Edmund Purdom's fling at Hollywood stardom was brief. The young Englishman shot to the top when Mario Lanza was dumped by MGM and a replacement was needed in a hurry for their lavish version of *The Student Prince* in 1954. Lanza had prerecorded the Sigmund Romberg songs and, over Lanza's objections, Purdom was brought in to mouth them. MGM's gamble paid off, and the result was a greatly profitable picture. As Prince Karl, a Heidelberg University student, Purdom was required, by the code of the German aristocracy, to perform with the saber to prove his sense of honor and his bravery. Here he acquits himself against the nasty Count von Asterburg (John Ericson). At this juncture Purdom seemed like a good bet for action-and-costume films. But luck was not with him. MGM loaned him to Twentieth Century-Fox to play the lead in their gargantuan flop *The Egyptian* and it did Purdom more harm than good.

The King's Thief (MGM, 1955) might have done something for Edmund Purdom's career had it been a brighter, more exciting film. It contained some fine stuntwork and swordplay but the obvious lack of flair, so essential to tales of swashbuckling, sabotaged both the picture and Purdom's chances of continuing success in Hollywood. He left a year later to live and work in Europe. The King's Thief was produced at a time when the studio had its eye on economy—the mid-1950s were an off period for film profits. The film might have been better had it hewed more closely to history; Purdom's character was remotely based on the adventurous Captain Thomas Blood, who managed to steal the Crown Jewels from the Tower of London in 1671. Instead, it invented, having Purdom curtail the murderous ambitions of the Duke of Brampton (David Niven), seeking to advance himself as the minister nearest the throne by liquidating the opposition on false charges of treason. Here Purdom makes a point with Niven as heroine Ann Blythe and monarch George Sanders look on. This was Sanders's second stab at playing King Charles II, but here he did so with less vitality than he had in Forever Amber. Possibly Sanders was overly influenced by John Wilmot's estimate of Charles, used in the foreword to the film: "He never says a foolish thing nor ever does a wise one."

Tom Jones (United Artists, 1963), Henry Fielding's eighteenth-century scamp, was most winningly brought to life by Albert Finney in a saucy romp directed with a swift pace by Tony Richardson. It gave evocation of period and life style. The story of a handsome young lad of adventurous spirit and healthy curiosity underwent many spicy convolutions, as Tom overcame the spiteful resentment of certain relatives who doubted his background and his right to inheritance, and dallied with a variety of ladies—all of them quite willing to dally. *Tom Jones* is memorable for several marvelous episodes, among them the most erotic eating scene ever filmed, a fox hunt filmed at dazzling pace over the rolling hills of Somerset, and a sequence that stunningly depicts the horror and squalor of the old Newgate Prison. Filmed in actual manor houses and gardens of England's West Country, and using a large cast of expert actors, *Tom Jones* is a gem in the filming of comic-historical romance. As for Finney's Tom, only an irate husband could take offense, unless he found the young rogue a better swordsman.

Start the Revolution Without Me (Warners, 1970) was a satire on the Dumas-Sabatini brand of costume heroics—and a brilliant one. Swashbuckling can be satirized effectively only if the quality of swordplay, the costumes, the settings, the dialogue, and the characters are as good, if not better, than they were in the original vehicles. Here was proof positive. Gene Wilder and Donald Sutherland played two identical sets of twins—one set aristocrats and the other dumb Parisian peasants. When the aristocrats, one a limp-wristed fop and the other a neurotic, are brought from their estate in Corsica to take part in a plot against the king, it can only be a matter of time before their dim-witted look-alikes become involved in multiple cases of mistaken identity. Using actual French locations—along the Seine by Notre Dame, and in the palace at Versailles—*Start the Revolution Without Me* manages with humor and exuberance to amuse, rather than offend, the devotees of historical romance. As Wilder and Sutherland and hundreds of extras dash off in epic confusion at the end of the picture, they might well be yelling, "Start the next cycle of swashbuckling movies without me."

INDEX